Praise for the book

"A remarkable compendium. The topics Arora tackles here—India's formidable caste, class, and gender inequalities, and how its leaders, writers, and thinkers have engaged with them—have been tackled before, but mostly in dense academic volumes. What's unique here is Arora's seamlessly accessible and personable language, rich with autobiographical context, so we feel that the author has a stake in what he speaks of, above all, as an engaged citizen. From ancient scriptures to Dalit literature, reservations to violence against women, Arundhati Roy's controversial views on Gandhi and Ambedkar to Perry Anderson's controversial views on Indian history, these essays are essential reading for anyone who wants to understand contemporary India."

Arun P. Mukherjee, Professor Emerita, York University.

"Namit Arora writes with envy-inspiring clarity and erudition about the central role in our lives of the many random inequalities we begin life with, such as class, gender, and, especially important in the Indian context, caste. This brilliant book is an immensely useful corrective to the conservative notion that people get more-or-less what they deserve, based on their own 'merit' and hard work. Read it. If nothing else, it will surely soften your attitude toward the disadvantaged in our midst, which is never a bad thing."

S. Abbas Raza, Founding Editor, 3 Quarks Daily.

The Lottery of Birth

On Inherited Social Inequalities

Namit Arora

Three Essays
C O L L E C T I V E

First Edition April 2017

ISBN 978-93-83968-19-0

Three Essays
COLLECTIVE

B-957 Palam Vihar, GURGAON (Haryana) 122 017 India
Tel: 91-124 236 9023, +91 98681 26587, +91 98683 44843
info@threeessays.com Website: www.threeessays.com
Printed and bound at Chaman Offset Printers, New Delhi

To my parents,
Shrinath Arora and Lata Arora,
for giving me a childhood most can only dream of.

Contents

Introduction

The idea of equality may be as old as the human imagination. We remain in thrall to it, even as we continue to argue over what sort of equality we want: of rights, opportunities, results? The most foundational of these, equality of *rights*, is perhaps something that most people today agree on—a rather wondrous thing—as evidenced by their broad support for equal political and civil rights, or formal equality before the law, for all.

Most people today might also agree that equality of *results* (meaning equality of socioeconomic outcomes) is not a worthy goal. They're disenchanted with far-left politics. Achieving equality of results in individual lives, it appears, comes with other undue costs, such as repressive curbs on liberty and a devaluing of the natural differences between people—a loss both to society and to individual flourishing.

But the same people may also agree that the results should not be spread out too wide—out of a concern for social stability, if not also for justice and individual flourishing. Most people seem to want the results to fall within a 'reasonable spread', though how wide the spread ought to be, around what median—and what moral arguments could justify it—remains an area of lively debate and a fault line in our politics today. Yet, in recent decades, wealth distribution has grown more extreme even as an unprecedented number of people have emerged out of abject poverty.

What about equality of *opportunity*? This refers to the idea of a 'level playing field' where people compete with others on equal terms, without being disadvantaged by bias, discrimination, or socioeconomic disability. Most people might agree that this is not only good but a necessary goal. With genuine equality of opportunity, the accident of one's birth in any particular social stratum would cease to be a major predictor for outcomes in one's life—or at least much less than it is today, especially in India—and there would be high social mobility, with people moving both up *and* down based on a fair set of rules.

But people often don't agree on when and where equality of opportunity is lacking, or how best to increase it. Indeed, a great blindness, apathy, and doublethink often descend on people when discussing this topic, especially if they are ahead. Furthermore, how are we to achieve equality of opportunity while permitting inequality of results? Wouldn't those who are ahead also invest their material and cultural capital in keeping their progeny ahead? Wouldn't they find creative ways to pull the ladder up behind them and to lower it selectively only for 'their own people', undermining both equality of opportunity and social mobility?[1] Wouldn't this soon create an entrenched social class that would monopolize the ranks of the 'meritorious', possibly for a very long time?[2]

---

1 For more on this phenomenon, see Christopher Hayes. 2012. *Twilight of the Elites: America After Meritocracy*. Crown.
2 Research by two Italian economists has revealed that in Florence, Italy, the top earning families today 'were found to have already been at the top of the socioeconomic ladder six centuries ago'. Gug-

Not surprisingly, equality of opportunity remains a formidable battleground and a major goal of social justice movements. What are the psychological, social, and ideological barriers to advancing the equalities of opportunity and results everywhere, including in India? I'll briefly discuss three such barriers in this introduction, leaving a fuller exposition to emerge from other essays. These barriers include (a) our psychological disposition to believe in a just world, (b) our social organization in moral communities, and (c) the ideology of the dominant class. All three are intertwined and reinforce each other to discourage an egalitarian order.

The Belief in a Just World

A leading ideological fiction of our age is that worldly success comes to those who deserve it. Per this fiction, the smarter, more talented and disciplined men and women, with some unfortunate exceptions, come out ahead of the rest and morally deserve their material rewards in life. The flip side of this belief is of course that, with some unfortunate exceptions, those who find themselves at the bottom also morally deserve their lot for being—the conclusion is inescapable—neither smart nor talented nor disciplined enough.

Such a view partly derives from what social psychologists call 'belief in a just world' (usually amplified by ideology, more on that soon).[3] This widely held belief presumes that humans live under an overarching moral order—whether based on divine providence, karma, destiny, social cause-effect, or another principle—which tends to produce fair and predictable consequences for our actions. It's a belief in

lielmo Barone, Sauro Mocetti. 2016. 'What's your (sur)name? Intergenerational mobility over six centuries', *VOX*, May 17.
3   See Melvin Lerner. 1980. *The Belief in a Just World: A Fundamental Delusion*. Plenum: New York. Also see this article for an overview, Oliver Burkeman. 2015. 'Believing that life is fair might make you a terrible person', *The Guardian*, Feburary 3.

just deserts that, to varying degrees, all of us subscribe to. It's evident in phrases like 'chickens coming home to roost' or 'what goes around, comes around'. This deep-seated belief may well be essential for human self-preservation. It enables us to make plans, engage in practical goal-oriented behavior, and take pride in the outcomes of our efforts. Many aspects of our world even help validate this belief. Indeed, it seems like a natural instinct among people in all societies.

Yet this belief also clashes with the daily evidence of a capricious natural and social world that randomly and un-justly shapes individuals' outcomes in life. A strong belief in a just world has a dark side. When something threatens the comforting cocoon of this belief, it can lead us to either deny the evidence, or to explain it away using tactics like victim blaming or discounting others' hardships—especially in the face of systemic injustices and other situations that we can do little about. This often arises from our need to avoid the pangs of guilt we might feel for our good fortune, or to help justify our apathy, or perhaps to get over the emotional dis-comfort of empathizing with the victim.

In other words, belief in a just world is easier to sustain if we can blame, even if subconsciously, the victims of pov-erty, illnesses, traffic accidents, sexual and domestic violence, police brutality, alleged discrimination, employment termi-nation, and drone strikes in faraway places. Pause to think about how common such tendencies are. We imagine with-out evidence, or based on the slightest of cues, that 'it must be partly their fault' or 'they brought it upon themselves'. This move has big psychic advantages: it releases us from worry-ing too much about injustice in the world and brings more calm to our worldly pursuits (many Indians, under a spell of karmic fatalism, tend to oppress, tolerate, and explain away a lot more than they ought to). Alas, it can also bias us against remedial measures—such as welfare schemes to help the poor, marginalized minorities, or women—because it biases us to think that others must have done something to deserve their (unhappy) lot.

So we have a paradox. In the absence of any belief in a just world, we'd see the world as unruly, without a reliable payback for our efforts, where striving for specific outcomes would seem futile. That would make life unbearable. This is why at least some belief in a just world is helpful. Yet the same belief can lead us to indulge in victim blaming and to rationalize inequalities that favor us, including those created by unjust social institutions.

Belief in a just world spans cultures and social locations, though, not surprisingly, the belief is weaker among the least powerful members in a society. It is the penchant of the strong to see the world as just and their place in it rightfully deserved. Belief in a just world is further amplified by powerful social narratives and practices, such as of racism, sexism, Brahmanism, social Darwinism, libertarianism, meritocracy, and more.

Above all, our belief in a just world can prevent us from seeing how random and undeserved our own success and rewards are—that we could just as easily have been in another person's shoes—a very threatening idea especially to those among us who have come out ahead. It questions our identity of being 'self-made' and having truly 'earned it' through merit and hard work (even as we habitually blame bad luck for our own failures, not the lack of merit or hard work!). Such willful blindness and double standards can, in turn, lead us to support and defend, often subconsciously, narratives that preserve our unearned advantages and rewards in social life.

An example might help here, so let me look at my own life. In 1985, I got into the Indian Institute of Technology (IIT), Kharagpur. Being among the leading engineering institutes of India, it's well known for giving its graduates a running start in life. Most people around me saw my All India Rank of 190 as a reward for my academic merit and hard work in school, and bestowed on me enough awe and respect to embarrass a minor god. I had prevailed, or so it was held, in a competition open to all, for which I, Namit Arora, deserved all the thunder and applause. After graduation, I received financial aid for a master's degree from an American university, worked hard in Silicon Valley, and was justly rewarded for my knowledge and labor. This is how most people still see it. It is the default narrative.

But this is not how I analyze my own success. If I'm honest with myself, I can't take much credit for it. A great deal of my success was not my own doing, but was accidental or due to my being at the right place at the right time. What catapulted me ahead was achieving a high score on the IIT entrance exam, which on any given day, for any examinee, involves a fair bit of luck. But exam luck was only the tip of the iceberg. As psychologist and Nobel Laureate Daniel Kahneman has noted, 'luck plays a large role in every story of success; it is almost always easy to identify a small change in the story that would have turned a remarkable achievement into a mediocre outcome.'[4] For starters, the IIT entrance exam itself was a rigged competition. Its selection criteria favored certain Indians over others, largely based on socioeconomic factors that are arbitrary and derive from accidents of birth. The runners on the racetrack to the IIT—i.e., other kids my age—couldn't begin at the same starting point. How proud should I feel for prevailing in such a race?

In my case, I happened to be born in an upper-caste household, inheriting eons of unearned privilege over 80 percent of all other Indians. I was a fair-skinned boy raised in a society that lavished far more positive attention on fair skin

---

4   Daniel Kahneman. 2011. *Thinking Fast and Slow*. Farrar, Straus and Giroux, p. 11.

and boys. My parents fell somewhere in the middle- to up-per-middle-class range, had university degrees, and valued professional education.[5] My birth in this family was *entirely* random, inducting me into the advantages of the so-called 'lucky sperm club'. In other words, I randomly inherited a fairly decent place in the hierarchy of status and dignity. I was born in a kid-friendly township with parks, playgrounds, and even a staff clubhouse with sports facilities. I attended an English medium school, a huge advantage in taking the IIT exam conducted only in English. I also had role models and access to a library, coaching classes, and peers preparing for engineering careers.

I neither suffered any caste discrimination, nor faced any social and physical restrictions on account of my gen-der, nor was troubled by my sexual orientation. My growth wasn't stunted by malnutrition, nor did I have any physical or mental disabilities (at least none that I know of). My par-ents weren't among the 60 percent illiterates in 1970s India. I wasn't raised in a village, nor lived in a noisy and crowded urban slum. I didn't have to defecate in the open fields or by the railway tracks, as most Indians did back then. My mother didn't walk miles or queue at a public tap to fetch water every morning. I never had to go to bed hungry, nor had to wash dishes or clothes at home, or clean our toilet (until I went to America). I never had a parent or sibling die when I was young (though both my parents had witnessed sibling deaths in childhood). I was never catcalled or sexually harassed, nor did anyone mock my accent or physical appearance. No one hurled abuses or sent cues to me or my family to stay within our *aukaat* ('status'). My social class ensured that I was taken seriously in shops, offices, and hospitals; in such spaces, I

---

5   For more details, see Namit Arora. 2014. 'A Place Called Home', *3 Quarks Daily*, September 22.

didn't have to deal with suspicious stares or an implicit diminishing of my concerns.

Clearly, hundreds of millions didn't have my kind of start in life. My background gave me a sense of security and self-confidence that put me ahead of perhaps 96 percent of Indians—the odds that I would excel in standardized college entrance tests were huge from the start, even as the lack of certainty permitted me the illusion that I had won based on my own merit. But how much of it was *me* versus *my inherited background* that won?

I got lucky in other ways too: I lived in a time and place where my natural aptitude for science and mathematics was much in demand. Would I have done as well in an earlier age when rewards favored those with an aptitude for trade or administration or art? My random aptitude served me well in an India looking to industrialize and the US facing a shortfall of engineers, which eventually secured me an H1-B visa and a lucrative job in Silicon Valley.

But what about the personal drive and hard work I put into it? Do I not deserve credit for my diligence? Hard work is certainly important to get ahead in life, but while it's usually necessary, it's hardly sufficient: many of my peers who didn't make it worked no less hard than I did. Besides, countless factors beyond my conscious choices also shaped my ambition and drive to work hard and succeed—my parents' work ethic, parental and peer pressure, my childhood experiences, personal insecurities, career fads, role models, available life paths, lucky breaks, and other contingent factors. So how much of it was *me* versus *my socially conditioned ambition and drive* that won?

As I began seeing through the fiction—that I'm the sole, or even primary, author of my success and so I morally deserved my rewards—I also began to see the ways in which I was setting myself apart from others. I had to undo a fair bit of my social programming. It led me to start recognizing our common humanity and to desire a social order that more justly doled out its successes and rewards. What especially bothered me were life outcomes that depended on the lottery of birth, where people were, so to speak, marked in the womb for worldly success and failure, based on their accidental inheritance of caste, class, gender, region, religion, sexuality, language, and more. This was a screaming negation of belief in a just world. I also saw that the biggest beneficiaries of inherited inequalities everywhere, as also in India, tend to be least aware of them, nor wish to be reminded of them. Instead, they tend to hold to a narrow 'merit'-centric stance in public life that breeds apathy, perpetuates their inherited advantages, and stifles equality of opportunity.

We could call those with a strong belief in a just world ignorant or deluded, and while it may make them behave very badly indeed, it would be a stretch to call them all willfully evil. Their behavior is more an instance of what the philosopher Hannah Arendt called the 'banality of evil', which refers to the tendency of ordinary people, who, as cogs in an oppressive system, unthinkingly inflict great violence on others and normalize and perpetuate the system, all while believing that they're leading a good and moral life.

Knocking down these oppressive systems would therefore reduce the ready justifications people find for their unthinking behaviors. If some belief in a just world is inescapable—with both its positive and negative consequences—we should at least aspire to a world where this belief is not sustained by an unjust social order, that at least our social institutions and dominant ideologies aren't the ones furnishing many justifications for victim blaming. Among other things, *The Lottery of Birth* is my attempt to understand the powerful and often covert social forces that furnish exactly such justifications in India, forces that help sustain the fiction of 'deserved' successes and rewards, perpetuate inherited privileges, and obstruct equal opportunity for all.

The Role of Moral Communities

A moral community is a concept from social ethics, popularized by the sociologist Émile Durkheim in the context of religion. We could define it as a community with certain shared social attitudes, beliefs, and practices. Its members implicitly accord equal—or at least 'more equal'—moral worth and consideration to each other. Humans have long lived in moral communities, often marking themselves off as superior to the excluded.

Moral communities arise out of certain shared identities based on factors like ties of blood, race, caste, region, religion, language, culture, class, shared history, occupation, sexuality, politics, and more. These help define in-groups and out-groups, 'us' and 'them'. Examples include White Europeans, Brahmins, Americans, Vaishnavites, Muslims, Serbs, communists, nationalists, Arabs, urban professionals, Catholics, and patriarchal men. Since a person can be many things—such as a villager, a Brahmin, a Tamil, a man—he can be part of intersecting and overlapping moral communities, some more dominant than others.

Almost by definition, those within our moral community evoke more of our empathy and seem more real to us. We instinctively root for them in a conflict with others, or feel for them in a tragedy. For instance, the Sandy Hook Elementary School shooting of 20 children in the United States (2012) provoked massive outrage in the media and the public, including among heartland Americans who seem hardly perturbed by news of American jets and drones killing civilians overseas, including children. Is there any doubt that this outrage owes much to the ability of every soccer mom and dad in America to relate to a tragedy affecting 'their own kind'? Likewise, upper-caste, middle-class folks in Delhi are more outraged by a woman's rape if they see her as 'one of us', and less outraged if she is a Dalit in a neighboring Haryana village, an urban maid, or a hijra in a slum.

A moral community can be strong or weak in its binding power, be small or large in its size, and contextually vary in importance in a person's life. It can also expand or contract its membership over time. The ancient Buddhists expanded theirs to include women and outcastes in their *sanghas*. Americans expanded theirs to include slaves and women as equal citizens of the republic. Many humanists imagine theirs to include all humans. Even animals may be accorded partial membership in a moral community, as is common with Jains, Buddhists, and vegans; so many others already do this with dogs and cats. A moral community may also contract in response to certain communal conflicts, real or imaginary existential fears, and other social turmoil, as people fall back on their more primal bonds and identities.

Since humans primarily evolved in small tribes, our tribal instincts—though a bit attenuated in the modern era—still remain strong in us. Moral communities rely on such instincts to provide the binding glue. They promote a sense of roots and belonging and a psychological support system. They help create reciprocal obligations and motivate us to act in the interests of a collective, or for causes larger than ourselves, which can lead to greater common good—as with some forms of patriotism and community service.

Alas, what binds us with some also divides us from others. We're more likely to be cavalier towards those outside our moral community. And herein lies another paradox: the division of humans in distinct moral communities tends to undermine the egalitarian ethos, because moral communities tend to look after their own at the expense of outsiders. Recall the moral communities of Catholics and Jews in Medieval Europe, of Native Americans and Spaniards in the

Americas, or the imagined moral community of nationalists in which others who don't fit their fervent idea of the nation are demonized. Patriarchy has long excluded women from the moral community of men.

Caste, or *jati*—of which thousands exist today—emerged as a leading marker of moral communities in India. There were other markers too, such as economic and social class, gender, region, and language. The relative mix of these markers shaped one's overall place in the social hierarchy, both at the time of birth and how far one went later in life. What's striking about the Indian experience is its division of people, *even co-religionists*, into permanent groups of high and low spiritual status, each with separate rights and obligations, with no possibility of social mobility for individuals. This was justified with scriptural authority, reproduced through endogamy, and enforced—if not by the 'consent' of the mentally colonized—by coercive physical, social, and economic force. A caste-based moral community made it easier for its members to diminish the travails and humanity of those 'beneath them' and to see nothing immoral about perpetuating their misfortune or enabling their oppression (using rationalizations like, 'these people are used to it', or 'they are like that only'). Victim blaming became easier, since one's place in the hierarchy was linked to karma, destiny, and divine order—so one could go on believing in a just world and perpetuate the privileges of one's moral community without guilt or remorse.

So while it's true that the egalitarian instinct has not exactly flourished around the world for much of the historical era, Indians seem to have evolved—or at least more fully developed and longer maintained—some unique forms of and justifications for inequality, 'dividing not simply, as in most cases, noble from commoner, rich from poor, trader from farmer, learned from unlettered, but the clean from the unclean, the seeable from the unseeable, the wretched from the abject, the abject from the subhuman … hard-wired with religious force into human expectation.'[6]

Social progress can't occur if moral communities don't become more porous. But their members resist change and rarely yield without a fight. Progressive change requires new narratives that raise human consciousness and humanize the excluded. Some aspects of modernity, globalization, and mass communication are enabling just that in India. Other aspects, driven by the rapid pace of social and cultural change today, have unleashed new fears and disruptive ideas of the self, religion, nation, and culture that are either morphing older moral communities or reconstituting newer ones. How egalitarian will these be?

Much work is needed here. Attaining flatter, more in-clusive moral communities in India will require more robust liberal education and institutions, reasoned public debate, better childhood socialization, new welfare measures and safety nets, and much else in a continual process of social and moral regeneration. It needs vigilance against the strong centrifugal forces in our social psyche that are always in play and can swiftly transform social relationships into zero-sum games. But we can dream, and do the best we can.

The Ideology of the Dominant Class

So much of our social outlook is shaped by the ideas of the dominant class. This may well be a feature of all organized societies. 'The ideas of the ruling class are, in any age, the ruling ideas', wrote Marx and Engels in *The German Ideology*. Whatever its mix of progressive and regressive ideas, the dominant class, above all, promotes that which perpetuates its own dominance. It does so using various overt and cov-

6 Perry Anderson. 2012. *The Indian Ideology*. Three Essays Collective, pp. 111-112.

ert means: elevating one historical narrative over others; the making of heroes and villains; yardsticks of truth and justice in social and economic life; standards of beauty; canons of art, literature, and music; and so on. It relies on propaganda and rewards obedience. Dominance, after all, is much easier to sustain if the masses come to 'willingly' subscribe to the worldview of the dominant class (but when all else fails, there is always repression and violence to maintain the *status quo*). In the words of Ngugi wa Thiong'o, Kenyan author of *Decolonizing the Mind*, 'Economic and political control can never be complete or effective without mental control.'

In time, mental colonization—spread by the dominant class through its control of the mass media, education, cultural institutions, economic resources, and more—turns the masses into willing servitors of the dominant ideology. They are the uncritical followers, who not only internalize but even defend it as their own. In the US, for instance, a great many of the poor and working-class citizens willingly vote to cut taxes for the rich. The dominant class, in order to preserve its status and privileges, invests in the message that markets are mostly fair and allocate their rewards based on merit; that the rich know best how to create good jobs with their surpluses; that there is substantial equal opportunity in America, where, barring exceptions, all kids are given the same chance of making it big—and those who don't make it are 'losers' and have only themselves to blame, not the system. This message is further reinforced by conservative Christianity, patriotic slogans like 'the greatest nation on earth', and motivational rags-to-riches stories that extol individualism, hard work, and the self-made man who pulls himself up from the bootstraps—while stigmatizing the idea of help from the government (coded in the call for 'small government' and disdain for 'tax-and-spend liberals' who redistribute wealth to the 'undeserving'). No wonder inequality in America has increased sharply in recent decades, and its lack of equal opportunity and just deserts is plainly evident in its worsening social mobility, now 'among the lowest of major industrialized economies'.[7] Yet, a considerable proportion of its poor and working-class citizens not only see the rich as deserving of their rewards, they don't want the rich to pay more taxes, which further hurts their own social mobility. They learn to blame themselves, failing to recognize that the system is rigged against them.[8] Worse, economic disempowerment and anxieties only raise their vulnerability to demagogic ideas, conspiracy theories, and narratives that demonize others in *their own* economic strata, such as immigrants said to be stealing 'their jobs' or the so-called 'welfare queens'. Such is the modus operandi of the dominant ideology.

Likewise, with women's struggle for equality. Some fairly stiff resistance to it has come from other women who seem to have internalized the idea that they are inferior to men, or are meant only to be wives and mothers, rather than leaders or explorers. Many people of color, too, internalize that they're inferior to Whites and even help preserve the status quo: Black policemen in South Africa attacked the early anti-Apartheid protestors; racist colonial laws in India were mostly enforced by Indians. Many Indians in the caste order still 'bow their heads to the kicks from above and ... simultaneously give a kick below, never thinking to resist the one or refrain from the other.'[9] Most Indian-Americans are very sensitive to the racism they face from White Americans yet are themselves quite racist towards Blacks. Many upper-class

---

7   Alana Semuels. 2016. 'Poor at 20, Poor for Life', *The Atlantic*, July 14. Also see Elise Gould. 2012. 'U.S. lags behind peer countries in mobility', *Economic Policy Institute*, October 10.

8   For more on this phenomenon, see Victor Tan Chen. 2016. 'The Spiritual Crisis of the Modern Economy', *The Atlantic*, December 21.

9   According to Marathi poet Govindaraj as quoted by Sudhir Kakar and Katharina Kakar. 2012. *The Indians: Portrait of a People*, Penguin Books India, p. 27.

English speakers in India look down on their own mother tongue as unsophisticated. Such is the powerful spell of a dominant ideology. It uses power and 'knowledge' to set up norms and hierarchies, and naturalizes a particular way of looking at the world—to the point where we even forget that it's just one of many ways of being.

Any social ideology can arguably become oppressive when it combines prejudice with power, creating a systemic or structural pathology.[10] The dominance of an ideology, however, is never complete. Resistance from another ideology always lurks around the corner. Because such ideological contests usually spring from a conflict of moral values, they're unlikely to be settled by facts. In democratic polities, the art of persuasion may be the best vehicle for change but the changemakers need to better understand what they're up against. To be more persuasive, it's always best to take one's adversaries seriously and to see them in human terms, as manifestations of unexceptional historical and psychological forces.

Jonathan Haidt, an American social psychologist, has posited six innate moral foundations that, he argues, all humans possess and build their culture on: Care/Harm, Fairness/Cheating, Liberty/Oppression, Loyalty/Betrayal, Authority/Subversion, and Sanctity/Degradation. Liberals and conservatives differ on how they interpret and relate to them. Haidt has shown that whereas liberals fixate on the first three much more than the latter three, conservatives emphasize all

---

10 This formulation was developed in 1970 by the academic Patricia Bidol-Padva. It follows from it that while some women may well be deeply prejudiced against men, their attitudes don't amount to sexism. Prejudice is necessary but insufficient. Prejudice *plus* social power (dominance vested in the prejudiced person's group) is what makes it sexism—a systemic or structural pathology worse than personal prejudice. Much the same holds with racism.

six more equally.[11] This leads to very different social and political priorities, and dialog between the two camps can be
fraught and even bitter. Since they have different goals and
yardsticks, neither is *objectively* 'right' or 'wrong', however
much we believe one to be better than the other. Their differences in values may well be largely shaped by things like their
relative openness to new experiences and their different degrees and kinds of fear of the world. Love of nation, religious
faith, and sanctity of marriage are more important to conservatives than to liberals. To conservative women, gender
equality (an aspect of the Fairness foundation) may not be
as paramount as it is to liberal women because conservative
women try to balance it with their greater regard for things
like patriarchal authority, traditional family values, and loyalty to the social order.

In other words, it is important to recognize that most
people who subscribe to a social ideology don't usually do
so out of compulsion or malice. Most often they are simply
born into it, come to identify with it, and do not question it
enough. Yet, in their own way and despite their blind spots,
they try to live a righteous life in accord with that ideology,
which may nevertheless be tied up with the oppression of
others or with undermining their own interests. This, once
again, is Arendt's 'banality of evil' territory. So, to affect positive change, the offending social ideology, which may be the
dominant ideology, itself needs to be dissected, debated, and
challenged.

Brahminism and patriarchy are the two most endur-
ing and formidable pillars of the dominant ideology that
perpetuate inherited inequalities in India. They're reflected
in, and reproduced by, our spiritual texts and social institutions. Most upper-class folks today on both the Left and the

---

11 Jonathan Haidt. 2012. *The Righteous Mind: Why Good People Are
Divided by Politics and Religion*. Pantheon.

Right might disagree over aspects of the economy or culture, but they tend to wistfully imagine the history of India in a particular way: as largely non-violent, spiritual, and tolerant, brimming with unity in diversity and respect for women, lived in once-idyllic, prosperous villages. They tend to conveniently whitewash the violence of caste, in particular, but also of feudalism and patriarchy—and the long resistance against them—while subscribing today to a religio-cultural nationalism and being 'casteless', promoting a de facto perpetuation of caste.

None of this can be upended without a shift in public consciousness and a wider awakening that interrogates the dominant ideology and forges new social narratives. This is a monumental task that touches every aspect of social life, including history, economics, language, and religion, which codify much of its moral corruption. The task should aim not only to restore greater humanity in social life—including to the oppressors trapped in their own prison of inhumanity—but also to prevent the oppressed from becoming the new oppressors, as the Brazilian educator Paulo Freire cautioned in *Pedagogy of the Oppressed*.

Such an emancipative task, wrote Freire, is not led by members of the dominant class but emerges from below, as it did in India, most notably with the 'Bhakti' thinkers in medieval times and with Dr. BR Ambedkar and feminists more recently. To achieve scale, however, this task requires enough people from the dominant class to also introspect, step forward, and join forces with the oppressed out of a spirit of solidarity, as in the struggle for Civil Rights in America. True solidarity, as opposed to a patronizing generosity, requires a great deal of empathy, humility, and courage. It requires one to examine the many dark corners of one's own soul, and the many meanings and contexts of 'oppression'. This is rare, since even the most rigorous thinkers—and not just of the dominant class—continue to harbor various unexamined biases, intellectual evasions, and moral blind spots. But perfect need not be the enemy of good. Progress is still possible as long as enough of us appeal to the better angels of our nature and, without feeling too self-righteous, wage a battle that, in Ambedkar's words, 'is in the fullest sense spiritual ... a battle not for wealth or for power [but] for freedom [and] the reclamation of the human personality.'

In time, new social narratives enter our collective consciousness (such as on class, race, caste, gender, sexuality); more of us stop looking at language as a neutral vehicle of communication; religious texts are less often seen as mere expressions of spiritual quest and yearning, and more as outcomes of certain social and political processes; our ideas of 'merit', and the rewards we 'deserve', become more sophisticated. Isn't this sort of change and self-awareness worth striving for in our personal and social milieus, even though its gains always remain contingent and reversible?

A Note About This Book

I'm not much of a 'social activist' in any conventional sense. My writing is driven, above all, by an urge to comprehend my world—how it works and my place in it—and the desire to not be caught on the side of the executioners, understanding that it is not always obvious who they will turn out to be. I also believe that no quest for social justice ought to be detached from a quest for truth and beauty. My writing, like all writing, is subjective and intertwined with my own ideological and psychological dispositions and blind spots, many that I'm not fully aware of, nor ever will be. My reward in writing this book is intrinsic to the writing itself and in finding an audience that might make it a part of their own journey of comprehending their worlds.

Most of these essays first appeared in various venues between 2010-16. For this collection, I've considerably revised and expanded most of them, and added more detailed annotations. Each essay still stands on its own, though I've ordered them in such a way that each essay, I hope, builds on preceding ones. But readers may just as well hop around non-linearly to topics that interest them more.

To me this collection is a snapshot of a project that's best thought of as always 'in progress'. It is not without a certain idealism, as in the belief that while morality is largely relative, some moral ideas are contextually better than others in reducing human suffering, and that we can, in each time and place, uncover these ideas through reasoned analysis and introspection. Alternatives divorced from this approach seem to me decidedly worse.

Our age rightly presumes that a writer's analysis and assessments are shaped by his specific identity, ideology, and privilege. But the same writer is also shaped by his specific empathy, experience, knowledge, curiosity, intellectual courage, and compassion. And so, clearly, much depends on what the writer, with his unique and subjective conscience, actually says.

Still, hasty, reductive judgments abound, proving that good critics are as rare as good writers. I've taken on many charged and sensitive topics in these essays, which means almost everyone will find something to dislike in them! This is fine with me. I'm not trying to win a popularity contest. I can only hope that readers will evaluate my arguments in the right context and in light of the whole. But some, I suspect, will respond very selectively, picking on this or that argument they object to (or support) and making it stand for the whole. This approach may gratify the critic but it is not likely to advance the conversation. It may not be obvious from my writing but I greatly admire, in principle if not always in practice, the task of persuading others in the manner of Socrates: with 'no complacent self-righteousness of the Pharisee', nor with 'a scowling face and an upbraiding voice'.[12]

I hope this book will also amplify the aspiration that has moved countless Indians to seek a more egalitarian world. We may never be able to remove all systemic biases in our social institutions—as new ones often replace the old—but things can usually be made better than they have been (without subscribing to crude notions of linear progress, promised lands, or utopias). I believe a mark of our humanity is to not abandon this effort, even though, as with our ancient yearning to give love, it may not amount to much after all.

---

12 From *Encyclopedia Britannica*. 2008. Entry on Socrates.

SECTION 1
The Experience of Inequality

Joothan: A Dalit's Life[1]

I grew up in the central Indian city of Gwalior until I left home for college. This was the 70s and 80s. My father worked as a textile engineer in a company town owned by the Birla Group, where we lived in a middle-class residential quarter for the professional staff and their families. Our 3-BR house had a small front lawn and a vegetable patch behind. Domestic helpers, such as a washerwoman and a dishwashing woman, entered our house via the front door—all except one, who came in via the rear door. This was the latrine cleaning woman, or her husband at times. As in most traditional homes, our squat toilet was near the rear door, across an open courtyard. She also brought along a couple of scrawny kids, who waited by the vegetable patch while their mother worked.

My mother often gave them dinner leftovers, and sometimes tea. But unlike other domestic helpers, they were not served in our utensils, nor did the latrine cleaners expect to

1   Omprakash Valmiki. 2007. *Joothan: A Dalit's Life*. Translated from the Hindi by Arun Prabha Mukherjee. Samya. This review appeared on 3 Quarks Daily on March 29, 2010. It also won the top award in the 3 Quarks Daily 2011 Arts & Literature Contest.

be. They brought their own utensils and placed them on the floor; my mother served them while they stood apart. When my mother turned away, they quietly picked up the food and left. To my young eyes this seemed like the natural order of things. These were the *mehtars*, among the lowest of the so-called 'untouchables'. They worked all around us, yet were 'invisible' to me, as if part of the stage props. I neither gave them much thought during my school years, nor recognized my prejudices as such. I, and the kids in my circle, even used 'untouchable' caste names as playful epithets, calling each other *chamar* and *bhangi*.

It's possible that I first reflected on the idea of untouchability only in college, through art house cinema. Even so, upper-caste Indian liberals made these films and it was their viewpoint I saw. It is hardly a stretch to say that the way even the most sensitive White liberals in the United States knew and described the experience of Black Americans is partly why one had to read Frederick Douglass, Zora Neale Hurston, Ralph Ellison, Richard Wright, James Baldwin, and other Black authors. A similar parallel holds for Native Americans, immigrants, and women, as well as the 'untouchables,' now called Dalits ('the oppressed'), numbering one out of six Indians. For some years now, they have been telling their own stories, bearing witness to their slice of life in India. Theirs is not only a powerful new current of Indian literature, it is also a major site of resistance and revolt.

Joothan by Omprakash Valmiki is one such work of Dalit literature, first published in Hindi in 1997 and translated into English by Arun Prabha Mukherjee in 2003 (she added an excellent introduction in the 2007 edition). It is a memoir of growing up 'untouchable' starting in the 1950s outside a typical village in Uttar Pradesh. Told as a series of piercing vignettes, *Joothan* is also a remarkable record of a rare Indian journey, one that took a boy from extremely wretched socioeconomic conditions to prominence as an author and social critic.

* * *

Valmiki was born into the Chuhra caste (aka Bhangi), whose ordained job it was to sweep the roads, clean the cattle barns, get shit off the floor, dispose of dead animals, work the fields during harvests, and perform other physical labor for upper-caste people, including the Tyagi Brahmins. The Tyagis didn't address them by name, only called out, 'Oe Chuhre' or 'Abey Chuhre.' It was alright to touch cows and stray dogs but touching a Chuhra inflicted instant 'pollution' on the Tyagis.[2] During his boyhood, his entire family worked hard, yet they 'didn't manage to get two decent meals a day,' not the least because they often didn't get paid for their labor and instead 'got sworn at and abused.'

The Chuhras were forced to live outside the village reserved for upper-caste people. A high wall and a pond segregated their brick houses in the village from the Chuhra *basti*, or cluster of shanties. Upper-caste men and women of all ages came out and used the edge of the pond as an open-air lavatory, squatting across from the Chuhra homes in broad daylight with their private parts exposed. 'There was muck strewn everywhere,' writes Valmiki. 'The stench was so overpowering that one would choke within a minute. The pigs wandering in narrow lanes, naked children, dogs, daily fights, this was the environment of my childhood.'

In the rainy season, these narrow lanes of the *basti* filled up with muddy water mixed-in with pigs' excrement; flies

---

2   Compare with Langston Hughes in the United States of America, 1952: 'I saw [WHITES ONLY] signs when I first went South in the 1920s. I see them still there today.... A dog can sit on a WHITE bench in a WHITE park and, if his legs are long enough, lick water out of a WHITE fountain. I cannot. I will be put in jail. My color makes me less than a dog to those who run the South.'

and mosquitoes thrived. Everybody's arms and legs became mangy and developed itchy sores. There was one drinking well in their *basti* for about thirty families, and despite a guard wall around it, it became full of long worms during the rainy season. They had no choice but to drink that water, as they were not permitted to use the well of the upper-caste folks. Their homes were made of clay that sprang leaks all over. During heavy rains, the ceilings or walls often collapsed, as it did for Valmiki's house more than once. One season most of their homes collapsed; as always, there was no outside help or insurance, and they had to rebuild on their own.

What Valmiki had going for him was a headstrong set of parents, determined to give him a better future. In 1955, despite Gandhi's work on 'upliftment' and the new anti-discrimination laws on the books, his father had a hard time getting him admission into a primary school. When the boy finally got in, he was not allowed to sit on the benches but on the floor, away from the upper-caste boys, at the back by the door, from where he couldn't see the blackboard well. Other boys hurled epithets and beat him casually, turning him into a cowering introverted kid. Even the teachers looked for excuses to punish him, he writes, 'so that I would run away from the school and take up the kind of work for which I was born.' In fourth grade, a new headmaster arrived, who thrashed him almost daily and one day asked him to take a broom and sweep all the rooms and the playground in school. The hapless boy spent two full days sweeping, hoping it would soon be over.

> The third day I went to the class and sat down quietly. After a few minutes the headmaster's loud thundering was heard: 'Abey Chuhre ke, motherfucker, where are you hiding … your mother …' I had begun to shake uncontrollably. A Tyagi boy shouted, 'Master Saheb, there he is, sitting in the corner.'
>
> The headmaster had pounced on my neck. The pressure of his fingers was increasing. As a wolf grabs a lamb by the neck,

he dragged me out of the class and threw me on the ground.
He screamed: 'Go sweep the whole playground … Otherwise
I will shove chillies up your arse and throw you out of school.'

Frightened, I picked up the three-day-old broom [now only
a cluster of] thin sticks. Tears were falling from my eyes. I
started to sweep the compound while my tears fell. From
the doors and windows of the schoolrooms, the eyes of the
teachers and the boys saw this spectacle. Each pore of my
body was submerged in an abyss of anguish.

As it turned out, his father was passing by that day and
saw him sweeping the grounds. Sobbing and overcome by
hiccups, the boy told him the story. Father snatched the
broom and with eyes blazing, began to scream, 'Who is that
teacher, that progeny of Dronacharya, who forces my son to
sweep?'[3] All the teachers stepped out, including the headmaster, who called his father names and roared back, 'Take
him away from here … The Chuhra wants him educated …
Go, go … Otherwise I will have your bones broken.'

On his way out, his father declared in a loud voice, 'I am
leaving now … but this Chuhre ka will study right here … In
this school. And not just him, but there will be more coming
after him.' His father's courage and fortitude left a deep and
decisive mark on the boy's personality. His father knocked on

---

3 Arun Prabha Mukherjee notes that 'Valmiki places his and his
   Dalit friends' encounters with upper-caste teachers in the context
   of the Brahmin teacher Dronacharya tricking his low caste disciple
   Eklavya into cutting his thumb and presenting it to him as part of
   his *gurudakshina*, or teacher's tribute. This is a famous incident in
   the *Mahabharata*. By doing this, Dronacharya ensured that Eklavya,
   the better student of archery, could never compete against Arjun,
   the Kshatriya disciple. Indeed, having lost his thumb, Eklavya
   could no longer perform archery. In high caste telling, the popular story presents a casteless Eklavya as the exemplar of an obedi-
   ent disciple rather than the Brahmin Dronacharya as a perfidious
   and biased teacher. When Valmiki's father goes to the school and
   calls the headmaster a Dronacharya, he links the twentieth-century
   caste relations to those that prevailed two thousand years ago.'

the doors of other upper-caste men he had worked for, hoping they would support him against the headmaster, but the response was the opposite. He was plainly told: 'What is the point of sending him to school?' 'When has a crow become a swan?' 'Hey, if he asked a Chuhra's progeny to sweep, what is the big deal in that?' When his father had all but given up, one village elder yielded to his tearful beseeching and intervened to get the boy reinstated. A close call, else he would have ended up illiterate like the rest of his family.

Most of his family worked at harvest time. For a hard day's labor, which included harvesting lentils, cutting sheaves of wheat in the midday sun, and transporting them via bullock carts, each person got one out of 21 parts produced—about two pounds of wheat—as wages. For the rest of their labor in the cowshed, they got paid in grain and a leftover roti each day ('made by mixing the flour with the husk since it was for the chuhras'), and at times scraps of leftovers from their employer's plates, or *joothan*. The Hindi word *joothan*, explains Mukherjee, 'literally means food left on an eater's plate, usually destined for the garbage pail in a middle-class, urban home. However, such food would only be characterized *joothan* if someone else besides the original eater were to eat it. The word carries the connotations of ritual purity and pollution as *jootha* means polluted.' Words like 'leftovers' and 'leavings' don't substitute well, 'scraps' and 'slops' work better, though 'they are associated more with pigs than with humans.' *Joothan* is also unfit for consumption by anyone in the eater's family or in his own community. Mukherjee writes:

> The title encapsulates the pain, humiliation and poverty of Valmiki's community, which not only had to rely on *joothan* but also relished it. Valmiki gives a detailed description of collecting, preserving and eating *joothan*. His memories of being assigned to guard the drying *joothan* from crows and chickens, and of his relishing the dried and reprocessed

joothan burn him with renewed pain and humiliation in the present.

The word actually carries a lot of historical baggage. Both Ambedkar and Gandhi advised untouchables to stop accepting *joothan*. Ambedkar, an indefatigable documenter of atrocities against Dalits [and an 'untouchable' himself], shows how the high caste villagers could not tolerate the fact that Dalits did not want to accept their *joothan* anymore and threatened them with violence if they refused it.

Valmiki describes one such incident, among the most powerful in the text. His community looked forward to marriage feasts in the village when they would gather outside with big baskets. After the guests had eaten, 'the dirty *pattals*, or leaf plates, were put in the Chuhras' baskets, which they took home, to save the *joothan* sticking to them.' At the end of one such marriage feast, Valmiki's mother requested the Brahmin host for additional food for her children, only to be humiliated and told to mind her place, be satisfied with what she already had collected, and to get going. Valmiki writes:

That night the Mother Goddess Durga entered my mother's eyes. It was the first time I saw my mother so angry. She emptied the basket right there. She said to Sukhdev Singh, 'Pick it up and put it inside your house. Feed it to the *baratis* [marriage guests] tomorrow morning.' She gathered me and my sister and left like an arrow. Sukhdev Singh had pounced on her to hit her, but my mother had confronted him like a lioness. Without being afraid. [p. 11]

His family fell on even harder times when his oldest brother and wage earner got a high fever, and without access to a clinic, died. Valmiki had finished fifth grade but their deepening poverty—they didn't even have enough food—meant that he could not continue with school. He dropped out and began tending buffaloes in the field, watching with a heavy heart his schoolmates going to school. Over the protests of others, his brother's widow pawned the only piece of

jewelry she had, a silver anklet, to pay for Valmiki's school—
yet another close call.

Back in school, Valmiki continued to face severe discrimination. Though he consistently did well in his studies,
his memories of school are suffused with pain and humiliation: from taunts and beatings by schoolmates and teachers
in a 'terror-filled environment', to his exclusion from extra-
curricular activities like school plays; during exams, he was
not allowed to drink water from a glass when thirsty. He had
to cup his hands, and 'the peon would pour water from way
high up, lest our hands touch the glass.' At times, he writes, 'I
feel I have grown up in a cruel and barbaric civilization.' He
does remember fondly a couple of boys who befriended him
and didn't let caste come between them.

Remarkably enough, Valmiki was determined to make
full use of the school library; by the time he reached eighth
grade, he had read Saratchandra, Premchand, and Rabindranath Tagore, and relates this poignant vignette.

> I had begun to read novels and short stories to my mother
> in the faint light of the wick lamp. Who knows how often
> Saratchandra's characters have made a mother and son cry
> together? This was the beginning of my literary sensibility.
> Starting from *Alha*, the *Ramayana* and the *Mahabharata* to
> *Sur Sagar, Prem Sagar*, Premchand's stories, *Kissa Tota Mai-
> na* ... whatever I found, I, the son of an untouchable illiterate
> family, read to my mother. [p. 16]

He studied in the light of a lantern in his intensely noisy
neighborhood. 'I was the first student of my caste,' writes Valmiki, 'not just from my *basti* but from all the surrounding
villages of the area, appearing for the high school exams,' and
he felt the pressure that came from their pride in him. His
graduation became an occasion for a feast in his community.
He remembers that even one of the Tyagi Brahmins came to
his *basti* to offer congratulations, and later took him home
and fed him lunch in their own dishes while sitting next to

him. Valmiki's example inspired other children to show more interest in education, and for a while he even ran evening classes in his *basti*.

* * *

Unlike in the dominant Hindu tradition—which Valmiki pointedly denigrates and wants no part of—widow remarriage was even in the 60s an accepted norm in his community. He describes in some detail how their gods were utterly different from Hindu Brahminical gods and how different their religious rituals were.[4] Around Janmashtami, for instance, they worshipped not Krishna but Jaharpir, a folk deity, and 'during Deepawali it is not the goddess Lakshmi but Mai Madaran who is worshipped and offered a piglet' and a bottle of liquor. He also describes lots of family drama and interpersonal politics in his community, not shying from reproach where it is due, especially on their rank superstitions. He writes about their jobs, suffering, and everyday struggle for dignity, acknowledging that the women had an even rawer deal than men.

Many Hindi writers and poets had written about the charms of village life, observes Valmiki, but its 'real truth,' depicting the 'terrible suffering of village life has not even been touched upon by the epic poets of Hindi.' In this he echoes Ambedkar's own views: 'What is a village but a sink of localism, a den of ignorance and narrow mindedness.' Valmiki also recounts other changes that were beginning to take place in his village. The young men of his community had begun to refuse to work without wages. This soon escalated into an open confrontation with the upper-caste men who couldn't tolerate their nerve, and even got the local police

---

4 Kancha Ilaiah outlines a range of sociocultural differences between the twice-born Hindus (of the top three *varnas*, namely, Brahmin, Kshatriya, and Vaishya) and the Shudras and Dalits in his trenchant book, *Why I Am Not a Hindu*.

to beat them up. Valmiki calls this a turning point of sorts; young men began departing from their *basti* to nearby towns and cities.

Valmiki too left to pursue college education in the city of Dehradun, where his brother and uncle worked. They all shared a single room in a Bhangi *basti*. It was here that he encountered the works of Ambedkar, which shook him up; he 'spent many days and nights in great turmoil.' He grew more restless; his 'stone-like silence' began to melt, and 'an anti-establishment consciousness became strong' in him. Ambedkar's books, he writes, 'had given voice to my mute-ness,' and raised his self-confidence. His rage grew sharper and he became more active in college events, until his penury made him quit college and seek technical training in an ordnance factory, with its promise of a shop floor job that would judge him only for his work. But quitting college made no dent whatsoever in his love of reading.

After a year of training, he got posted to the city of Jabalpur in 1968, moving in the ensuing years to Bombay and Chandrapur, Maharashtra. The last third of his memoir is on this phase of his life. Now he really came into his own: he met a bunch of Marxists, read Chekov, Turgenev, Dostoevsky, Hemmingway, Zola, and other Western writers. He joined a local theater group, saw Vijay Tendulkar's plays, 'read the entire works of Tagore and Kalidasa,' was drawn to the Buddha's teachings, and discovered Marathi Dalit literature, the most sophisticated in all of India, which energized him and forged his literary consciousness. He began to publish poems and write a column in a local weekly, later also plays and short stories. Almost two decades later, he published *Joothan*. In its last two paragraphs, he anticipates his critics:

> Times have changed. But there is something somewhere that continues to irk. I have asked many scholars to tell me why Savarnas [caste Hindus] hate Dalits and Shudras so much? The Hindus who worship trees and plants, beasts and birds,

why are they so intolerant of Dalits? Today caste remains a pre-eminent factor in social life. As long as people don't know that you are a Dalit, things are fine. The moment they find out your caste, everything changes. The whispers slash your veins like knives. Poverty, illiteracy, broken lives, the pain of standing outside the door, how would the civilized Savarna Hindus know it?

Why is my caste my only identity? Many friends hint at the loudness and arrogance of my writings. They insinuate that I have imprisoned myself in a narrow circle. They say that literary expression should be focused on the universal; a writer ought not to limit himself to a narrow, confined terrain of life. That is, my being Dalit and arriving at a point of view according to my environment and my socioeconomic situation is being arrogant. Because in their eyes, I am only an SC, the one who stands outside the door.[5]

Valmiki's narrative voice brims with a quiet sense of outrage at what he has had to endure as a human. Indeed, I'm inclined to see his memoir as a form of Satyagraha: in reflecting back to others their own violence and injustice, it attempts to shame them into introspection. This is the kind of book that becomes 'the axe for the frozen sea inside us.'[6] More Indians ought to read it and let its hard edges get to work inside them.

---

5 SC stands for Scheduled Caste, the administrative term for the former 'untouchables'.

6 Franz Kafka, on the books we ought to read, from a letter to Oskar Pollak, January 27, 1904.

The Terrain of Indignities[1]

'Indian writing' is often equated in the West with its small subset: the work of a tiny class of Indians that thinks and writes in English. Salman Rushdie, introducing *Mirrorwork: 50 Years of Indian Writing 1947-97*, which he co-edited, fueled this conceit when he declared the work of such Indians a 'more important body of work than most of what has been produced in the '16 official languages' of India'. Of the 32 works of fiction and non-fiction chosen for this anthology, 31 were written in English and one in Urdu, i.e., only one translation made the cut. Some of this lopsidedness can be explained by the paucity of translations into English, but is Rushdie's judgment defensible in a country where, even today, less than one percent of Indians consider English their first language, less than ten percent their second,[2] and 80 percent of all books are put out by hundreds of vernacular

---

1   Ajay Navaria. 2013. *Unclaimed Terrain*. Translated from Hindi by Laura Brueck. Navayana.

This review and a conversation with its author appeared on 3 Quarks Daily on Oct 7, 2013.

2   Based on the 2001 Census of India.

language publishers,[3] including from authors with far greater Indian readership than most who write in English?[4] Rushdie doesn't even speak most of these languages. Isn't his claim, then, an instance of linguistic prejudice? Aren't the dynamics of class in India, and the power of English language publishing in the West, speaking through him?

Ajay Navaria's *Unclaimed Terrain*—a collection of seven short stories translated from Hindi to English by Laura Brueck—shows from its first page how different its world is from those imagined by the Indians in Rushdie's anthology. Navaria, a faculty member in the Hindi department in Jamia Millia Islamia, Delhi, may well be the first Dalit to teach Hindu religious scriptures at a major university. He is also the author of a novel and two books of short stories. In *Unclaimed Terrain* the protagonists of most stories are Dalit men who have clawed their way into the urban middle-class through their wits and education, sometimes with the help of reservations. Many harbor episodic memories of social life in ancestral villages, memories in which bigotry and abuse overwhelm kindness and beauty. They love the anonymity of the big city, even as they live in fear of being 'found out' and reminded—in the artful ways of the metropolis—of their 'proper place'.

In the story *Subcontinent*, for instance, the protagonist, as a boy, has seen village men abuse and assault his groveling father and grandma—returning after a stint in the city—for breaking caste taboos. As a boy, he has seen a Dalit wedding party attacked by thugs because the groom has dared to ride a horse in the village, and later that day, a woman of the party being raped: 'I saw, beneath the white dhoti-clad bottom of a pale pandit-god, the darkened soles of someone's feet flailing

3   Shri Nath Sahai. 2009. 'Publishing industry on a roll', *Business Standard*, May 17.
4   From a review of Rushdie's *Mirrorwork* by Sunil Khilnani. 1997. *LA Times*, September 14.

and kicking'. Rather than file a complaint, the village policeman mocks them, 'They say she was really tasty. Lucky bitch,
now she's become pure!' In his middle age, the protagonist,
Siddhartha Nirmal, Marketing Manager in a government
enterprise in the big city, exults at the distance he has traveled in the world: 3BR flat; car; eating out at Pizza Hut and
Haldiram's, where the counter-boys call him Sir. He can hire
the services of a Brahmin doctor, keep a Garhwali Brahmin
driver who bows at him, and employ a Bengali music teacher
he found on the Internet for his daughter, who goes to an
expensive convent school. But such welcome anonymity that
the city affords him disappears in familiar spaces, such as his
office, which has 'the same snakes. The same whispers, the
same poison-laden smiles. Our 'quota is fixed'. I got promoted only because of the quota ... that's it. Otherwise ... otherwise, maybe I'm still dirty. Still lowborn. Like Kishan, the office janitor. Like Kardam, the clerk. Because I am their caste.'

Yes Sir, the most delightful story in this collection, presents a historic role reversal in a government office. Narottam, a Dalit, has risen to become Deputy General Manager
and has inherited as his peon an older Brahmin man, Tiwari. Narottam has picked up all the haughtiness of the office babu class towards subordinates. He is patronizing and
sometimes rude to Tiwari, who burns with resentment and
inwardly swears at him—even organizes Satyanarayan puja
to get rid of him and considers polluting Narottam's coffee
with his spit—but his need for a job and Narottam's place in
the office hierarchy keep him in check, leading to a brilliantly
comical end. In *New Custom*, an urban middle-class Dalit
arrives in a village to attend a wedding. At the bus stand, a
chai-seller, impressed by his demeanor and attire, takes him
to be a Thakur, i.e., high-caste, and treats him with deference.
When the truth is indirectly revealed, the deference turns
into rudeness. The chai-seller asks him to rinse his glass be-

fore returning it. In a powerful scene, the visitor buys the glass and smashes it on a stone platform.

The story *Sacrifice* sensitively depicts the emotions of a boy who had to help his father slaughter Piloo, a kid goat he loves. As an adult, the protagonist, a Dalit Ambedkarite, recoils from and confronts his father's prejudice against the protagonist's wife, who is from a caste even lower than theirs. A death at home and revelations of a romantic affair in father's youth bring hope for mutual understanding. In *Scream*, a Dalit schoolboy is raped by a Patel boy in the village. He escapes to Mumbai, does sundry jobs, tastes the intoxication of money, and ends up working as a gigolo, even as he pursues an MA and prepares for the civil services exam. Now wealthy, he visits his village, donning a fat gold chain and two gold rings. Coming face to face with the boy who sodomized him, he gloats: He 'couldn't even speak. He couldn't even smile. Next to me, he seemed like a beggar. I saw the defeat in his eyes.' Back in Mumbai, his life twists and turns with two of his female clients, through scenes evoking vintage film noir, until he meets a harrowing end.

Navaria is deeply political but rarely simplistic. There is truth in his fiction, the kind that's best revealed in story-telling. He has a keen eye for hypocrisies that lurk in Indian hearts, across caste and class locations. His Dalits are flesh-and-blood humans: sympathetic because flawed, not nobler than others, not above ordinary vanities and prejudices. They love and suffer and do what it takes to survive their often-hostile situations. Nor are his upper-caste characters black and white. *Unclaimed Terrain* offers sharp vignettes of the psyche of urban North India, from a vantage point that's both new and indispensable—and largely missing from the work of Indians who think and write in English.

* * *

I meet Navaria at a cafe near Lodi Gardens, Delhi, where we grab a corner table and slip into leisurely conversation. He is soft-spoken, thoughtful, and likes to talk. I relish his polished Hindi, including words that vanished from my active vocabulary during my years of living in the West. Navaria, 41, one of five siblings, grew up in Madangir, Delhi. His father was a gardener and daily wage laborer who later opened a small general store. Navaria's Hindi medium school was mostly attended by Scheduled Caste children. He did well in school, went to college and finished his MA at 22, got a job, returned to JNU at 28, emerged with a Ph.D. at 34, and has been an Assistant Professor for seven years.

How did he end up teaching Hindu religious scriptures (HRS)? His interest began early, with Amar Chitra Katha comics, and grew organically. Reading Ambedkar's analyses of HRS further fueled his interest and he began spending time in a library to learn more. How critical is he of the scriptures in the classroom? He follows an 'analytical approach', he says, orienting his mostly-*savarna* students to the basic content and social context of the *Vedas*, *Upanishads*, *Puranas*, *Gita*, *Ramayana*, etc. Does he not feel anger at all the caste biases in these scriptures? No, he says, because anger at such biases doesn't help in any concrete way. He keeps his Dalit activism separate from his teaching, though he does mention some alternative interpretations to his students. 'I have to choose my battles,' he says. Despite his restrained approach, fierce debates sometimes erupt in his class, often with students choosing sides along caste lines. Inevitably, someone raises the issue of reservations and tempers really flare up; he then has to manage and pacify both sides. He mentions with evident pride that his students, knowing full well that he is Dalit, nevertheless love him. Some even walk up to him on campus and touch his feet, which he dislikes and discourages.

Is the future of Hindi bleak, I ask, what with the urban middle-class *savarnas* chasing English *en masse*? He demurs and calls this an exaggerated fear. He believes this class's median English proficiency is still very poor but, he says, it's quite true that they are disinvesting in Hindi because it is no longer aligned with social power structures, higher class aspirations, or good jobs—'a 10th-pass who speaks English has better job prospects than an MA who doesn't'. However, another demographic shift is happening. In North India, a vast new generation is coming into literacy for the first time, and it is doing so in Hindi. This will probably go on for decades, and like new entrants everywhere, they will take Hindi language and literature to new places—the linguistic counterpart of the changes that the rise of the 'lower castes' has brought into politics. He is hopeful that these new entrants, and their more self-confident, middle-class descendants, will not only evolve Hindi but also other hybrid cultural forms that emphasize their own creative traditions, much like African-Americans have done. It's only later that I reflect on Navaria's optimism. Why wouldn't the future middle-classes continue to migrate to English like the current middle-classes? What else would have to change for them to abandon their sense of hierarchy, including among languages? (More on this in the essay, 'Decolonizing My Mind'.)

I ask Navaria if he has a religious identity. He isn't religious but calls himself Hindu, partly because his identity documents say so. He grew up with the usual Hindu pujas, gods, and festivals. He believes conversion to Buddhism, or any religion, is futile for Dalits. At the Jaipur Literature Festival 2013, he disagreed with Kancha Ilaiah, public intellectual and Ambedkarite, who advocates conversion to Buddhism. The problem, Navaria explains, is that in social terms, Dalit Hindus turn into Dalit Buddhists (or Dalit Christians, etc.) after conversion. Nor are the converts willing to give up caste-based reservations. What, then, is gained? Perhaps some self-respect, I suggest, via the radical personal act of quitting a religion that denies them equal humanity. Further, I argue, shouldn't the converts continue to get reservations for their historical disabilities that don't disappear overnight with conversion? Navaria seems unmoved by my reasoning. 'No religion in the Subcontinent is free of caste.' Freedom from caste discrimination, he asserts, will come not by changing one's religion, but through secular-democratic struggles. He would like to see Hinduism reformed from within, which he believes is entirely possible—already some regions and communities are further ahead on that path than others. Instead of converting to Buddhism, why not embrace the egalitarian values of the Buddha? Why do Dalits decry the casteism of the upper castes but keep practicing it among their own sub-communities without much self-reflection? This reminds me of my own observation about Indians in America, who resent any whiff of White racism but are themselves racist concerning African-Americans.

How bad is caste prejudice in Delhi today? As long as he remains anonymous, he says, all is good. He can get the services he needs; his wife, also a Dalit, can visit any beauty parlor and get a pedicure from an upper-caste woman. Fortunately, his last name, Navaria, doesn't reveal his caste, unlike, say, Valmiki. Anonymity enables self-respect. None can understand the benefits of *gumnamiyat*, or anonymity, as Dalits do, and therein lies the eternal pull of the city for them. However, excluding a few pockets, the old structures of caste still remain in Delhi. They come into play when one's identity is revealed. In rural areas, he says, discrimination is more open and often physical, whereas it's covert and psychological in the metros (Mumbai, he says, is more progressive than Delhi). In offices, business dealings, and rental housing, others are always trying to suss you out through your surname, color, customs, father's profession, watching visitors to your home. In the office, Dalits often face social exclusion, greater scrutiny than others, and get fewer chances for failure. When they do fail, it's more likely to be attributed to their caste. Some acts of harassment that professional Dalits he knows have faced include stealing of their keys, defacement of walls, assigning them the least desirable time slots or tasks, and even maliciously blocking the exit for one's parked vehicle.

In his fictional themes, he says, he tries to hew close to the larger experiences of Dalits. He tells me about two harsh incidents in these stories that come from his own life. His primary readership has been more Dalit than non-Dalit, but *Unclaimed Terrain* has brought him both national and global visibility. 'Power of English!' he notes. He likes the translation and is grateful to Laura Brueck, and to S. Anand at Navayana, his supportive publisher. Who are his key literary influences? Bhisham Sahni, Nirmal Verma, Uday Prakash, Kamleshwar, and Rajendra Yadav (a patron who has also given him opportunities with the literary magazine *HANS*). Also Chekhov and Pushkin. He is drawn to literary works that explore the inner lives of individuals: how they shape, and are shaped by, their social milieus.

A giant influence on him is Ambedkar, who, he says, has sadly been rendered beyond criticism and turned into a god by 'Ambedkarites'. This is contrary to the spirit of the man, a pragmatist who disliked idolatry and hero worship. He has great respect for Ambedkar as a thinker and emancipator of Dalits, but he doesn't take his words as the gospel truth. Approaching him rationally is the best way to honor and enhance his legacy. Were he alive today, Navaria speculates, wouldn't he have done some things differently? I ask if Ambedkar's rising tide in recent decades, mirroring the rise of the 'lower castes' in politics, means that he is also gaining in stature among the 'upper castes'. Not yet, he says. Ambedkar's estimation among the upper castes rarely goes beyond his negative association with reservations. In pockets where some appreciation exists, it is mostly done for show, for political correctness, to tell themselves they've changed. That said, genuine admiration for Ambedkar will likely arise among their later generations.

I ask what he's working on nowadays. Two novels and a couple of short stories, alongside teaching three courses each weekday, grading, and preparing for conferences. His early-teen kids also demand his time. He has persuaded them to give up TV, he says cheerfully. Instead, they watch two movies each week. They just saw the Hollywood movie *Oblivion*. The boy is in a Bruce Lee phase and enjoys playing the guitar; the girl paints. They understand that this is the time to explore their talents. He wants to write a novel focusing on the unique challenges of Dalit middle-class urban kids, something that's going to be increasingly relevant. But then he sighs: 'will I ever have time for that?'

Beyond Man and Woman
The Life of a Hijra[1]

Most Indians encounter hijras at some point in their lives. Hijras are the most visible subset of transgender people in South Asia, usually biological men who identify more closely as being female or feminine. They often appear in groups, and most Indians associate them with singing and dancing, flashy women's attire and makeup, aggressive begging styles, acts and manners that are like burlesques of femininity, a distinctive hand-clap, and the blessing of newlyweds and newborn males in exchange for gifts.

Most modern societies embrace a binary idea of gender. To the biologically salient binary division of humans into male/female, they attach binary social-behavioral norms. They presume two discrete 'masculine' and 'feminine' identities to which all biological males and females are expected to conform. These two gender identities are imbued with ideal, essential, and distinct social roles and traits. In other words,

---

1   A review of a memoir by A. Revathi. 2010. *The Truth About Me*. Penguin Books. This essay first appeared on 3 Quarks Daily on April 18, 2016.

the binary schema assumes a default alignment between sex, gender, and sexuality. In reality, however, gender identities and sexual orientations are not binary and exist on a spectrum, including for people who identify as transgender—an umbrella term for those whose inner sense of their gender conflicts with the presumed norms for their assigned sex (unlike for cisgender people). Transgender people often feel they're neither 'men' nor 'women'.

According to biologist Robert Sapolsky, 'Gender in humans is on a continuum, coming in scads of variants, where genes, organs, hormones, external appearance, and psychosexual identification can vary independently, and where many people have categories of gender identification going on in their heads (and brains) that bear no resemblance to yours'.[2] Many cultures have granted a distinct identity to various types of transgender people, including South Asian, Native American, Indonesian, Polynesian, and Omanese cultures.[3] A landmark Supreme Court ruling in 2014 legalized a *third gender* in India, including hijras and other transgender people.

Hijras in popular culture date back to ancient times. The fact that procreation underpins the social and familial order in all societies may partly explain why in some societies transgender (and homosexual) people have been seen as useless, perhaps even a threat. What likely helped the hijras survive is that since ancient times, they have been endowed with certain spiritual powers, including to confer blessings and curses, as with ascetics. Perhaps it also helped that even Gods and heroes manifest transgender traits in Hindu mythology: Shiva has an androgynous form, half male, half female; Arjuna disguised himself as a eunuch during the Pan-

---

2　Robert Sapolsky. 2016. 'Caitlyn Jenner and Our Cognitive Dissonance', *Nautilus*, April 14.
3　Jessie Guy-Ryan. 2016. 'In Indonesia, Non-Binary Gender is a Centuries-Old Idea', *Atlas Obscura*, June 18.

dava exile; the goddess Yellamma has the power to change one's sex; Krishna turned into a woman, Mohini, to marry and spend the last night with the warrior Aravan before his final battle; and so on. The hijras even have a patron goddess, Bahuchara Mata, whose temple in Gujarat is a pilgrimage site for both hijras and others.

In short, while Hindu mythology and scriptures see human equality as unnatural—and uphold a caste hierarchy—they largely accept transgenderism (and homosexuality) as natural, if not socially desirable. And while the Mughals held the status quo and even patronized the hijras—especially a minority among them, the eunuchs, as harem keepers—the British were utterly scandalized by the hijras.[4] They saw in the hijras 'a breach of public decency', 'the vilest and most polluted beings', and sought to curtail 'the abominable practices of the wretches.' They outlawed the hijra practice of castration, took away their legal right to collect alms from peasant households that had been granted to them by many Indian states, and classified them as a 'criminal tribe'. This also transformed the attitudes of Indians, strengthening the more reactionary strands in their midst. The net result was a long, multi-generational decline for the hijra community.

For the first time ever, the census in 2011 counted transgenders using an 'other' gender category. But due to the social stigma and shame attached to being trans, they're likely quite underreported, and overrepresented by trans men, the most public group among trans people. Estimates vary from half-a-million transgenders reported by the census[5] to over six million for just the ones who identify as trans men, a subset of transgenders.[6] Whatever their social status in earlier

4   Onni Gust. 2014. 'Hyperbole and horror: hijras and the British imperial state in India', *Notches*, January 6.
5   Rema Nagarajan. 2014. 'First count of third gender in census: 4.9 lakh', *The Times of India*, May 30.
6   UNDP India. 2010. 'Hijras/Transgender women in India: HIV, Human Rights, and Social Exclusion', December.

eras—including acceptance and even respect of sorts—hijras today are shrouded in an aura of fear, secrecy, rumor, prejudice, and 'magical powers'. They mostly slink in the shadows, in the margins of social life where discrimination and abuse rule the day. What are their lives like? What are their common struggles? What social structures and customs mark their communities?

A few ethnographies on hijras exist—the most significant being Serena Nanda's *Neither Man nor Woman*—but even fewer unmediated testimonies have come from the hijras themselves. One extraordinary example is *The Truth About Me: A Hijra Life Story* by A. Revathi (2010). Translated from Tamil by V. Geetha, a writer, social historian, and activist, this is apparently the first hijra autobiography to appear in English. (Translators remain unsung heroes even as they play a pivotal role in bridging cultural divides and raising mutual understanding.) In Revathi's own words, her memoir aims 'to introduce to the readers the lives of hijras, their distinct culture, and their dreams and desires.' What follows are a few glimpses from her life and of others in the hijra community.

From Doraisamy to Revathi

Revathi was born a boy, Doraisamy, the youngest of four brothers and a sister, in a working class family of Gounders, an intermediate caste, in a small village in Tamil Nadu. His father was a lorry driver who ran a milk delivery business. His mother worked in their fields and tended to their goats and cows. By the age of ten, Doraisamy 'would go to the village school along with the girls from the neighbourhood and return with them.' At school he played with the girls and 'longed to be like them'. Returning from school, he'd wear his sister's long skirt and blouse, a cloth braid, and walk like 'a shy bride, eyes to the ground'. His family would laugh, thinking he'd outgrow this silliness in due course.

At school Doraisamy was bullied and punished for behaving like a girl, for speaking and holding his 'body coyly like one'. He was caned for 'not being brave like a boy'. For not playing boys' games, the PT instructor would box his ears and yell, 'Are you a girl or what? Pull your trousers down, let me check.' This made him cry. She knew she behaved like a girl, writes Revathi, 'It felt natural for me to do so. I did not know how to be like a boy.' Doraisamy's confusion grew further: 'I felt drawn to the boys who did not tease me, and I imagined I was in love with them … Was this right or wrong?' The harassment grew so much that Doraisamy often skipped school (he'd eventually drop out in high school).

During a village festival, when other boys in the neighborhood dressed like bears, tigers, policemen, and gods, Doraisamy disguised himself as a female gypsy. But he was afraid of being discovered by his brothers, who had started beating him for his behavior, which they felt was shaming their family. He was thrilled when others complimented him for looking like a real woman. 'To the world, it appeared that I was dressing up and playing a woman, but inside, I felt I was a woman,' writes Revathi. 'As I re-emerged in my man's garb, I felt that I was in disguise, and that I had left my real self behind.' In the mid-eighties, around the time Doraisamy reached class 10, Revathi writes,

> I experienced a growing sense of irrepressible femaleness, which haunted me, day in and day out. A woman trapped in a man's body was how I thought of myself. But how could that be? Would the world accept me thus? I longed to be known as a woman and felt pain at being considered a man. I longed to be with men, but felt shamed by this feeling. I wondered why God had chosen to inflict this peculiar torture on me, and why He could not have created me wholly male or wholly female. Why am I a flawed being, I wondered often. I might as well die, I thought. I could not study, yet pretended to, and all the time I was obsessed, confused and anxious.

Still in high school, Doraisamy discovered a few young men who assembled every evening on a hill by the village. They addressed each other as women and sang and danced. From them he learned of 'people like us—who wore saris and had had an 'operation''. A famous 'amma' in a nearby town had had this 'operation'. One day he and his friends snuck away to meet amma, who received them warmly. They changed into saris, put on wigs and jewelry, and learned the social customs of amma's hijra community. Doraisamy was 14 or 15, tall and slim, with no facial hair. Someone complimented him that he looked like the movie actress Revathi. The name stuck and Doraisamy henceforth became Revathi, a hijra. 'I looked at myself in the mirror and felt a glow of pride. I did look like a woman. It was at that moment that I was convinced I was indeed one.'

A New Family and Escape to Delhi

But to become a 'real woman', Revathi learned at amma's, she needed an operation called *nirvaanam*, or castration, where her penis, scrotum, and testicles would be removed (only a minority of hijras undergo this operation). That was usually arranged by a guru. Hijras, she learned, almost always lived in a household resembling a commune, comprising *chelas* (disciples) and a guru. A guru was like a mother to 'daughters' like Revathi, and ceremonially adopted her *chelas*, provided shelter, clothing, food, security, and arranged their *nirvaanam*.[7] The *chelas* too had obligations, of working and giving all or part of their earnings to the guru, respecting her

---

7   In her ethnographic study on hijras, *Neither Man nor Woman*, Serena Nanda describes *nirvaanam* as 'a rite of passage, moving the *nirvan* (the one who is operated on) from the status of an ordinary, impotent male to that of a hijra. Through the operation, the former, impotent male person dies, and a new person, endowed with sacred power (*shakti*), is reborn', one, ironically, with the power to bless infertile women.

wishes and of other elders in her family, and caring for their guru in old age. It was like joining a family whose members were all trans women, who, unlike their own biological families, supported each other through thick and thin. In the face of their greater adversities, caste and religious distinctions tend to collapse in hijra communities.

At amma's place, Revathi found a guru she liked and ceremonially became her *chela*. Unfortunately, her guru had to go to Delhi for six months. In just a day, Revathi had become deeply attached to her affectionate guru and pleaded to be taken along but the guru advised her to go home until the guru could return from Delhi. Revathi spent a month with her guru's hijra family in a nearby town—dressing and living like a woman—before returning home.

Revathi's biological family was not amused by her disappearance. Her elder brother beat her mercilessly with a cricket bat, declared her unfit for school, and put her to work on the family business, cleaning lorries. She had to wear a lungi again and live like a man. 'I doubt if words quite capture the anguish I experienced at having to be a man,' she writes. 'I was like a worm, out in the sun, squirming and ready to die. I wanted to run away, but feared that if my brothers caught me, they would surely kill me.' With the help of a friend, she mustered enough courage to catch a train to Delhi to find her guru—she hadn't even *seen* a train until then—with a mere 80 rupees in her pocket. She was not yet 16. (Running away from insensitive, shame-ridden families is a remarkably common story among hijras.)

> With some luck, she found her guru in Delhi and joined her community, starting at the bottom of the hierarchy, doing chores like washing clothes and cleaning spittoons. She learned the social customs of her new community and even some Hindi. She pierced her ears and nose and was soon inducted into begging—about the only livelihood open to hijras besides prostitution and dancing at ceremonies. Many shopkeepers considered an early morning visit by a hijra aus-

picious and gave them alms. Revathi's guru told her to not flirt with men and risk losing their goodwill. Using a friend's address, Revathi wrote a letter home saying she was safe. One day she ran into a lorry driver from her village, who likely went back and told her family about her ways. Some days later a telegram arrived: her mother was seriously ill. Revathi decided to rush home, this time dressed in a sari and traveling in the ladies' coach, though she changed into a man's dress before going home.

The telegram was a trap. The moment she got home, her middle brother attacked her with a cricket bat. 'Let's see you wear a sari again, or dance, you mother-fucking *pottai* [hijra]!' Revathi recalls, 'He beat me hard mindlessly, yelling that he wanted to kill me … I felt my hands swell. I was beaten on my legs, on my back, and finally my brother brought the bat down heavily on my head … there was blood all over, flowing, warm.' She even heard her mother say, 'That's right. Beat him and break his bones. Only then will he stay at home and not run away.' Her brother stopped only 'when he was tired and his arms ached'. She had greatly shamed her family. 'How can someone from a good family do that?' her mother asked. 'Do you know who we are and what caste we belong to?'

The next day they took her to a temple to shave off her long hair and implore the goddess to banish 'that seducing female demon who even now has a hold on him.' Her hair, which hijras are obliged to grow long, was now so central to her identity that its shaving caused her more emotional pain than her brother's beating (in rare cases, if a hijra severely flouts the rules of her commune, her guru may order her hair cut to publicly shame her). In ensuing days, nosey neighbors would stop by and offer free advice: why not rub holy ash over her body to 'cure her'? Soon she was forced to wear a man's dress and work again, 'loading and unloading milk cans as before'. Some workers at the cooperative would tease and pinch her chest and caress her bum. Every day was an ordeal. She wanted her hair to grow before returning to Delhi, 'for one with a shaven head has no standing amongst [hijras].' Three months later she escaped to Delhi again. For her safety, her guru decided to send her to Mumbai, to join another house of hijras.

The Mumbai Blues

Mumbai was a whole new world of discovery, joy, and suffering for Revathi. Hijras in Mumbai, too, lived in ghettos and were organized in seven clans, or houses, each with a *naik* at the helm. Every guru-*chela* relationship had to be approved by a *jamaat*, or council, comprising the *naiks* of all seven houses. Gurus in each house had exclusive rights to work in certain territories—whether begging, prostitution, or ceremonial dancing—and didn't take kindly to trespassing from members of other houses, or by independent hijras. Revathi chose a new guru and was consecrated. Six months later, her guru arranged for her *nirvaanam*. Rather than the painful and illegal traditional method—which apparently raises a hijra's esteem in her community—it was to be done under anesthesia by a medical doctor. Revathi was overjoyed and set off for a small-town hospital in Tamil Nadu that performed this operation. Her surgery was successful but her aftercare was poor, causing her great physical suffering that lasted many weeks.

Forty days later, her house hosted a big ceremony for her—a rite of passage similar to certain puberty rites done for girls after their first menses—with all the trappings of puja, incense, flowers, gifts, chanting before the goddess, *haldi-mehndi* rituals, feet-touching of elders, sermons, and more. In her own eyes, Revathi had now 'truly become' a woman. (Not all hijras consider castration as central to their gender identity as does Revathi. Other hijras, such as rights activist Laxmi Narayan Tripathi, hold contrary views, that what makes one a hijra is only the soul—inner feelings—not surgical or hormonal alterations.[8])

Revathi continued to earn her living by begging in the market. But she was 20 and troubled by sexual desire. 'It seemed as natural as hunger, this hankering of the flesh.' She felt drawn to some of the men she met. 'Till I had my *nirvaanam*,' she writes, 'I had not acknowledged my sexual feelings … I had learnt to suppress desire and had told myself that it was important for me to become a woman first.' As is common among hijras, Revathi even longed to 'marry and settle down' with a husband—like the presumed trajectory of all good Indian women—but she wondered 'who would want to marry a hijra?' The few such marriages she knew of had mostly ended badly, with much physical and mental abuse for the hijras. It struck her then that perhaps she could fulfill her sexual urges if she joined 'a house for sex work.' One day she walked out of her guru's house and found a guru in another house whose *chelas* did sex work. 'I became a *chela* to my new guru because of my desire for sexual happiness, in order to fulfill my sexual longings.'

Her heart sank when she discovered that she'd have to live in, and do sex work from, a couple of decrepit shanties by a railway track, which rattled whenever a train passed. Her customers turned out to be 'mostly drunks and men who could not afford to spend more than fifty rupees.' She didn't like most of them but couldn't turn anyone away. Her guru sat outside, collected the money, and tried to shield her from the rougher sorts as best as she could. Rather than finding sexual happiness, Revathi found herself 'having to treat sexual experiences as work'. But in other ways, she felt freer and more valued by her new family. 'Though we lived poor-

8   Shanoor Seervai interviews Laxmi Narayan Tripathi. 2015. 'India's Third Gender', *Guernica*, March 16. Also see Vaishali Raode. 2013. 'Lakshmi's Story', *Words Without Borders*. Translation © 2013 by R Raj Rao and P G Joshi.

ly and in a hut, I was indulged by all, and was the darling of the household, chiefly because I was fair and pretty and spoke nicely.' It helped that she also fetched the highest price among the lot.

But some rowdies often came to terrorize and steal money from them. One night, a large rowdy chased away her guru, pulled out a knife, and raped Revathi. She'd never had anal sex before. 'He spat abuse at me and forced me into the act … I was hurting all over, and yet had to give in and do as he told me. The skin down there felt abraded and I was bleeding.' He stole her purse too. It had been only two months since she started sex work. 'I was beginning to discover the horror and violence of this choice. I cried and confessed that I wanted to go home to my parents, that I would fall at their feet and beg to be taken back.' Within a few days, she was on a train to see her parents.

For the first time, Revathi entered her home in a sari. Her mother began wailing and her brother flared up again. This time Revathi was more assertive, 'Look! I've had an operation and I'm a woman now. From now on, I'll live as I wish…. If you dare hit me, I'll go to the police.' She lifted her sari and showed them. This only raised her mother's sense of family shame, and she promptly fainted. When the brother insisted that she change into a man's clothes, Revathi refused firmly. Before the matter escalated into violence, her father came home. He seemed calmer and invoked fate. 'It seems this is his destiny. Who can change what has been ordained? ... Let him be and eat of our food.' Tempers cooled. She was told to not roam around the village or attend public events. She thought it 'remarkable that they had accepted me wearing a sari and being a woman.'

People in the village were curious about her and stared at her. Some women were even eager to talk to her and wondered if she had real breasts (she had started taking hormones). 'For such people, I was a thing to be looked and

laughed at, an oddity, a comic figure.' Her family began to accept her for who she had become but her mother worried in-
cessantly about her future. Revathi visited the local Mariam-
man temple and thanked the goddess for helping her realize
her wish, and for uniting her with her family. Three months
later, she was back in Mumbai.

Once again, to earn a living she began sex work but in
a different house on a busy street known for its prostitutes,
both hijras and women. Revathi had to solicit customers on
the street. She vividly describes a Hobbesian world unlike
any she'd seen before, where hijras fought over clients and
were cheated by their mistress, where many hijras had con-
tracted STD and even died, where clients often 'paid them a
mere fifteen or fifty rupees' and 'used them as they wished,
brutally, and left them with bite marks on their bodies, as if
they had been bitten and abandoned by mad dogs'. She describes some hijras who were 'carried away by the police for
no fault of their own, who were beaten with whips and lathis
and stamped upon by police boots, had electric current run
through their bodies, who could only leave after paying the
police a hefty bribe.' She got introduced to alcohol and soon
began drinking every day. Her pleasant memories from this
phase of life in the early 1990s are few, and include memories
of rain, watching Tamil films, and visits to her two 'favour-
ite shrines every week—to the Haji Ali dargah on Thursdays
and the Mahalakshmi temple on Fridays.' She eventually
fought with the mistress of the house and quit.

She went back to her parents and spent the next year
with them. The villagers and the family began accepting her
more, and she felt grateful for it. After more horrid family
drama, she even got a share of the property her parents had
sold, and so now had about one lakh rupees. She bought a
scooter and rented a home to live by herself in the village.
Briefly, she even had a half-fling with a man, which severely
tested her family's tolerance and provoked the wrath of her

brothers. She lamented, 'If society scorns us, then we turn to our families … But if family scorns us, who do we turn to? Is this why people like me do not stay in touch with their families?' She had heard of a *hamam*, or bath house run by hijras in Bangalore, and she decided to pack her bags and go there.

Moving to Bangalore

She was warmly received in Bangalore. Some hijras worked in the *hamam* for low wages, others, as usual, begged or did sex work. Here too, life was harsh. People frequently threw stones at their door at night. 'When I went to buy groceries and vegetables in the vegetable market, people sometimes threw rotten tomatoes at me.' She became a *chela* to a new guru. She had seen that 'In this world, it is enough that one has money. Respect and regard follow.' To get money, she decided to take up sex work again, soliciting customers on the street. This came with the usual troubles: rude and violent clients, harassment by rowdies, police beatings, bribes. One time a policeman locked her up in a cell, forced her to strip, and stuck a *lathi* into her anus. 'Sometimes, I wondered if I should continue to do sex work at all. But what else was I to do? I had no choice but to suffer it.' She even sent money home to help her father rebuild their house. Respite from sex work came whenever she got hired to dance at weddings and temple festivals. She went home often, but her family's shame and people's reactions to her meant that she couldn't bear to stay for long. 'I think this is why God makes sure that people like me seek out others of my own kind.'

One day she was approached by three young city-bred, college educated hijras, who didn't live in traditional hijra communities, and even had their *nirvaanam* done on their own. They pleaded with her to become their guru. Revathi agreed, and decided to forge a more open and nurturing guru-*chela* relationship than what she came to see as the norm:

overly hierarchical and often economically exploitative, a world full of 'rules and tenets' with 'all its particular sorrows and joys.' They introduced her to Sangama, an organization that fought for the rights of sexual minorities. Sangama was looking to hire a transgender person, and Revathi made a bid for it. She joined Sangama as an office assistant for a meagre salary, quit sex work, and moved into her own place—rented to her on the condition that no hijra would visit her. At least, she writes, her landlord thought of her as a woman and didn't discriminate against her. The year was 1999.

She soon became involved with activism and social work at Sangama, participating in events 'about hijra culture, hijra ways of living, and the violence and discrimination that we faced.... As a spokesperson for hijra rights, I also gave interviews to newspapers and spoke at public meetings.' At first she didn't talk about her sex work out of fear and shame. But this changed as she realized that the fault lay not with her but with 'the way the world perceived me and refused to accept me, the manner in which it snatched away my rights and made it difficult for me to earn a living except through begging and sex work.' She spoke in colleges on sexual identity and even approached her own community to educate them about their rights. But, she adds, 'fear and suspicion lurked large among hijras. It was only when they faced violence because they were hijras and Sangama helped them get out of the false cases foisted on them, that they began to come to us.' She writes:

> Just as how dalits have come to oppose the violence inflicted on them, why cannot we hijras get together and fight for our rights? Do we not have the right to change our sex? Aren't we human too, born of mothers, as others are? We have not descended from the sky, have we? We have rights, just like the others. We are citizens of this nation. Don't we want all those rights that are granted to other citizens: the right to have a ration card, to hold property, to have a passport, the right to work, to marry, adopt or raise a child?

In the course of her work and travels at Sangama, Revathi and a senior colleague, a bisexual man, grew close and she started falling in love with him. He reciprocated too, and they soon began living together in an apartment, sharing their household expenses. Revathi did all the house work, laundry, and cooking. She felt happy, for she was 'leading a normal family life, much like other women' (curiously, as seems common with other trans women, her idea of being 'womanly' harks back to a 'traditional' ideal that many modern cisgender women in urban India may find regressive). She was thrilled when the man proposed to her. Since he didn't believe in priests, circling the fire, or the *thali* ('auspicious thread'), the marriage was simple: an exchange of garlands at a temple next to the *hamam*, with her hijra family and four of his friends. Marital life began well but soon cracks developed. He didn't tell his parents about their marriage, even when they visited. He grew less romantic, more aloof, and immersed himself into work. He rebuffed her overtures of love. 'Living by his whims and desires, I felt my own retreat till there was nothing left,' she wrote. Perhaps class divides between them played a role too. Their marriage ended a year later, leaving her utterly heartbroken.

'But my work turned out to be the healing balm that I needed,' she writes. She began collecting testimonies from other hijras to write her first book, *Unarvum Uruvamum*. Many of them 'sobbed and screamed when they recounted stories of their mothers, lovers, husbands … My difficulties were nothing compared to some of the things I heard.' Then came two shocks in quick succession: one of her *chelas* committed suicide, and some rowdies stabbed and killed Revathi's guru at the *hamam*. This unsettled her greatly. After the mourning period, she left her activist work, went home, and stayed for many months to care for her ailing mother. She looked for a job at home but no one would hire a hijra.

Back in Bangalore and finding herself pushed back into poverty, she briefly turned to sex work again (social activism, she writes, didn't pay enough), which hurt her a lot. Now in her mid-30s, clients called her 'aunty' and chose younger hijras. 'Unable to make a living, I wondered if I should end my life,' she writes. Her activism had changed her too much and she could no longer flourish in the hijra community. At the end of this memoir, we find Revathi returning to work at Sangama again.

Postscript

Revathi's story is almost too painful to read. It portrays, vividly and honestly, the vulnerability of a young person struggling to reconcile the gap between her inner sense of gender and society's presumed norms for her. She faces hurdles and indignities at every step. What she confronts may be worse than most social oppressions because even her own family turns hostile against her, which must count among the most intimate of traumas and betrayals. Her testimony, highly representative of the hijra experience, holds a mirror to our social world, which dehumanizes and is frequently violent towards those who do not fit the mould. It also exposes some more limits of the 'famed Indian tolerance'.

The Indian Supreme Court ruled in 2014 that 'it is the right of every human being to choose their gender' and legalized a *third gender*, granting hijras and other transgender people the same legal rights as others. Application forms for many government IDs, such as the passport, voter identity card, and Aadhaar card, no longer force them to choose 'male' or 'female' and include a 'transgender' option. The court's ruling also paved the way, via the *Rights of Transgender Persons Bill* of 2015, for their inclusion under Other Backward Classes (unless they're SC/ST), reservations in public-sector jobs and college admissions, and tougher prosecution of certain crimes against them. For transgender rights activists in India, this was the culmination of a long struggle.

But while changing the laws and providing reservations are obvious first steps, changing minds is the ultimate and harder endgame. Revathi's memoir reveals the distance yet to be traveled on that front. Not many want to provide employment, housing, education, or healthcare to the hijras. Sexual prurience and degrading myths surround them. For instance, many Indians believe that they abduct and forcibly castrate children, that they have bizarre nighttime funeral rites, etc. However, even their sporadic public displays, or threats thereof, of their (post-*nirvaanam*) sexual anatomy are survival tactics—meant to extract money from a discriminatory society by pushing its norms of sexual decency. The reality is that the hijras have one of the worst socioeconomic indicators across all social groups. The majority are still illiterate (they drop out of school or don't regularly attend due to harassment and shame) and aren't even aware of their rights.[9] That said, a handful of hijras of the new generation are breaking barriers and gaining social mobility through education and activism.[10]

But Revathi represents only one kind of transgenders in India: trans women. A lot more stories of hijras and of other transgender people—of those who are born female but identify as male (trans men), who consider themselves agender, who variously identify with both genders, and who inhabit

---

9   For instance, the literacy level in the hijra community is just 46% versus 74% in the general population. Source: Rema Nagarajan. 2014. 'First count of third gender in census: 4.9 lakh', *The Times of India*, May 30.

10 Read the perspective of another hijra and rights activist, Laxmi Narayan Tripathi, interviewed by Shanoor Seervai. 2015. 'India's Third Gender', *Guernica*, March 16. Also see article by Shikha Kumar, Nidhi Choksi and Neeta Chhatwani. 2016. 'Banker, model, mayor: Transgenders forge a new identity in India', *Hindustan Times*, April 27.

yet other permutations of gender identity—are yet to be written. What will keep emerging from such testimonies is that the 'sickness' or 'defect' is not in their authors, but in those who continue to deny them an equal humanity.

SECTION 2
The Architecture of Inequality

The Blight of Hindustan[1]

An egalitarian ethos has not been a prominent feature of Indian civilization for at least a thousand years, when Buddhism began losing ground in South Asia. The dominant Hindu sensibility has long held that all men are created unequal, constituting not a single but separate moral communities, and possess varying natural rights and duties. The anthropologist Louis Dumont saw hierarchy as so central to Indian lives, whether in the family, the workplace, or the community, that he titled his 1966 treatise on Indian society, *Homo Hierarchicus*.[2] Indeed, a host of hierarchical relationships—framed by traditional norms of deference, authority, and obligation—shape most Indians throughout their lives. In the Indian social realm, the primary institution of hierarchy is caste, or *jati*, of which thousands exist today. But where does caste, a blight of modern India, come from?

---

1 An earlier version of this essay appeared on 3 Quarks Daily on March 1, 2010.
2 Louis Dumont. 1998 (original 1966). *Homo Hierarchicus: The Caste System and Its Implications*. Oxford India Paperbacks.

The Origins of Caste

How the institution of caste took root and spread is still a hotly debated question among scholars, but its story begins c. 1500 BCE with the arrival of the Indo-Aryans into what is now Pakistan. Data from disciplines like linguistics, philology, and archaeology strongly suggests that these bands of nomadic pastoralists came from further west. Upon arrival, they encountered long settled rural communities, which were perhaps divided into subgroups based on occupation, much like guilds—they were not hierarchical, hereditary, or endogamous. The Indo-Aryans, whose culture became dominant, introduced into the region their social pyramid with three classes, or *varnas* ('color'): the Brahmins (priests and teachers), the Kshatriyas (warriors and rulers), and the Vaishyas (traders and merchants). They added a fourth *varna* after their arrival: the Shudras (laborers and artisans). All four divisions appear in the earliest known Indo-Aryan text, the *Rig Veda* (though not the word '*varna*'), and were no doubt a feature of the emerging Vedic society. 'According to the *Mahabharata*, the 'colors' associated with the four [*varnas*] were white, red, yellow and black; they sound more like symbolic shades meted out by those category-conscious Brahminical minds than skin pigments.'[3]

As the settled indigenous communities became part of the early Vedic society, they also adopted its principle of hierarchy—interwoven as it was with its cosmology, gods, and rituals—turning their own occupational subgroups into castes, or *jatis*. The main organizing principle of this hierarchy, proposed Dumont, had to do with ritual 'purity' and 'pollution' that members of each occupational subgroup were assigned at birth. The highest 'purity' points went to those associated with religious, intellectual, and administrative pursuits, the lowest to workers associated with dead bodies, human waste,

---

3   John Keay. 2000. *India: A History*. Atlantic Monthly Press, p. 54.

tanneries, butchery, street cleaning, and such—most of these were in fact deemed too low to be part of the *varna* system at all, i.e., they were considered outcastes. Stated differently, 'purity' became a means of codifying social power relations using Brahminical 'knowledge'.

As this new social order spread in the first millennium BCE, it encountered more settled peoples as well as forest dwelling clans. Whether by force, persuasion, or mutual advantage, more groups were brought into its fold. They too found themselves plugged into its hierarchy, perhaps loosely at first, and gradually gave up their more egalitarian ways. In doing so, they used the same principle of relative 'purity' to make *jati* and *varna* decisions for various units within their own societies, and by extension, to divide power and resources.[4] To sweeten the deal, the Vedic social order became flexible enough to absorb indigenous gods into its ever-growing pantheon—including perhaps even gods like Shiva and Krishna—giving rise to a syncretic religious culture. In some cases, a whole endogamous tribe could become one *jati*, often regarded as outcastes. *The Laws of Manu*, written about 2,000 years ago, mentions many such communities: the Medas, Andhras, Chunchus, and Madgus who live off 'the slaughter of wild animals', the Pukkasas by 'catching and killing [animals] in holes', etc. In time, new dietary regimes would get associated with each new *jati*. For instance, beef and alcohol would become taboo for those accorded a higher caste.

Many modern thinkers, including Tagore, have argued that while far from perfect, this was back then a practical way of bringing together highly diverse peoples, through which 'men of different colors and creeds, different physical features and mental attitudes settled together side by

---

4   Romila Thapar. 2002. *The Penguin History of Early India*, pp. 62-68.

side.'[5] In *The Discovery of India*, Nehru, struck a stronger
note of apologia: 'Thus at a time when it was customary for
the conquerors to exterminate or enslave the conquered
races, caste enabled a more peaceful solution which fitted in
with the growing specialization of functions.'[6] He saw caste
as 'necessary and desirable in its early forms, and meant to
develop individuality and freedom'. Such thinkers argued
that by assigning religious, political, and economic power
to three different classes—the Brahmins, the Kshatriyas, and
the Vaishyas—the system prevented their concentration in
a single dominant racial or ethnic group, thereby creating a
basis for cooperation and avoiding far greater friction, open
slavery, and even genocidal wars. Historian John Keay, while
calling this new social order 'systematised oppression', added
that 'it should also be seen as an ingenious schema for har-
nessing the loyalties of a more numerous and possibly more
skilled indigenous population.' In recent decades, many Hindu nationalists, keen to boost Hindu self-respect and pride,
have whitewashed their social history and invented a rosier
one. The four *varnas*, they claim, were wholly meritocratic

---

5   Rabindranath Tagore, *Selected Essays*. Rupa. From the essay titled
    'Race Conflict', p. 343.
6   Jawaharlal Nehru. 1946. *Discovery of India*, p. 85. Nehru's social af-
    finities and romanticization of Brahmins are also visible in this ex-
    tract from his autobiography, *Toward Freedom* (1936): 'Today [our
    old culture] is fighting silently and desperately against a new and
    all-powerful opponent, the *bania* civilization of the capitalist West.
    It will succumb to this newcomer, for the West brings science, and
    science brings food for the hungry millions. But the West also
    brings an antidote to the evils of this cut-throat civilization – *the
    principles of socialism, of co-operation, and service to the community
    for the common good. This is not so unlike the old Brahman ideal
    of service*, but it means the brahmanization (not in the religious
    sense, of course) of all classes and groups and the abolition of class
    distinctions. It may be that when India puts on her new garment, as
    she must, for the old is torn and tattered, she will have it cut in this
    fashion, so as to make it conform both to present conditions and
    her old thought.' (Italics mine.)

in ancient times, based on personal choice, aptitude, and conduct—i.e., one's varna depended on individual qualities, not on the accident of birth in a household. Some even go as far as saying that it was the invading Muslims and the British who perverted the *varna* system into the caste system that's with us today.

Modern genomic research has shown that endogamy became widespread about seventy generations ago, at least 'among upper castes and Indo-European speakers', replacing the earlier pattern of widespread admixing of extant populations.[7] Over time the institution of caste grew rigid and restrictive, becoming, as BR Ambedkar said, not a division of labor but a division of laborers. Any mixing of castes via intermarriage came to be frowned upon and often harshly punished. Social mobility got severely curtailed and the upper castes conveniently linked one's place in the hierarchy to karma and destiny; even their epics and mythologies helped perpetuate this social order (though it would be simplistic to read them as doing nothing more, or to not contain contradictory views). The *Ramayana* contains strong expressions of hierarchy, the *Bhagavad Gita* extols the sanctity of caste, and *The Laws of Manu* attempts to codify its operation, declaring a crime against a Brahmin much worse than one committed against a 'low-caste' person.

The caste system eventually took on beliefs and social practices that have trampled on some of the most basic tenets of human dignity and inflicted untold misery, humiliation, and injustice on too many for too long. Among its worst victims are the Dalits ('the oppressed')—formerly 'untouchables'—numbering one out of six Indians. Injury and prejudice are in fact so integral to the functioning of the caste

---

7   Analabha Basua, Neeta Sarkar-Roya, and Partha P. Majumder. 2015. 'Genomic reconstruction of the history of extant populations of India reveals five distinct ancestral components and a complex structure', *PNAS*, December 17.

system—doesn't the extreme 'purity' of one caste require the extreme 'impurity' of another, and all that this entails?— that it's hard to imagine today what a plausible defense of it by an insider or a cultural pluralist might look like.

How old is untouchability? Historians report a few instances of it in pre-Gupta times, some as early as 400 BCE when Panini mentions it. From around the same time, one of the Jataka Tales—which contain stories about the Buddha's past lives—mentions the *Chandala*, whose mere sight sully a merchant's daughters and a priest. The *Laws of Manu* also advises that the impure *Chandala* must live outside the village and must not look at Brahmins when the latter are eating. If a Brahmin happens to touch a *Chandala*, he must bathe to regain purity. Historian Romila Thapar therefore dates the appearance of untouchability to over 2,000 years ago.[8] Ambedkar likely got it wrong when he stated that 'Untouchability was born some time about 400 A.D.'[9] Untouchability however became a *socially significant* phenomenon only in the early medieval period,[10] not long after Buddhism had peaked in the Subcontinent in mid-first millennium CE. It was well established when the Persian traveler Al-Beruni visited India in early 11th century, and saw many groups of 'degraded outcastes' who lived outside upper-caste villages and were 'occupied with dirty work'.

By then, this 'dirty work'—the cleaning of other people's shit by hand, the disposing and skinning of dead animals, etc.—was entirely hereditary, aided by the deep internali-

---

8 Seema Chishti. 2016. 'Appearance of untouchability can be dated to over 2,000 years ago: Romila Thapar', *Indian Express*, New Delhi, April 15.

9 In *The Untouchables: Who Were They and Why They Became Untouchables*, BR Ambedkar analyzed various historical and religious texts and concluded: 'We can, therefore, say with some confidence that Untouchability was born some time about 400 A.D.'

10 RS Sharma. 2010. *Rethinking India's Past*. Oxford India Paperbacks, p. 7.

zation of one's own 'natural' place in the hierarchy, and enforced by the threat of verbal, physical, economic, and other violence. By late medieval times, bonded labor and sexual exploitation of the outcastes was common too. In some regions, the feudal landlord was even entitled to spend the first night with the newlywed wives of the 'untouchable' men in his employ, as in the infamous system of *dola*.[11]

The caste system also worsened the plight of other women beyond the inequities inherent in all patriarchies. The desire to preserve upper-caste 'purity' created anxieties over miscegeny (intercaste breeding), including extra horror and penalties for hypogamy, where an upper-caste woman marries a lower-caste man. This demanded more stringent control over female sexuality, which then encouraged the custom of female child marriage. 'Women's cooperation in the system', writes historian Uma Chakravarti, 'was secured by various means: ideology, economic dependency on the male head of the family, class privileges and veneration bestowed upon conforming and dependent women of the upper classes, and, finally, the use of force when required.'[12]

The Anatomy of Caste

Castes are not a feature of Hindu society alone. A de facto caste hierarchy also exists among the Christians, Muslims, and Sikhs of India—even as people converted away from Hinduism, they couldn't abandon the caste mindset. Moreover, while caste is today most visibly associated with India, forms of it have either existed or still exist elsewhere, including in Japan (including an outcaste group, the Burakumin),

11 Indu Bharti. 1990. 'Dalits Gain New Izzat', *Economic and Political Weekly*, Vol. 25, Issue No. 18-19, May 5.
12 Uma Chakravarti. 2006. *Beyond the Kings and Brahmanas of 'Ancient' India*. Tulika Books. From the chapter titled 'Conceptualizing Brahminical Patriarchy in Early India', p. 140.

Korea, Europe, Hawaii, Arabia, and Africa, some with strikingly parallel notions of 'purity' and 'pollution'. Dumont however pointed out that despite the presence of caste-like forms in these societies, they lacked a proper caste system, which ensures that no member of the society is beyond its classification, as in the Indian Subcontinent. And while it's true that inherited inequalities are a part of the human story everywhere, many inequalities of caste in South Asia seem distinct in both scale and conception. Furthermore, 'the impassable trenches of the caste system', writes British historian Perry Anderson, created 'truly deep impediments to collective action, even within language communities, let alone across them'. According to Anderson,

> Hereditary, hierarchical, occupational, striated through and through with phobias and taboos, Hindu social organisation fissured the population into some five thousand jatis, few with any uniform status or definition across the country. No other system of inequality, dividing not simply, as in most cases, noble from commoner, rich from poor, trader from farmer, learned from unlettered, but the clean from the unclean, the seeable from the unseeable, the wretched from the abject, the abject from the subhuman, has ever been so extreme, and so hard-wired with religious force into human expectation.[13]

Prejudice invariably feeds upon culturally constructed ideas of human difference, including of caste, race, gender, beauty, reason, civilization, and so on. In *The Indians*, Sudhir and Katharina Kakar point out that psychological training to associate 'purity' with clean and 'pollution' with dirty begins early on in Indian households:

> For the upper-caste child, a dalit is a member of a group that is permanently and irrevocably dirty. The child's knowledge is not anthropological or religious-textual but a *knowledge-feeling* that is pre-verbal and has, so to speak, entered the

---

13 Perry Anderson. 2012. *The Indian Ideology*. Three Essays Collective, pp. 111-112.

child's very bones. Many a time while growing up, the child
has sensed the sudden kinesthetic tension in the body of his
mother, father, aunt, uncle, when a dalit has come too near.
He has registered their expressions of disgust, unconsciously
mimicking them in his own face and body at any threatened
contact with an untouchable. Given the child's propensity to
place himself at the center of all experience, he effortlessly
links the family's disapproval and revulsion toward the untouchable to those times when he has been an untouchable
himself, that is, the times ... above all, when he has been filth-
ily, gloriously dirty.[14]

Regarding others as impure and dirty, and therefore subhuman, is also commonplace outside the context of caste. It
is a universal trick designed to withhold empathy from and
to dominate antagonistic groups, especially during ethnic
conflicts. As the Kakars write,

'Dirty nigger' and 'dirty Jew' are well-known epithets in the
United States. The Chinese regard Tibetans as unwashed and
perpetually stinking of yak butter, while Jewish children in
Israel are brought up to regard Arabs as dirty. In the Rwan-
dan radio broadcasts inciting the Hutus to massacre the Tut-
sis, the latter were consistently called rats and cockroaches,
creatures associated with dirt and underground sewers, ver-
min that needed to be exterminated. [p. 32]

Many historians have criticized Dumont's pioneering
analysis of caste in India, accusing him of overstating the
power of the Brahmins and of the 'purity' principle in shaping caste. They claim that norms, inter-caste relations, and
social practices were more fluid and diverse than Dumont's
schema suggests, with the Brahmin not the only reference
point (royalty could be more powerful, for instance, but this
led scholar Gail Omvedt to raise an important question: did
the secular power tussles between the royals and the Brahmins resist the ideological frame of Brahmanism itself? If

14 Sudhir Kakar, Katharina Kakar. 2007. *The Indians: Portrait of a
People*. Penguin Books India, pp. 31-32.

not, the point about royal power may be a red herring[15]). Today's caste system, these historians argue, was heavily shaped
by the social, administrative, and economic changes that
began in early colonial times—until then, a lot of Indians
'were still comparatively untouched by the norms of *jati* and
varna as we now understand them.'[16] Census classifications
and differential state policies also hardened caste identities
in modern times. In *Castes of Mind*, Nicholas B. Dirks accused Dumont of treating 'the political and economic aspects of caste as relatively secondary and isolated.' Dirks argued that from the late 19th century, British ethnography and
resulting knowledge became a potent evolutionary force on
caste—via hierarchical ranking of castes using 'racial-types'
and anthropometry as factors among others, criminalization
of entire caste groups, instituting caste-based regiments and
the concept of 'martial races' in the army, 'implementation
of legal codes that made the provisions of law applicable on
caste lines,' and more. According to Dirks, 'Caste emerged,
stronger than ever, from the legacy of Orientalist forms of
knowledge.'[17]

A complementary view, articulated by scholar-activist
Anand Teltumbde, is that British judicial and administrative
practices, seemingly based on equality before the law, 'under-
mined the importance of caste.' The institutions of the British
Raj, which seeded modernity in India, created 'an enabling
environment' for the 'emerging anticaste ethos', 'opened opportunities for economic betterment, particularly for the
untouchables, and allowed both untouchables and shudras

15 Gail Omvedt. 2008. *Seeking Begumpura: The Social Vision of Anti-
    caste Intellectuals*. Navayana, pp. 142-146.
16 Susan Bayly. 1999. *Caste, Society and Politics in India: from the Eigh-
    teenth Century to the Modern Age*. Cambridge University Press, p.
    25.
17 Nicholas B. Dirks. 2001. *Castes of Mind*. Permanent Black, pp. 58,
    45, 41.

access to modern education.'[18] It was only later, Teltumbde holds, that certain dubious 'modernist policies' of the Indian State and a harsher capitalism, while erasing 'certain caste divisions', gave rise to new political and economic contestations—especially between a newly ascendant shudra class of peasant landowners and landless Dalits in rural India.[19] This 'reinforced caste and accentuated its viciousness as never before.' For both Dirks and Teltumbde, then, caste has been far more malleable, dynamic, and responsive to mundane (non-religious) causes than in Dumont's portrait.

Other critics who see Dumont's view of caste as monolithic argue that to a certain extent, social mobility has existed all along—a lower-caste group could change its way of life and move up within a generation or two, a process that has been called 'Sanskritization'. The sociologist MN Srinivas has defined it as a process through which 'a *low or middle* Hindu caste, or tribal or other group, changes its customs, ritual ideology, and way of life in the direction of a high and frequently *twice-born* caste.'[20] It might invent an 'Aryanized' version of its past and a link with an old royal dynasty. In late 19th century, for instance, the Yadavs of north India began claiming descent from Krishna himself. Within a generation or two, a caste could 'rise to a higher position in the hierarchy by adopting vegetarianism and teetotalism, and by

18 Anand Teltumbde. 2010. *The Persistence of Caste*. Zed Books, pp. 20-22, 31, 47-48, 50, 151, 185.
19 At least on U.P., historian Christophe Jaffrelot has a similar view: 'The OBCs and Dalits class interests are clearly antagonistic in Uttar Pradesh since the latter are often landless laborers or cultivators with very small plots who work for the former' and conflicts have become 'more frequent since the Dalits and the OBCs grew more assertive following the 1993 elections. These bones of contention partly explain the increasing number of atrocities against the Dalits.' Christophe Jaffrelot. 2011. *Religion, Caste and Politics in India*. Hurst & Company, p. 502.
20 As quoted in N. Jayapalan. 2001. *Indian Society and Social Institutions*. Atlantic Publishers & Distributors, p. 428.

Sanskritizing its ritual and pantheon. In short, it took over, as far as possible, the customs, rites, and beliefs of the Brahmins, and adoption of the Brahminic way of life.' However, it is also easy to overstate the actual incidence of Sanskritization, for it was resisted by the gatekeepers of tradition and remained rare, more an aspirational idea in the lower rungs of the hierarchy. 'Srinivas normalizes, even glorifies, caste and Brahmanism,' according to Braj Ranjan Mani, author of *Debrahmanising History*. 'Implicit in his theory and his overall scholarship is that caste is amazingly fluid and fair'.[21]

Notably, Sanskritization not only didn't challenge the caste system, it strengthened and legitimized the pursuit of what Ambedkar has called its 'ascending scale of reverence and a descending scale of contempt'.[22] In effect, 'By adopting the most prestigious features of the upper castes' ethos, the lower castes explicitly acknowledge their social inferiority'.[23] Historian Christophe Jaffrelot has observed that the incidence of Sanskritization was higher among the so-called dominant castes, a term that describes 'peasant Shudras who have occasionally risen to power because of their hold over land and their sheer number.' Throughout history, he adds, the dominant castes that were 'most successful in their attempt at conquering power managed to be recognized as Kshatriyas by Brahmins who invented genealogies for them.' For recent examples, he points to Marathas (Maharashtra), Lingayats and Vokkaligas (Karnataka), and Kammas and Reddys (Andhra Pradesh). Citing Srinivas, he writes that 'the Kshatriya category was the most open of the caste system.' To Jaffrelot, 'the very existence of 'dominant' castes shows

---

21 Braj Ranjan Mani. 2015. *Debrahmanizing History: Dominance and Resistance in Indian Society*. Manohar, p. 57.

22 BR Ambedkar. 1946. *Who were the Shudras?* Thacker and Co., Ltd.

23 Christophe Jaffrelot. 2011. *Religion, Caste and Politics in India*. Hurst & Company, p. 487.

that the Brahminical view of society may describe (or pre-
scribe) an ideal-type in the Weberian sense, but not [always]
the reality of power relations: *swarnas* [those of the top three
varnas] may not [always] be at the top of the socio-political
hierarchy',[24] despite being at the top in terms of ritual status
and its privileges. Even social reform movements and policies of state sometimes provoke a shift in power relations and
collective identities. The Jats of north India, for instance, have
opportunistically claimed to be both Kshatriya and OBC in
different contexts, first under the aegis of Arya Samaj's missionary drive to Sanskritize lower castes and then in response
to positive discrimination programs initiated by the Mandal
commission.

Notably, Marxist historians like Irfan Habib have argued that 'purity' was a rationalization for class interests
and existing social exploitation,[25] and further, that the material impact of colonialism and capitalism is what turned
caste into the potent force that it became in modern India.
Caste endogamy and heredity were shaped, too, by its function as a provider of community and a means of preserving
specialized artisan skills and knowledge; Habib argues that
thrusting lowly status on some castes, such as iron smiths,
carpenters, and weavers, can easily be explained by the primary desire to keep their wages low, and their low 'purity'
score may have arisen out of this desire. Others note that
Dumont conveniently ignored the individualistic and egalitarian aspects of Indian life that have coexisted all along. At
times, a whole stratum of lower castes, led by egalitarian ideologies espoused by charismatic figures, has even fused into
one ethnic identity. In the south, for instance, Periyar's non-
Brahmin (or Dravidian) movement coalesced around an ide-

---

24 Christophe Jaffrelot. 2011. *Religion, Caste and Politics in India.*
    Hurst & Company, p. 413.
25 Irfan Habib. 1995. *Essays in Indian History: Towards a Marxist Per-
    ception.* Tulika Books.

ology that saw Brahmins as Aryan invaders, and Dravidians as the original inhabitants of India and ancestors of all non-Brahmins. But Dumont's theory, despite its shortcomings, still remains indispensable, an essential starting point for understanding caste.

The Persistence of Caste

In the last 2,500 years, many Indians have rejected and attacked the caste system. 'Egalitarianism is neither alien to India nor the gift of the West,' writes Braj Ranjan Mani. 'Common people everywhere have a tradition of aspiring to build an egalitarian world,' a tradition that includes the Jains, the Buddhists, and the Carvakas in ancient times; Basava and Bhakti thinkers and poets like Namdev, Janabai, Ravidas, Kabir, and Tukaram in the medieval period; Phule, Iyothee Thass, Ambedkar, and Periyar in the colonial era. But the caste system has survived them all. Others, such as Gandhi, Vivekananda, and Ram Mohan Roy, did not reject it but advocated major reform. Gandhi, in particular, naively defended the idea of caste itself, imagining it could be made free of discrimination through education and 'upliftment', clashing bitterly with Ambedkar, an 'untouchable' who wrote *The Annihilation of Caste*, perhaps the sharpest critique of the caste system in modern times (more on this in the essays, 'Ambedkar in the Indian Imagination' and 'The Rationalist and the Romantic').

Under British rule in the early 20th century, most Indian nationalists loudly debated the problem of caste and what to do about it, including the debate on what was worse: Western racism or Indian casteism. Gandhi, Lajpat Rai, Tagore, and Bose condemned the practice of untouchability while calling it not as bad as slavery in America. This came out especially in response to the question posed in 1929 by an American journalist: 'Is the plight of the untouchable as hard as that of

the Negro in America?' No, argued most Indian leaders, citing the history of slavery, dehumanizing Jim Crow laws and
the lynch mobs to make their case, but their stance was also
shaped by their desire to deflate 'superior' westerners all too
convinced of the White man's burden. Ambedkar however
argued the reverse, invoking not the *de jure* but the *de facto*
position of the 'untouchables'.[26] In juridical terms, ownership
of a person, he conceded, made slavery worse than untouchability. But in practice, the slave, being property with value,
gave the master an incentive to take 'care of the health and
well being of the slave'. Whereas, 'No one is responsible for
the feeding, housing and clothing of the untouchable.' Furthermore, 'slavery was never obligatory', it only 'permitted'
one to hold another as slave. 'But untouchability is obliged',
he wrote. A Hindu 'is 'enjoined' to hold another as untouchable', a 'compulsion [that the Hindu] cannot escape'.[27] In
one of his many debates with Gandhi, Ambedkar forcefully
pointed out that 'the outcaste is a byproduct of the caste system. There will be outcastes as long as there are castes. Nothing can emancipate the outcaste except the destruction of the
caste system.' Many have asked the questions that Ambedkar
begins with in this passage from *The Annihilation of Caste*:

> Why have the mass of people tolerated the social evils to
> which they have been subjected? There have been social
> revolutions in other countries of the world. Why have there
> not been social revolutions in India, is a question which has
> incessantly troubled me. There is only one answer which I
> can give, and it is that the lower classes of Hindus have been
> completely disabled for direct action on account of this
> wretched Caste System. They could not bear arms, and with-
> out arms they could not rebel. They were all ploughmen—or

26 Nico Slate. 2006. 'Race, Caste, and Nation: Indian Nationalists and
   the American Negro, 1893-1947'. Paper presented at the annual
   meeting of the *American Studies Association*, Oct 12.
27 BR Ambedkar in an essay titled 'Which is worse? Slavery or Untouchability?' *Babasaheb Ambedkar Writings and Speeches* (*BAWS*),
   Vol. 12. Ed. Vasant Moon.

rather, condemned to be ploughmen—and they never were
allowed to convert their ploughshares into swords. They had
no bayonets, and therefore everyone who chose, could and
did sit upon them. On account of the Caste System, they
could receive no education. They could not think out or
know the way to their salvation. They were condemned to
be lowly; and not knowing the way of escape, and not having
the means of escape, they became reconciled to eternal ser-
vitude, which they accepted as their inescapable fate. ...The
existence of Caste and Caste Consciousness [also] prevented
solidarity [between the oppressed castes].[28]

In *Homo Hierarchicus,* Dumont wrote that 'untouchability will not truly disappear until the purity of the Brahmin is itself radically devalued'.[29] This devaluation remains a
work in progress. Or, as the scholar Gopal Guru has noted,
although Indians have embraced 'one person, one vote', they
are nowhere close to embracing the larger ideal of democracy: 'one person, one value' (that is, *equal value at birth,* ir-
respective of caste, class, gender, language, sexuality, religion,
and more).[30] The mindset of hierarchy goes beyond caste to
sustain other forms of domination and control. Whether
couched as etiquette, custom, or respect, its legacy persists
in a range of silences, submissions, and subordinations. For
instance: wives are to obey husbands; one mustn't question
family elders; employees are to meekly follow orders; and so
on. Hierarchy still has a tenacious hold on too many Indians
who, in the words of the Marathi poet Govindaraj, 'bow their
heads to the kicks from above and who simultaneously give
a kick below, never thinking to resist the one or refrain from

28 BR Ambedkar. 1936. *Annihiliation of Caste*, Section 17. Columbia University website, http://ccnmtl.columbia.edu/projects/mmt/
ambedkar/web/index.html
29 Louis Dumont. 1998 (original 1966). *Homo Hierarchicus: The Caste
System and Its Implications*. Oxford India Paperbacks, p. 54.
30 Gopal Guru, 'Dalit Critique of Liberal Democracy', YouTube,
March 1, 2012.

the other.'[31] Omprakash Valmiki wrote in *Joothan* that not just among the 'upper castes', even Dalit social activists in Maharashtra's Dalit *bastis* in the 1970s, 'although they talked outwardly of forgetting the differences between Mahars, Mangs, Chamars and Mehtars, [they were internally] caught in the clutches of these beliefs.' As a witness to this reality, Valmiki's 'heart would break. One could clearly perceive the hesitation of the [mostly Mahar] activists when they entered the Mehtar bastis', which in turn made the Mehtars 'suspicious of the Dalit leadership.'[32]

The Indian Constitution of 1950, in Articles 15-17, outlawed untouchability and other forms of caste-based discrimination, proclaimed equality of opportunity in public employment, and asserted the right of the State to make special provisions 'for the advancement of any socially and educationally backward classes of citizens or for the Scheduled Castes and the Scheduled Tribes.' From the start, the State reserved 22.5% of seats in public-sector jobs, higher education, and central and state legislatures for SC/ST communities, and would later extend caste-based reservations in jobs and education to other communities as well (more on this in the essay, 'The Dance of Indian Democracy'). In 1955, the Parliament also enacted *The Untouchability (Offenses) Act*, later called the *Protection of Civil Rights Act*. Given its weaknesses, it was supplanted in 1989 by a stronger hate crime legislation called the *Scheduled Castes and Tribes (Prevention of Atrocities) Act*.

However, in this deeply conservative country, passing legislation is one thing, enforcing the laws and changing minds is quite another. Discrimination in housing, marriage, and employment is commonplace, even in the modern

---

31 Quoted by Sudhir Kakar and Katharina Kakar. 2007. *The Indians: Portrait of a People*. Penguin Books India, p. 27.
32 Omprakash Valmiki. 1997. *Joothan: A Dalit's Life*. Translated from Hindi by Arun Prabha Mukherjee, 2007. Samya, p. 109.

sectors of the economy. Especially outside the major cities, caste-based violence is still rife, ranging from bonded labor to rapes and murders that frequently go unpunished, not the least because casteism also abounds in the institutions of State that deal with crime and punishment. Even the *Prevention of Atrocities Act*, writes Teltumbde, is 'oblivious of village dynamics' in some ways. For instance, it's oblivious to realities like collective punishment to members of a caste, 'social and economic boycott and blackmail'. In recent decades, he writes, changes in the political economy of rural India have given the landowning castes 'unprecedented wealth but failed to empower dalits to a comparable degree, thereby accentuating between the two groups the power asymmetry that is the prime mover behind atrocities.' He attributes the post-1960s upsurge of caste violence in rural India to three factors: (1) the rise of a large, new class of shudra oppressors who have now 'assumed the brahminical baton' (2) 'the relative progress' and 'assertiveness' of Dalits, and (3) moral corruption, including Brahminism, in 'the lowest rungs of the police and the bureaucracy' that mediate 'between the state and society'[33] (rungs that typically also include Dalits but who, barring exceptions, often learn to mimic the dominant institutional attitudes and norms rather than defy them at great risk to themselves[34]). Unfortunately, Brahmanism

33 Teltumbde, in *The Persistence of Caste*, also argues, less than persuasively I think, that the rise in atrocities against Dalits is significantly caused by neoliberal globalization that began in the 1990s. It's less than persuasive because the impact of neoliberal globalization has been strongest in urban India and relatively weak in rural India, the site of most atrocities. More likely, as Christophe Jaffrelot as argued, the atrocities are a dominant caste reaction to the greater Dalit assertion in rural India following the rise of Dalit politics and the Bahujan Samaj Party in the early 1990s.

34 In his memoir, *An Untouchable in the I.A.S.*, Balwant Singh documented this sort of social reality in the administrative ranks in the 1960s, but which no doubt continues; reported by Gyanendra Pandey in *A History of Prejudice* (p. 69). Cambridge University Press.

also pervades the higher echelons of State administration, ensuring that this systemic problem doesn't get the attention it deserves. It's true that 'society perpetrates atrocities against dalits,' adds Teltumbde. 'But when dalits approach the police with grievances against such a society, they invariably encounter an equally repugnant and hostile force.' State governments have often used violence to repress even Dalit protest marches and calls for justice following gruesome incidents, as in Khairlanji, Maharashtra.

The broad trends, fortunately, are not without hope. 'Dalit', writes feminist writer Urmila Pawar, 'means people who have been oppressed by a repressive social system, and [who] challenge the oppression from a scientific, rational and humanitarian perspective.'[35] In recent decades, those on the lowest rungs of the social pyramid have been politicized and have made their presence felt in the Indian democracy, even commanding high political offices. Poverty and illiteracy among them, though still significantly higher than average, have declined. A few Dalits have chosen the path of militant resistance, some of principled activism, many of conversion to a different religion, others are navigating new avenues of social mobility offered by the modern economy, at times through reservations in public jobs and education. A few have even chosen art and literature to tell their own

---

Kindle Edition. Balwant Singh wrote, 'For officers from the low castes things were... complicated. They were acceptable if they accepted the prevailing... social norms.' Pandey adds, 'Balwant Singh might have made the point more strongly still, for it is probably fair to say that such officers were tolerated if they accepted upper-caste ways and attitudes and yet [were] never fully accepted as social peers. Low-caste officers suffered from much social indignity and humiliation. Expressions of grievance on their part were commonly met with the response that these were 'trivial', 'inconsequential' matters.'

35 Urmila Pawar. 2003. *Aaydaan*. Granthali. Translated by Maya Pandit. 2008. *The Weave of My Life: A Dalit Woman's Memoir*. Stree, p. xii.

stories, bearing witness to their slice of life in India. Dalit literature, explains author Sharankumar Limbale, is 'writing about Dalits by Dalit writers with a Dalit consciousness'. It has added 'to Indian literature fresh experiences, a new sensitivity and vocabulary, a different protagonist, an alternate vision, and a new chemistry of suffering and revolt.'[36] To novelist, feminist, and politician, P. Sivakami, Dalit literature is the 'rebellious expression of a new awakening among educated Dalits.'[37] Dalit creativity, wrote the scholar DR Nagaraj (1954-1998), 'is marked by specific forms of contestation; it challenges the hegemonic modes of segregation [of works into, say, folk and classical, and other 'hierarchized opposites']. It also celebrates the capacity of the human mind to uphold the essential spiritual dignity of being.'[38]

Last but not the least, a new breed of scholars is contesting the dominant historical, cultural, and religious narratives of India, including those forged in recent centuries by a convenient collusion of the power and knowledge of Europeans and Brahmins. These scholars include Ambedkar in his large and lucid body of work, Kancha Ilaiah, author of *Why I Am Not a Hindu*, DR Nagaraj, author of *The Flaming Feet and Other Essays*, Gail Omvedt, author of *Seeking Begumpura: The Social Vision of Anticaste Intellectuals*, Gopal Guru, author of *Humiliation: Claims and Context*, Anand Teltumbde, author of *The Persistence of Caste*, Braj Ranjan Mani, author of *Debrahmanizing History: Dominance and Resistance in Indian Society*, and many others.

---

36   Sharankumar Limbale. 2004. *Towards an Aesthetic of Dalit Literature*. Orient Longman, pp. 19, 37. The Marathi original of 1996 was translated into English by Alok K Mukherjee.
37   P Sivakami. 2012. 'Tamil Dalit Literature - Some Riddles', *Cross / Cultures*, No. 145, Jan 1.
38   DR Nagaraj. 2013. *The Flaming Feet and Other Essays: The Dalit Movement in India*. Permanent Black. Kindle Edition, Locations 2791-2793.

More than ever, Dalits now understand that 'Freedom is never voluntarily given by the oppressor; it must be demanded by the oppressed.'[39] But as Sivakami has written, the 'relative silence on the part of non-Dalits on issues of caste amounts to an assumption that confronting casteism and untouchability is the sole responsibility of Dalits, just as it was assumed that confronting gender inequalities was the job of feminists.'[40] As Teltumbde points out, 'Castes cannot be annihilated by Dalits alone for the simple fact that they have not created it. Unless the larger society owned up to this task, castes will not be annihilated.'[41]

---

39 Quote by Martin Luther King, Jr.

40 P Sivakami. 2012. 'Tamil Dalit Literature – Some Riddles', *Cross / Cultures*, No. 145, Jan 1.

41 Anand Teltumbde. 2013. 'To the Self-Obsessed Marxists and the Pseudo Ambedkarites,' *Sanhati.com*, April 2.

The Dance of Indian Democracy[1]

The Republic of India began life as an unlikely nation. Gaining independence in 1947, India adopted a democratic form of governance, a liberal constitution, and secular public institutions (at least in intent if often not in practice). None of these sprang from a living indigenous tradition.[2] Rather, they were chosen by an elite class of Indians that had developed a taste for them via its exposure to the West, and had even acquired some experience in representative self-rule in the closing decades of the British Raj. Many observers thought the experiment was doomed to failure. Among them was the stodgy imperialist Winston Churchill, who felt that if the British left, India would 'fall back quite rapidly through the centuries into the barbarism and privations of the Middle Ages.'[3] Indians were unfit to govern themselves, and needed 'the sober and resolute forces of the British Empire.'

1   An earlier version of this essay appeared on 3 Quarks Daily on May 24, 2010.
2   Ancient India did have many democratic republics. Steve Muhlberger. 1998. 'Democracy in Ancient India'. https://faculty.nipissingu.ca/muhlberger/HISTDEM/INDIADEM.HTM
3   Winston Churchill. 1931. 'Our Duty in India', March 18. Speech delivered at Albert Hall, London. http://www.winstonchurchill.org/

Doubters abounded for decades after independence. Unlike so many post-colonial nations, including those in South Asia, the continued existence of democracy in India—its fair elections and peaceful transfers of power—puzzled not just the lay observers, but it also became, according to historian Ramachandra Guha,

> an anomaly for academic political science ... That India "could sustain democratic institutions seems, on the face of it, highly improbable," wrote the distinguished political scientist Robert Dahl, adding: "It lacks all the favorable conditions." "India has a well-established reputation for violating social scientific generalizations," wrote another American scholar, adding, "Nonetheless, the findings of this article furnish grounds for skepticism regarding the viability of democracy in India." [4]

The naysayers rightly saw democracy as an outgrowth of a particular historical experience in the West, rooted in a consciousness we now call modernity. They spoke of the conditions thought to be necessary for the flourishing of democracy: an egalitarian social order, an ethos of individualism, and a culture of secular politics and pluralist tolerance. India had mostly the opposite: a deeply hierarchical social order, subservience of the individual to family and community, and a culture of political quietism, though it did have a kind of tolerance (more on this below). Only a tiny class of Indians saw themselves as citizens of a nation-state, or could lay claim to political participation. Nor had the masses agitated to be rid of the hundreds of kings in as many princely states of British India, though discontent did exist in pockets. Indians were notoriously diverse, with identities spanning caste, class, region, custom, language, religion, and more, all impediments to a shared ideal of citizenship. Indeed, how was democracy expected to survive in such inhospitable terrain?

---

resources/speeches/1930-1938-the-wilderness/our-duty-in-india
4   Ramachandra Guha. 2007. *India after Gandhi*. Harper Perennial, p. 598.

Democracy, With Reservations

One Indian who anticipated these contradictions and worried about them was Dr. BR Ambedkar, the architect of the Indian Constitution. In his essay, *Caste, Class and Democracy*, Ambedkar astutely argued that once the British left, an Indian elite from the upper castes would simply step into their place. The right to universal adult suffrage alone wouldn't make India a democracy—except in a narrowly technical sense—if the 'servile classes' in this deeply stratified society found no political representation. Ambedkar noted that the Indian political establishment, almost exclusively from the upper castes, despised the 'untouchables', and would neither strive to represent their interests, nor put up 'untouchable' candidates. Instead, they would hog all the power and resources and serve their own class interests. Ambedkar believed that 'self-government and democracy become real not when a Constitution based on adult suffrage comes into existence but when the governing class loses its power to capture the power to govern.'[5]

Ambedkar realized that the Indian soil had to be fertilized to make democracy bloom. The 'people' in its definition—of the people, by the people, for the people—had to mean *all people*, not just the privileged classes. Further, what was needed for a healthy democracy was not just political equality but also substantial social and economic equality. Indeed, the former was not achievable without the latter—and would never be unless a society offered substantial equality of opportunity to all. With an eye to a fair deal and a level playing field for the 'servile classes', to which he himself belonged, Ambedkar argued for reservations—a form of positive discrimination, called 'affirmative action' in the

---

5   BR Ambedkar. 2002. *The Essential Writings of BR Ambedkar.* Edited by Valerian Rodrigues. Oxford India Paperbacks, pp. 132-148.

United States—in public institutions, government jobs, and even in central and state legislatures.

Jawaharlal Nehru, the first Prime Minister of India, is often, and for many good reasons, held up as a great liberal democrat, who did a lot to inculcate and entrench democratic impulses in India. In his own words, he was 'eager and anxious to change her outlook and appearance and give her the garb of modernity.' Nehru was, however, opposed to the idea of reservations. He saw them as divisive—perhaps led by the view that the existence of separate Hindu and Muslim electorates was partly to blame for the bloody Partition. But he had other grounds to resist them as well. In 1961, he wrote:

> I dislike any kind of reservations ... I react strongly against anything which leads to inefficiency and second-rate standards. I want my country to be a first-class country. The moment we encourage the second rate, we are lost. ... [I]f we go in for reservations on communal and caste basis, we swamp the bright and able people and remain second rate or third rate. ... This way lies not only folly, but disaster. Let us help the backward groups by all means but never at the cost of efficiency.

Surely not *Chacha* Nehru's finest sentiment.[6] He, too, rather simplemindedly, sees reservations as something opposed to quality of work and efficiency (more on this soon). A decade earlier, however, he had agreed to reservations for the 'untouchables' and the tribal peoples, referred to in the Constitution as Scheduled Castes (SC) and Scheduled Tribes (ST), respectively. They made up nearly a quarter of the population and the Constitution reserved for them 22.5 percent

---

6   Historian Christophe Jaffrelot points out that Nehru 'did not regard caste as a relevant category for State-sponsored social change'. His Home Minister, GB Pant, also articulated the Congress party's view when he 'disapproved of the use of caste as the most prominent criterion for identifying the backward classes', hiding his prejudices behind the seemingly respectable argument that 'the recognition of the specified castes as backward may serve to maintain and even perpetuate the existing distinctions on the basis of caste.'

of the seats in the central and state legislatures. Reservation for Muslims and women was debated but rejected, a tacit acknowledgement that the plight of the outcastes and the tribals was uniquely bad. Beaten down and lacking self-confidence, the SC/STs now had a practical means of advancing themselves. Their political consciousness grew hand in hand with them realizing the power of the vote and their special rights under the Constitution.

A striking feature of the Indian democratic experiment has been the increasing use of reservations to achieve greater social justice and equality of opportunity. Much of this has occurred not due to the goodwill of the elites but due to the shifting balance of political power across demographics. Since the 1950s, at least in some states, political power has been shifting away from upper-caste Hindus to the rest, who are far more numerous. From a society where public politics has long been marginal and a preoccupation of the few, India has become an intensely political society. By the 1970s, following the green revolution, many Shudra castes had gained enough socioeconomic clout to aspire to, and agitate for, a larger share of administrative and educational opportunities, where they were clearly underrepresented. Some of the largest and best-organized Shudra castes were the 'Yadavs in Uttar Pradesh and Bihar, Jats in Haryana and Punjab, Marathas in Maharashtra, Vokkaligas in Karnataka, and Gounders in Tamil Nadu.'[7]

An artifact of this social change was the Mandal commission of 1979, tasked to 'identify the socially or educationally backward' communities of India, and 'to recommend measures, such as reservations in the administration, that could contribute to their social uplift.'[8] The commission des-

7   Ramachandra Guha. 2007. *India after Gandhi*. Harper Perennial, p. 598.
8   Christophe Jaffrelot. 2011. *Religion, Caste and Politics in India*. Hurst & Company, p. 494.

ignated these communities Other Backward Classes (OBC), and estimated them to be 52 percent of the population, including many socially backward Muslim groups. The report came out in late 1980 and was summarily ignored by the upper-caste leadership of the two Congress administrations in the 1980s. Its reservation policy recommendations had to wait until 1990 to be turned into law by Prime Minister VP Singh, an intellectual disciple of the anti-caste socialist Ram Manohar Lohia.

Since 1993 India has reserved 27 percent of government jobs for the OBCs (but no seats in the legislatures, as for SC/STs) and since 2008, 27 percent of admissions to institutes of higher education that are 'established, maintained or aided by the Central Government.'[9] Each educational institute was granted some leeway in choosing the eligibility cutoff for its admission, so they could strike the right balance between 'excellence' and 'social justice'. In practice, this has led the institutes to set the cutoff too high and the OBC quota has gone unfilled for years, reverting to the general category as per the law. The quota also excludes a 'creamy layer' of 'socially advanced' OBCs that's financially well off. A performance review in ten years will propose adjustments. Notably, OBC reservation in employment applies only to initial recruitment, not to promotions (there is some support to enable the latter, at least for SC/STs, through a constitutional amendment). Including the 22.5 percent SC/ST quota, total reservation in government jobs and college admissions rose to nearly 50 percent. Not surprisingly, this provoked a huge backlash from upper-caste minorities—constituting less than 20 percent of the population nationwide—who saw their opportunities shrink.

---

9   The Central Educational Institutions (Reservation in Admission) Act, 2006.

Contrary to popular belief, reservations in India predate the Constitution by decades. Many socially conscious rulers of Princely States in south India—starting in 1902 with the Maharaja of Kolhapur, Chhatrapati Shahuji Maharaj, who dreamed of a caste-free society—had reserved public-sector jobs for marginalized groups in their domains. Others followed: The Maharaja of Mysore in 1921, the Bombay Presidency in 1931, the Maharaja of Travancore in 1935, and soon thereafter, the Maharaja of Cochin. In short, large parts of the South already had some form of reservations in public-sector jobs before 1947. Another common misbelief is that the Constitution limited all reservations to 10 years, whereas it did so only for political reservations (in state assemblies and the Lok Sabha), not for reservations in jobs and education, where the timeframe was kept open-ended and to be determined by outcomes.

The Reservations Debate

> To treat unequals as equals is to perpetuate inequality. When we allow weak and strong to compete on an equal footing, we are loading the dice in favour of the strong and holding only a mock competition in which the weaker partner is destined to failure right from the start.[10]

In societies rife with entrenched inequality and discrimination, it is the penchant of the privileged to speak of open competition and difference-blind policies as virtues. Many, if not most, upper-caste Indians dislike caste-based reservations (with a bit more tolerance in the case of Dalits than for OBCs) and support only income-based reservations. However, they never seem to ask: if caste is a distinct vector of exclusion and oppression, how will income-based reservations counter it? Or consider another situation: let's say our goal

---

10 Report of the Backward Classes Commission (aka Mandal Commission), 1980.

is to counter gender-based exclusion and oppression and to increase the representation of women in public life. Can income-based reservations achieve that goal, or will we need to provision gender-based measures? The same logic extends to caste. In short, each vector of disability that we intend to tackle requires positive discrimination along that vector.

Clearly, there are better and worse ways of structuring reservations. But, above all, we need to stop thinking of caste-based reservations as a benefit only for Dalits, Adivasis, or OBCs. Reservations also benefit the upper castes by making the society they belong to more inclusive, one with greater social trust and cooperation. Per enlightened self-interest, if reservations make our institutions more representative and diverse, and our society more egalitarian, don't we all benefit? Does it not behoove us to build a reservations regime—alongside other measures—to help achieve this goal?

In recent years, India has seen the entire gamut of critiques against reservations—from predictably shrill and crude takes on 'merit' and 'reverse discrimination' (discussed in the essay, 'On Caste Privilege'), to concerns that seem more reasonable but are often specious and no less crude. The latter include at least the following six variants:

(1) Divisive identity politics: Some critics claim that reservations fuel divisive identity politics. This argument tends to mix cause and effect. Identity politics primarily *reflects—not causes*—the serious social divisions and disparities that already exist, which won't just disappear if ignored. Often in politics, identity formation and assertion by a weaker group are preludes to the group's collective advancement, as in the Civil Rights struggle in the United States. In time and with sufficient assimilation, old identities tend to weaken or merge into new ones (a fear often cited here, exaggerated in my view, is that the lure of reservations may harden old identities, undermining the instrument's progressive intent, but this is less an argument against reservations, more a plea to design them right, with periodic, data-driven reviews and adjustments based on outcomes for various groups).

A variant of this concern is that considerations of 'caste good' are swamping those of 'common good', but did the latter ever exist in India? Won't considerations of 'caste good' remain paramount as long as there is casteist discrimination?

(2) **A permanent entitlement:** Other critics, including Sunil Khilnani, lament that reservations have become a permanent entitlement, rather than a temporary 'stimulus package' that needs periodic adjustments.[11] They wonder that when reservations have achieved the desired effect of 'equalization of castes', will the politicians have the wisdom and the courage to roll them back? This worry about the need for exit criteria seems legitimate, but it's hardly a good reason to oppose reservations today; more often, this worry is a symptom of upper-caste conservatism and their thinly veiled opposition to reservations.

In general, reservations along a dimension make sense as long as discrimination remains a significant barrier to equality of opportunity and a large results gap exists along that dimension, whether of caste, gender, or another social grouping. Needless to say, not all barriers to equality of opportunity, nor all of the results gap (such as in high school graduation rates), can be addressed by reservations in public-sector jobs and higher education. Many other prior systemic barriers to equality of opportunity—as in persistent disparities in childhood nutrition, family income, access to quality primary and secondary schools, etc.—require their own focused remedies, which, in turn, can only amplify the reach and effectiveness of reservations later.

---

11 Sunil Khilnani. 2010. 'From Representative Democracy', *Live Mint*, April 10.

(3) Reservations get hijacked by a handful of castes:
It's plainly true that among the wide range of OBC castes, not
all are equally disadvantaged. Some dominant castes among
the OBCs can, or may soon be able to, compete in the general
category. To keep reservations the sharp and effective instrument of social justice that Ambedkar intended it to be, Dalit
intellectual DR Nagaraj (1954-1998) emphasized the need
to periodically 'prepare a discriminating list of OBCs,' while
lamenting that it's 'a task few are willing to undertake.'[12] In
1993, soon after Nagaraj wrote that, the National Commission for Backward Classes (NCBC) was established to do just
that—to periodically revise the list of castes and other groups
eligible for reservations from over two thousand listed under OBC. The Commission's obvious dilemma is that if this
instrument of social justice lets a minority of eligible castes
dominate the reserved category (with no timebound or other
mechanism for them to make greater room for others who're
much worse off), it would not only have failed to advance
opportunities broadly, it may well cause infighting over its
'unfairness' and harm their collective interests.[13]

Indeed, to regard OBCs, or even Dalits, as a single group
here is problematic. The 'single group' view may have strategic value when contesting upper-caste hegemony—akin
to the nationalists representing 'Indians' as one group when
contesting colonial hegemony—but it can also obstruct social
justice in important ways. After all, if a reservation regime for
SC/STs and OBCs remains blind to their internal hierarchies
and levels of deprivation, it will most often propagate them.
For instance, by the 1990s in Andhra Pradesh, the Malas
came to dominate SC reservations at the expense of the Madigas and others. 'A reservation policy that did not recognize

---

12 DR Nagaraj. 2013. *The Flaming Feet and Other Essays: The Dalit
    Movement in India*. Permanent Black. Kindle Edition, Locations
    2497.
13 'Call for unity among Malas, Madigas', *The Hindu*, Dec 30, 2007.

disparities among the SCs of Andhra Pradesh actually reproduced the disparity,' wrote Dalit scholar K. Satyanarayana.[14]
Following a struggle by the Madigas, in which they claimed
a distinct caste and cultural identity—seeking, in effect, not
the annihilation of caste but equalization of castes—the state
subdivided the SC reservation quota among four new Scheduled Caste categories.

Even in U.P. and Bihar, post-Mandal OBC politics disproportionately benefited the Yadavs. Most coveted positions
went to members of this caste, causing resentment among
Kurmis, Lodhs, and other lower OBCs. 'Yadavization' of the
state administration took precedence over forging solidarity
and equality across OBC castes. According to scholar Braj
Ranjan Mani, Dalit-Bahujan politics 'remained tethered to
group representation, not structural transformation… Social
mobility, economic uplift, and political empowerment of a
section of dalit-bahujans took place without threatening the
existing hierarchies—as the fundamentals (the kernel of the
caste system that reproduces hierarchies) were left intact.'[15]
As Perry Anderson has observed, state elections 'readily become 'job auctions' in which castes, often conglomerates of
jatis cobbled together for the occasion, compete ferociously
with one another for the spoils of office, in disregard of any
logic of wider, let alone national solidarities.'[16]

But important as the beneficiaries' perception of fairness
is—*especially in a corrective instrument of social justice*—the
reality is that, even with a more finely tuned reservations regime and a nimbler NCBC, not all castes will be able to take

14 K. Satyanarayana. 2014. 'Dalit Reconfiguration of Caste: Representation, Identity, and Politics', *Critical Quarterly*, Vol.56, No.3, October, pp. 46-61.
15 Braj Ranjan Mani. 2013. 'The Crisis And Challenge Of Dalit-Bahujans', *Countercurrents.org*, December 17.
16 Perry Anderson. 2012. *The Indian Ideology*. Three Essays Collective, p. 155.

equal advantage of reservations. And invariably, the most privileged within a caste will benefit the most. This parallels how the admissions regime for foreign students in American universities, operating at the level of 'national quotas', disproportionately benefits the most privileged Indians. In 19th century India, when the British opened colonial schools for the locals, they disproportionately benefited the most privileged upper castes, mostly urban Brahmins. OBC and SC/ST reservations in India too, even without the nuisance of nepotism, may be able to reach only a few relatively privileged castes at first. *That's still better than reaching none.*

Alongside, the NCBC ought to actively minimize conflicts and implement periodic reviews and adjustments.[17] In March 2015, for instance, the Supreme Court upheld NCBC's ruling that Jats be excluded from OBC reservations nationwide, though they had previously availed of OBC reservations in two states and many political parties, led by political expediency, had promised them more in their election campaigns. The NCBC also intends to 'sub-categorize' the OBC quota to prevent its domination by a handful of stronger groups, and to keep identifying newer forms of backwardness for inclusion under the OBC list, such as being orphan or transgender. Similarly, to reduce the domination of the general category by rich members from a handful of urban upper castes, it would be only fair to set aside a portion of it for the poor that are not covered by any other reserved category (i.e., college admissions based on parental income).

(4) Use the market, not reservations: Some critics rightly point out how few public-sector jobs exist—a number that, in the post-1991 era of the market economy, keeps shrink-

---

17 In Nov 2016, for example, the central government approved an NCBC proposal to include 15 new castes in the Other Backward Classes (OBC) category. However, it remains a much harder task to *remove* any dominant castes from this category than to include new ones.

ing relative to the private and 'unorganized' sectors, down to about 3-5 percent of all jobs. Given this reality, reservations, even after decades, can reach only a small minority of Dalits, Adivasis, and OBCs, not the least because few even possess the minimum educational qualifications needed for these jobs, such as about 10 percent of Dalits.[18] These critics argue that the market economy (and English language proficiency) is doing more to improve the lot of Dalits than reservations in the public sector, so why not drop reservations entirely, which are needlessly distracting and increasingly ineffectual. I think this argument has multiple fallacies.

First, it uses either-or logic, i.e., either markets or reservations, whereas both are effective and complement each other. Reservations make our institutions more diverse and representative of the public they serve, making them more responsive and less oppressive. This is unlikely to happen via free markets alone. Such institutions span non-elected bodies across law enforcement, judiciary, academia, planning bodies, water and electricity boards, industrial development corporations, public service commissions, and other state bureaucracies in banking, healthcare, media, and more. Until our public institutions and universities see the benefits of diversity and commit to it in their ranks (as is increasingly common in the United States, though far from perfect), we need reservations to help reach that outcome.

Second, given how few public-sector jobs exist, it's a mistake to think of reservations as a job employment scheme. Rather, it's a way of giving hitherto excluded communities a say in running their own government. As Kanshi Ram, the founder of Bahujan Samaj Party, exhorting OBCs in 1991, said, 'reservation is not a question of our daily bread, reservation is not a question of our jobs, reservation is a matter

---

18 Anand Teltumbde. 2010. *The Persistence of Caste*. Zed Books, p. 70.

of participation in the government and administration.'[19] It helps politicize a caste's members, often a prelude to their collective empowerment. The few individuals who gain prominent public-sector jobs become sources of pride and role models in their communities. Concrete, material change comes thereafter, as some of these individuals translate their influence into new policies and actions.

Third, according to writer Chandra Bhan Prasad, former Naxalite who turned into an enthusiast of the market economy and is now an advisor to the Dalit Indian Chamber of Commerce and Industry, it was precisely these reservations in jobs and education that have 'given Dalits a launch pad' in the modern economy. According to Prasad's estimate, reservations had benefited about 5 million Dalit individuals by 2004. Counting the impact on their families and later generations, it may have brought 25 of 170 million Dalits into a higher socioeconomic class,[20] a modest but not an insignificant achievement. This despite the fact that in the early decades of the republic, SC/ST quotas in jobs and education largely went unfilled, whether 'due to a lack of qualified candidates [in U.P. only 7.1 per cent were literate in 1961] ... or a lack of willingness on the part of those in charge of filling them.'[21]

Finally, if public-sector jobs are shrinking, it may be time to also look at some form of reservations in the private sector, at least in corporations above a certain number of employees. India still has no legal provisions to combat discrimination in hiring, such as the Equal Employment Opportunity Act in the United States. Indian corporate managers have nominally

---

19 Quoted in Christophe Jaffrelot. 2011. *Religion, Caste and Politics in India*. Hurst & Company, p. 538.
20 Chandra Bhan Prasad. 2004. 'A Business Case for Reservations', *OneWorld South Asia*, November 16.
21 Christophe Jaffrelot. 2011. *Religion, Caste and Politics in India*. Hurst & Company, p. 520.

'moved beyond' caste only to employ euphemisms like 'family background'. Recent studies have 'shown that employment discrimination is substantial, especially in the private sector, and that discrimination occurs to a large extent in unequal access to jobs.'[22] Despite equal job qualifications, employers in the modern private sector respond differently to resumes that have recognizable Muslim and Dalit names compared to those with upper-caste names.

(5) Reservations lower excellence: A common view against reservations, one that Nehru held, is that quotas lower excellence. This of course relies on a silly, provincial idea of 'merit', based on test scores, degrees, or other 'objective' measures that do not take into account the subjective-social context of most jobs, especially public-sector jobs. A truly meritorious system, say, in public health, policing, or banking, is one that understands those it serves, and responds to their needs equitably and without discrimination. The most satisfying public services value no less the providers' social-emotional proximity to the served—not captured by standardized tests—than technical skills. In the United States, for instance, most cities no longer have a police force with predominantly White cops—a shift that has led not to a reduction in excellence but to its opposite: *it builds trust and makes policing more effective* (even as cell phone cameras suggest otherwise by revealing the still continuing, though broadly declining, abuses in policing, as in Ferguson, Missouri, 2014[23]). Ambedkar, a great believer in excellence himself, forcefully questioned simplistic ideas of merit with these words:

> Nobody will have any quarrel with the abstract principle that [the best person for a job should be preferred]. But Man

---

22 Sukhdeo Thorat and Katherine S. Newman. 2010. *Blocked by Caste: Economic Discrimination in Modern India.* Oxford, p. 143.

23 Peter Dreier. 2016. 'Caught on Camera: Police Racism', *American Prospect*, July 11.

is not a mere machine. He is a human being with feelings of sympathy for some and of antipathy for others. This is even true of the best man. He too is charged with the feelings of class sympathies and class antipathies. Having regard to these considerations the 'best' man from the governing class may well turn out to be the worst from the point of view of the servile classes.[24]

The same applies to all sorts of public services of the State. Can budget committees, planning commissions, or investment bodies make smart decisions without representative voices from a broad cross-section of society? Even the highly competitive Silicon Valley sees diversity as a key asset, because it leads to more creative, innovative, and successful solutions.[25] Reservations in our public sphere, by recruiting the best candidates from diverse social backgrounds, tend to improve overall excellence, not diminish it. Empirical evidence of this comes from a study on the Indian Railways, one of the largest public-sector employers in India. The study found 'no evidence whatsoever' that raising the proportion of SC and ST employees lowers 'productivity or productivity growth. On the contrary, some of the results suggest that the proportion of SC and ST employees in the upper (A and B) job categories is positively associated with productivity and productivity growth.'[26]

Finally, it is also worth noting that nearly every institution of post-independence India has been spearheaded by Brahminical elites. Their dismal performance in delivering even basic social services to the majority of Indians—of edu-

24 *Babasaheb Ambedkar Writings and Speeches (BAWS)*, Vol. 9, pp. 229-30.
25 'Fostering Innovation Through a Diverse Workforce', *Forbes*, July 2011.
26 Ashwini Deshpande. 2013. 'Social Justice through Affirmative Action in India', *PERI*, February 18. The study on Indian Railways is by Ashwini Deshpande and Thomas E. Weisskopf (2011): 'Do Reservation Policies Affect Productivity in the Indian Railways', Centre for Development Economics Working Paper No. 185, May.

cation, health, water, sanitation, and electricity—says volumes about their 'merit' and argues against leaving them in control of these institutions.

(6) Reservations distract from real work: Another critique of reservations calls it a mostly symbolic politics of vote banks—the worst manifestation of identity politics—that has masked genuine debate over reform and development. According to political theorist Bhikhu Parekh, '[s]ocial justice has come to be defined almost exclusively in terms of reservations, and the massive programme of redistribution needed to tackle the deep roots of historically accumulated disadvantages has been marginalized. Rather than fight for such a programme, the scheduled caste, scheduled tribe, and OBC representatives in powerful positions use their constituents as a vote bank to promote their own careers.' [27]

If Parekh is right and if reservations are little more than sops that distract from the larger task of social justice, we have a real problem and a failure of the political imagination on our hands. But is this a critique of reservations per se? Sure, there is an urgent need to 'fight for such a programme' but the fact is that the pursuit of social justice is not zero-sum. 'On the contrary, it can be argued that: 'the pursuit of justice in one dimension helps build a broader political culture that supports struggles for justice in other dimensions".[28] In other words, we can pursue reservations for historically disadvantaged groups *as well as* focus on redistributive socioeconomic justice by other means for the disadvantaged in all groups—these two goals are not mutually exclusive. Economist and politician, Meghnad Desai, has however identified one reason why this hasn't happened, especially in north India:

----

27 Quote by Bhikhu Parekh cited in Bidyut Chakrabarty. 2008. *Indian Politics and Society Since Independence*. Routledge, p. 71.
28 'Citizenship', *Stanford Encyclopedia of Philosophy*, April 2010.

The Indian State can deliver a nuclear bomb and launch satellites but not universal primary education or decent public health. This is not an accident. It is a choice made by the elite who have been in power for 60 years and reflects their values. [Even the] Indian socialists used the State to project elite power. The reason is that Indian society lacks a very basic element, which is present in most societies. This is the equality of respect, the basic idea that all human beings have equal status. Hindu society is a caste society and caste denies the simple idea of status equality. … The Indian State has been mainly manned by upper-caste elites and they do not consider the lower orders deserving of education and health.[29]

* * *

Supporters of reservations, including myself, argue that despite its design problems (e.g., the political difficulty of periodically scrubbing the list of eligible castes), instances of misuse (e.g., the upper castes using fake SC certificates), and implementation gaps (e.g., the upper castes finding ways to not fill quotas in education and jobs), reservations are still a valuable instrument of social justice, without which India will be even less likely to realize the full promise of democracy. Reservations are especially important in an India that has embraced Western models of economic development built on capital, professional education, and competition, thereby amplifying the historical advantages of the social elites. The debate on reservations may have added to the raucous unsettledness of the Indian polity, but it has also enabled more and more people from hitherto marginalized groups to participate in and fight for their idea of India. This is far more desirable than the reverse, and reservations remain an effective tool for redressing still-deep inequities and discrimination in Indian society.

In the same spirit, we should also applaud the ongoing initiative to reserve for women a third of the seats in the par-

29 Meghnad Desai. 2013. 'The Hindu rate of backwardness', *Indian Express*, July 28.

liament and state legislatures (including a third of the SC/ST seats), where their numbers have stubbornly hovered near or below 10 percent, though many (mostly upper-caste) women have made it to the very top. The women's quota is especially significant because a great many problems in India spring from the continued disempowerment of women. Curiously enough, the women's reservation bill has extensive support from upper-caste elites. One wonders why their vehemence against caste-based reservations does not extend to gender-based reservations, when both caste and gender are sources of systemic disadvantage in Indian society. Is it because sisters and daughters in their midst help them overcome their empathy deficit?

The debate over reservations has perhaps grown more intense because it has also become a touchstone for the fairness of our public policies and the moral affinities of our politicians. However, to Parekh's point, it is very important that Indians see reservations as only one in a bag of tricks to achieve greater social and economic equality. The stubborn persistence of inequalities that derive from illiteracy, hunger and malnutrition, lack of healthcare and sanitation, disparities in ownership of land in rural areas, uneven economic development, rising wealth and income gaps, and lax law enforcement suggests that India is nowhere close to realizing Ambedkar's inspiring vision of democracy.

The Subsoil of Indian Democracy

Even today, India lacks the classic ingredients of modernity said to be necessary for democracy, nor is India about to acquire them in a hurry. How indeed has democracy survived in India? What aspects of Indian culture made it hospitable to democracy? I think two factors soar above all others: tolerance and cultural diversity.

Given India's obsession with caste and other social hierarchies, it may strike some as strange to posit tolerance as an aspect of Indian culture. But tolerance comes in different flavors. Amartya Sen has called the Indian flavor of tolerance *swikriti*, or "acceptance', in particular the acknowledgement that [others] are entitled to lead their own lives.' [30] Part of this no doubt comes from the presence of thousands of self-absorbed endogamous castes, each with its customary way of life; another part comes from India's long history of cultural syncretism that has furthered many tolerant, pacifist, and private faiths, often alongside a gentle, dreamy, fatalistic detachment from the world. The tolerance of *Swikriti* is therefore different from the tolerance of modernity; the latter has its roots in egalitarian individualism. *Swikriti* may also have extended to political systems that came along, at least the relatively inoffensive kind, such as democracy. As long as political power didn't actively oppress, it was of marginal concern: rulers could come and go, dynasties rise and fall. To all but an elite class, democracy too began as yet another political experiment in a faraway city, later permeating the countryside and drawing sustenance from *swikriti*. There is, however, a fine line between *swikriti* and indifference. In *The Annihilation of Caste*, Ambedkar wrote:

> The Hindus claim to be a very tolerant people. In my opinion this is a mistake. On many occasions they can be intolerant, and if on some occasions they are tolerant, that is because they are too weak to oppose or too indifferent to oppose. This indifference of the Hindus has become so much a part of their nature that a Hindu will quite meekly tolerate an insult as well as a wrong ... Indifferentism is the worst kind of disease that can infect a people. Why is the Hindu so indifferent? In my opinion this indifferentism is the result of the Caste System, which has made *Sanghatan* and co-operation even for a good cause impossible.[31]

30 Amartya Sen. 2005. *The Argumentative Indian*. Farrar, Straus and Giroux, p. 35.
31 BR Ambedkar. 1936. *Annihiliation of Caste*, Section 11. Colum-

No less crucial to the survival of democracy in India was the extraordinary diversity of the newly independent republic. What, after all, did denizens of Ladakh or Mizoram have in common with natives of Kutch or Coorg? But what good is such diversity if it impedes people from coming together in common cause? India's history also shows that diversity has no causal relationship with material progress, rationalism, or social liberalism. Yet, cultural diversity, almost by definition, thwarts singular narratives of being, and acts as a formidable bulwark against political and religious fundamentalism. With so many competing claims and ways of life in India, democracy turned out to be particularly well suited as a practical means of resolving conflicts among various communities.

It's possible to argue that *swikriti* and cultural diversity are receding in India, not the least due to an intensifying competition for limited resources, Hindutva nationalism, and economic globalization. But alongside, a more widely shared secular identity—and a sense of imagined community—have also emerged, forged by things like cricket, popular music, movies and soap operas, TV and print journalism, railways, education boards, competitive exams, a unified market, state institutions and their administrative borders. Many progressive, modernizing ideas of self and community increasingly penetrate Indian culture and civil society. New forms of tolerance and sociocultural diversity—as in new art, music, lifestyles, vocations, and identities—have also arisen. More than six decades later, a different question looms large: Is India becoming a sicker or a healthier democracy?

bia University website, http://ccnmtl.columbia.edu/projects/mmt/ambedkar/web/index.html

On Caste Privilege[1]

An early goal of British imperialists in India was to create a class of local elites in their own image. They would be, wrote Thomas Macaulay, 'interpreters between us and the millions whom we govern; a class of persons Indian in blood and colour, but English in tastes, in opinions, in morals and in intellect.'[2] An elite class did emerge, not surprisingly from the socially dominant upper-caste Hindus of urban India.

As early as 1873, the social reformer Jotirao Phule had criticized the early colonial model of 'high class education' for creating a 'virtual monopoly of all higher offices … by the Brahmins.'[3] These elites, chin-deep in caste identities, saw themselves as innately superior to other Indians, mirroring the class- and race-based prejudices of the British. No

---

1 An earlier version of this essay appeared on 3 Quarks Daily on Aug 16, 2010.
2 Thomas Babington Macaulay. 1835. 'Minute on Indian Education', February 2. http://bit.ly/1d7GJE1
3 Jotirao Phule. 1873. *Slavery* (Gulamgiri). From *Collected works of Mahatma Jotirao Phule*. 1991. Translated by P.G. Patil. Published by Education Department, Government of Maharashtra. The quoted text is from the preface of *Slavery*.

wonder they got along so well. In fact, European Orientalists, armed with new theories about the origins of Sanskrit and the influx of light-skinned people into the Subcontinent, saw these caste elites as their long separated Aryan brethren. The latter, only too glad with this association, soon emerged as native informants and collaborators in interpreting 'Indian' society and culture, and in shaping a historiography that selectively glorified its past and framed it as largely 'tolerant', 'spiritual', and 'nonviolent', except when rudely disrupted by Muslim invaders.

Later, when these elites opposed the British, they used the same language of political rights and liberalism that the Europeans preached at home but didn't practice in their colonies. It was this class, led by Anglicized lawyers and bureaucrats, that succeeded the British. In the first Indian Parliament in 1952, Brahmins, who comprise less than 5 percent of the population, cornered almost 25 percent of the directly elected seats; altogether the upper castes, about 20 percent of the population, claimed over 85 percent of the seats.[4]

In a representative democracy, the idea of 'representation' implies that a politician, say, an upper-caste Hindu male, can and should fairly represent the interests of the entire electorate, including the lower castes, religious minorities, and women. But one can persuasively argue that this did not happen in the early decades of the Indian republic. Deep disparities along caste lines remained; religious minorities grew alienated and even declined socioeconomically; the vast majority of women remained marginal as before in political and economic realms. India was effectively a democracy of the few, by the few, for the few.

---

4   OBCs got 10 percent and Muslims 2 percent. Rajendra Vora, Suhas Palshikar. 2004. *Indian Democracy: Meanings and Practices*. Sage Publications, p. 25.

Since the 1970s, India has seen the rise of caste-based politics. Built overtly on the idea that only a member of your own (or proximate) caste can represent your interests, its primary driver was the failure of upper-caste politicians to represent the lower castes, and the latter realizing the power of their vote. Votes now openly began coalescing along caste lines, not the least because—besides being central to one's social identity—caste had long shaped one's share of opportunity, deprivation, and discrimination in life.

When the lower castes began mobilizing and putting up their own candidates, the elites grew anxious and began decrying the rise of caste-based politics and 'vote banks'. 'So regressive!' they complained, 'a betrayal of the spirit and ideals of democracy!' But of course, being founders and longtime practitioners of a supremacist politics of caste, with hardly an egalitarian bone in their bodies, they had played a rigged game all along, starting with language itself. 'Vote banks' were others, created by the new 'caste-based parties'; the elites didn't see their own upper-caste folk as a 'vote bank', though they all voted for upper-caste parties like the Congress and the Bharatiya Janata Party (BJP). A sense of entitlement prevented them from seeing that they had, contrary to a democratic ethos, long monopolized political power and opportunities based largely on caste. So now, their anxiety over the emerging caste-based politics betrayed, above all, a visceral fear—fear of the 'impure' masses, fear of losing their privileges, fear of being overrun by the boors. In no area is this anxiety more evident than in the debate on caste-based affirmative action, aka reservations, in public-sector jobs and college admissions.

Writing in *The Wretched of the Earth* (1961), Frantz Fanon lamented 'the unpreparedness of the elite, the lack of practical ties between them and the masses, their apathy, and, yes, their cowardice at the crucial moment in the struggle.'

These elites, he wrote, 'simultaneously resisted the insidious agenda of colonialism and paved the way for the emergence of the current struggles.'[5]

Fanon had in mind the post-colonial elites of North Africa, but his remark is no less apt for the Indians. India needed a real program of socioeconomic justice—via, say, land reform, universal education, and fighting caste discrimination. What legislation the elites did pass they didn't push far enough. Instead, they consolidated their domination over politics, the economy, education, cultural institutions, and the media—for instance, the richest 10 percent monopolize more land now than in 1951.[6] Having done quite well for itself, self-congratulation has come easy to this class. In an attempt to restore some balance, this insider, dear reader, will now relate to you its benightedness.

* * *

Walk into a relatively nice neighborhood in, say, Ahmedabad, Pune, or Jaipur, perhaps one of the burgeoning gated communities of flats owned by professionals, public-sector officials, and businessmen. This demographic will usually speak some English by choice, represent under 10 percent of the population but command far greater power in public life. Notice that nearly all mailboxes have upper-caste names. The average man here might profess to be modern and secular, but don't be fooled. His is an incipient modernity, without deep roots—more about clothes, gadgets, nuclear family, educating girls, and fewer food taboos. His idea of the individual, each with an equal human dignity, is terribly weak.

---

5   Frantz Fanon. 1961. *The Wretched of the Earth*. Translated from the French by Richard Philcox, 2004. Grove Press, New York, pp. 97, 145.

6   Manpreet Sethi. 2006. 'Land Reform in India: Issues and Challenges'. From Peter Rosset, Raj Patel, Michael Courville. 2006. *Promised Land: Competing Visions of Agrarian Reform*. Land Research Action Network.

Nor does he subscribe to the dignity of labor. If he lives in a walled high-rise complex, he would be at peace with its separate elevator for those not of his social class. Indeed, he would recoil at the very idea of inviting his sweeper to sit on his sofa to have a chai and samosa as a fellow human. Worse, he would never have wondered why none among his servants, maids, and sweepers share his last name, or what role his caste played in getting him where he is today. What prevents such ideas from crossing his mind is a deeply internalized hierarchy—and therefore entitlement—evident in the way he makes demands on those in his employ, and the deference he expects from them and their kind.

In this social class, middle-aged members might casually observe, 'I saw no casteism while growing up.' Of course, it's harder to see such things from above—which is part of their caste privilege—analogous to the legions of men who internalize their sexism so well they don't notice it at all. This is also the class that is prone to reminisce the 'unity' and 'harmony' of the olden days. Now it feels cheated by reservations. Not surprisingly, a good many champion the 'merit-only' line (implying that only test scores should be considered) and love to claim 'caste blindness' by asserting that their caste is 'Indian'. This 'caste-blind' stance has wide currency with those who somehow see it as totally fair and impartial. They don't recognize that while caste-based prejudice or discrimination is bad, a keen awareness of our different caste privileges is both good and necessary for positive change. In a caste-ridden society, their willful blindness to social pathologies only perpetuates them and does nothing to enhance social mobility. No wonder this class also largely opposed the 2011 caste census meant to assess the continuing socioeconomic disadvantage of caste.

Explain the premise of positive discrimination and see eyes roll. 'We don't treat them badly anymore,' one aunty told me, 'what are they agitating about?' Mention the benefits of diversity and question narrow ideas of 'merit', only to see hateful fear mongering spew out. 'Oye, what if a scheddu civil engineer built a bridge that collapsed?' ('Scheddu' is a derogatory reduction of Scheduled Caste, the administrative term for Dalits, formerly 'untouchables'.) 'What if a scheddu doctor killed a patient?' The instinct is to associate lower-caste with congenital stupidity. It doesn't occur to them that the beneficiaries of reservation have to pass the same course-work and training as all others. Besides, they have no empirical data on how many fallen bridges were built by 'scheddus', nor do they know that Dalit children routinely die due to discriminatory practices by 'merit' doctors.[7] What, if not prejudice, makes them assume that 'scheddus' build bridges that fall, rather than corrupt upper-caste engineers who steal public funds and use inferior materials? Nor do they hesitate in sending their own under-performing kids to engineering and medical colleges where admission is based solely on 'capitation fee'—on money, not 'merit'—as well as to obscure colleges in the former Soviet block countries cashing-in on the obsession this class has for 'foreign degrees'. Some years ago, through the media they dominate, they raised a storm over hate crimes in Australian cities against Indian students, clearly of their own social class. They even got the Indian State to flex its diplomatic muscle. Yet, in their own cities, they are quite oblivious to hate crimes against Dalit students (which also pushes many Dalit students over the edge to commit suicide), or African students, or students from north-eastern India.

Awed by the pop culture that trickles down from the West, this class knows little about the rest of India, nor has anything but condescending disdain for its tribal and folk

---

7   Sanghmitra S Acharya. 2010. 'Access to Health Care and Patterns of Discrimination: A Study of Dalit Children in Selected Villages of Gujarat and Rajasthan', *UNICEF*.

music, dance, and theater.[8] Of much greater concern is India's image in the West, the health of the IT sector, new consumer goods, the peril from Pakistan, emulating China. Utterly materialistic in its values, it equates education with technical training, success with money, and sneers at the idea of a career in the arts, social sciences, and the humanities. Its increasingly chauvinistic nationalism is built on an insecure pride in Hinduism. Members of this class may feel irked by Dalits decamping to Buddhism, Christianity, and Islam, but they know 'the problem' Dalits have: *their* problem is one of underdevelopment, to be fixed by more aggressive 'inclusive development'. Pieties and slogans aside, the members of this class make absolutely no demands on themselves. They never look at the mirror and see that they are squarely at the heart of 'the problem'.

* * *

I'm a graduate of the elite Indian Institute of Technology (IIT) system. At a recent dinner party, a Brahmin friend and a hostel mate at IIT Kharagpur, criticized reservations on the grounds that they are socially divisive and instigate disharmony. I had to laugh. Isn't the caste system all about social division, using graded notions of superior and inferior blood? Caste identities have been strong for ages; even today over 90 percent marry their own. If caste now also shapes political consciousness, it's because, in part, its members share the experience of discrimination and inherited disadvantage. If the decibels have gone up, it's because the lower castes no longer

---

8   An example comes from Professor Subramanium, Chennai Academy of Music, who said the following during a classical music recital: 'There is folk music and classical music. Carnatic music is scientifically organized, folk music is not so ... people who are not properly trained just sing out of emotion, enthusiasm. Folk music can be sung by any child. Quacks! Carnatic is not like this, you need a talent.' Source: Julian Silverman. 2003. 'Pariah Beats', *New Internationalist Magazine*, August.

tolerate the oppressive 'harmony' of the past. They want a piece of the pie, and they are seeking it via the ballot box. In another country, with the kind of inequities India has, the masses might have resorted to violent revolution long ago. They did not do so in India primarily because the caste system has also prevented unity for a common cause.

Why pursue reservations, my friend argued, when urbanization, capitalism, and industrial development are doing far better at defeating the inequities of caste. This is true up to a point, and a myth beyond. Caste has been updated and restructured by—and in some ways, attenuated by—capitalism, industrialism, urbanization, the Internet, and mass communication. It's true that cities offer greater anonymity and diverse jobs unrelated to traditional caste occupations, thereby weakening many, including some of the worst, forms of rural casteism. An office-going Brahmin is unlikely to worry about being polluted if he brushes against a Dalit in a crowded bus, or object to eating out lest a Dalit prepared the meal. But even as many old caste abuses have vanished or weakened in the face of urbanization, others have arisen or evolved into malignant forms. The so-called free markets of neoliberalism, scholar Gopal Guru has argued, have 'perpetuated casteism in new forms, making dalits participate in the perpetuation of casteism,'[9] even as neoliberalism has also created a few Dalit millionaires, who are then selectively cited to tout its 'success'.

---

9   Gopal Guru. 2012. 'Rise of the 'Dalit Millionaire'', *Economic & Political Weekly*, Vol. 47, Issue No. 50, December 15. Guru provides this example: 'The state's practice of outsourcing the management of urban governance or maintenance of sanitation has, in effect, created a set of 'garbage managers', contractors from within the dalit community. These new jobbers are said to be indulging in the worst kind of exploitation of ragpickers. Thus, globalisation has somehow led to the localisation of exploitation, which operates within the dalit community. Dalit ragpickers now have exploiters both from within and outside the community.'

In other words, capitalist industrialization is a turbulent force working upon the caste system, but it is not in itself a socially progressive force. Introduced in a society like India, with its entrenched inequities, capital and industry build on preexisting social privileges, discrimination, and kinship networks.[10] Furthermore, in an economic system that sanctions unbridled competition, groups with long-standing advantages of wealth and knowledge will continue to be its disproportionate gainers, increasing disparity along caste lines. Indeed, whatever political power the elites have lost to 'caste parties' in recent decades, they have more than made up for in economic power—which is now their backdoor entrée to political clout and control of the national agenda.

As many historians of caste have noted, caste in the urban milieu has morphed to behave more like an ethnic community, whose members not only harbor notions of 'ethnic' distinctiveness but also a strong consciousness of rank vs. other caste communities. This continuing lack of egalitarianism then poisons urban civic life. It impacts hiring decisions; access to rental housing, health care, and public services; response from law enforcement; judicial verdicts; etc.[11] According to a 2012 study, 'caste still remains a real axis of urban residential segregation in India's seven largest metro cities, [finding] residential segregation by caste to be sizeably larger than the level of segregation by socio-economic status. Caste has historically shaped the organisation of residential

---

10 See Amy Chua. 2004. *World on Fire*, Anchor, a very good study of many Asian, African, and Latin American countries (not India but lessons apply) that shows how neoliberal economics can worsen ethnic strife.

11 Such crippling negative discrimination can stymie most positive discrimination policies. But even for Black Americans, whose situation today is much better than that of Dalits, a 'results gap' continues to exist. For an explanation, see Orlando Patterson. 2010. 'For African-Americans, A Virtual Depression—Why?', *The Nation*, July 19.

space, especially at the village level, and it appears to continue to do so in contemporary urban India.'[12]

In our age of economic liberalization, even the Indian private sector oozes discrimination from all its pores. A recent and extensive compilation of studies, *Blocked by Caste*, decisively dispels the belief that the private sector is mostly caste-blind and hires based on 'merit'.[13] It shows that equally qualified Dalit and Muslim résumés are much less likely to get selected than upper-caste ones, and exposes other 'hidden nuances of caste prejudice in the language of globalisation that contemporary India speaks.'[14] In *The Grammar of Caste: Economic Discrimination in Contemporary India*, economist Ashwini Deshpande 'uses rich empirical data to uncover how contemporary, formal, urban sector labour markets reflect a deep awareness of caste, religious, gender, and class cleavages.' She 'argues that discrimination is neither a relic of the past nor is it confined to rural areas, but is very much a modern, formal sector phenomenon.'[15] Even things like upper-caste food taboos—and the feelings of nausea and disgust they provoke—adversely impact employment opportunities for even relatively privileged-class *Ashraf* Muslims

12 Trina Vithayathil, Gayatri Singh. 2012. 'Spaces of Discrimination: Residential Segregation in Indian Cities', *Economic & Political Weekly*, Vol. 47, Issue No. 37, September 15.

13 Sukhdeo Thorat and Katherine S. Newman. 2010. *Blocked by Caste: Economic Discrimination in Modern India*. Oxford. See a review by Madhura Swaminathan. 2010. 'Caste & the labour market', *The Hindu*, March 9. Among older studies is one by MN Panini, who showed that during the 'permit raj' era, the private sector was far from caste neutral or 'merit based' and routinely tapped into its caste networks. Susan Bayly. 1999. *Caste, Society and Politics in India: from the Eighteenth Century to the Modern Age*. Cambridge University Press, p. 322.

14 Latha Jishnu. 2009. 'The economics of caste inequity', *Business Standard*, December 18.

15 Ashwini Deshpande. 2011. *The Grammar of Caste: Economic Discrimination in Contemporary India*. Oxford University Press.

in urban India.[16] The obvious question such studies raise is: why shouldn't affirmative action, or at least strong anti-discrimination statutes and enforcement, be part of the strategy for equalizing opportunity in the private sector? Another implication is that such entrenched discrimination in public life is what ensures that even the beneficiaries of reservation can travel only so far (to be sure, factors other than casteist discrimination can also sometimes hold them back, such as the lack of a certain cultural capital deemed helpful for many jobs and promotions).[17]

My friend, whose attitudes are fairly representative of my other friends from IIT, had never even noticed that of the nine students in our IIT hostel wing, five were Brahmins, or the fact that our IIT faculty too was almost entirely drawn from the twice-born castes. This lack of awareness is another form of caste privilege. Even in 2015, only 11 of the 536 faculty members at IIT Chennai were SC (in 2001, SCs were only 2 out of 427; IIT Mumbai had zero).[18] In 2010, even in Jawaharlal Nehru University, Delhi, 'regarded as a bastion of progressive social scientists and historians—only 3.29 per cent of the faculty [was] Dalit and 1.44 per cent Adivasi, while the quotas are meant to be 15 per cent and 7.5 per cent, respectively.'[19] Each year, both during and since our time at IIT, the SC/ST quota had gone largely unfilled for the incoming students. Even then, my friend had internalized a dispro-

16 Sumeet Mhaskar. 2013. 'Indian Muslims in a Global City: Socio-Political Effects on Economic Preferences in Contemporary Mumbai', *MMG Working Paper*.

17 For an excellent survey of the reservations debate, see Jayati Ghosh. 2006. 'Case for Caste Based Quotas in Higher Education', *EPW*, Vol. 41, Issue No. 24, June 17.

18 Ajantha Subramanian. 2015. 'An anatomy of the caste culture at IIT-Madras', Open, June 12.

19 Arundhati Roy. 2014. 'The Doctor and the Saint', an introduction o BR Ambedkar's *Annihilation of Caste*. Navayana, p. 34.

portionate sense of the 'wrong' of reservations eating away at the system.

Notably, he supported income- and gender-based reservations. A votary of a technocratic idea of 'merit', he was nevertheless willing to trade some 'merit' for other social goods, except when it came to caste. He saw the disability of poverty and gender, but minimized the disability of caste, refusing to see how common it is even in urban life, let alone in rural India, where most Indians live. I wondered if he had ever really pondered the sting of casteism, or what Indian society might look like from Dalit perspectives, urban and rural. He seemed to embody all the ignorance, doublethink, and moral myopia of the social class we both belonged to. I saw in him the same empathy deficit that I had been ashamed to discover within myself.

* * *

It is often said that caste is to India what race is to America, so it may be instructive to compare their trajectories in both countries, and to see what India can do better. Though much work is still needed on race relations in America, debate on racial prejudice has been mainstream there since at least the 1960s, furthered by books like Ralph Ellison's *Invisible Man* (1952), James Baldwin's *Notes of a Native Son* (1955), and Harper Lee's *To Kill a Mockingbird* (1960). Whites joined Blacks in the Civil Rights movement and confronted other Whites in the public square.[20] Hollywood, the media, and the elites led the charge against racism. Urban civic institutions began combating it as a social evil. The courts cracked the whip on hate crimes (police violence against Blacks remains a problem today, but its incidence has evidently declined in recent decades; only its frequent documentation by phone

---

20 A good example here is Robert Jensen, Professor, School of Journalism, University of Texas at Austin. See his writings on race and White privilege. http://robertwjensen.org

cameras nowadays and subsequent media coverage, as in Ferguson, suggests otherwise)[21]. During the 1960s, the Civil Rights Act and the Fair Housing Act made it illegal to discriminate in employment and housing on the basis of race, color, sex, or national origin. This, combined with a fairly efficient legal apparatus, has considerably reduced such discrimination though it has by no means disappeared.[22]

Since the sixties, diversity and multiculturalism have become priorities in academic and cultural institutions. White readers widely read Black authors who write about their social milieus. Blacks are highly visible in popular culture, including sports, music, and films, and are fully integrated in the military. White majority areas have often elected Black mayors, senators, and governors; racist slurs by politicians are vigorously criticized in the media (though, clearly, such slurs still find support among sections of the public), and often lead to consequences (recall the 'macaca incident', said to have cost George Allen his re-election to the US Senate in 2006[23]).[24]

Now consider the situation in India. There is still no anti-discrimination statute in housing or employment in the private sector, nor effective prosecution for discrimination in housing and employment, which is rampant.[25] The media has

---

21 Peter Dreier. 2016. 'Caught on Camera: Police Racism', *American Prospect*, July 11.

22 For a nuanced and insightful portrait of race relations in the US, see Ta-Nehisi Coates. 2017. 'My President was Black', *The Atlantic Monthly*. January/February 2017.

23 Tim Craig and Micheal D. Shear. 2006. 'Allen Quip Provokes Outrage, Apology', *Washington Post*, Aug 15.

24 A counter-example here is Donald Trump, who won despite his many racist and sexist remarks in the 2016 presidential campaign, heralding an unprecedented and regressive new low in US politics, though most social elites were also vigorously critical of him.

25 Seema Chishti. 2015. 'Study shows NCR homeowners turn away Dalits and Muslims', *Indian Express*, 16 June. 'In both the methodologies, the home-seekers had the same credentials but for their

little more than superficial interest or insight into Dalit and Adivasi lives, nor hires Dalit or Adivasi journalists.[26] Major atrocities against Dalits still go unreported or misreported. Law enforcement is often indifferent or worse: policemen refuse to file FIRs, collude with the criminals, and obstruct justice in the courts. Of the hundreds of judges appointed to the Supreme Court of India, only three have been Dalit.[27] A Dalit politician, however qualified, has little chance of winning in a constituency that's non-reserved, even if it were in a relatively modern area like South Mumbai. Prime Minister and leader of the BJP, Narendra Modi, when he was Chief Minister of Gujarat in 2010, got away easily after coldly comparing Dalits to 'mentally retarded children' who gain 'spiritual experience' from manual scavenging.

Even among those few elites who read books, how many have read a single novel or memoir by a Dalit? In what is perhaps the most diverse country in the world, there is no commitment to diversity in the elite institutions that decide what is worthy art, music, and literature, or what is the content of history textbooks. None of the eighteen chairs thus far of the Indian Council of Historical Research, which funds historical research in India, has been Dalit. Brahminical thinking still deeply pervades scholarship about the past, creatively defanging and co-opting dissidents into its fold, as with the Bhakti thinkers and poets of the medieval period.[28] In book after book of stories for children, both the protagonist and the implicit audience are elite and upper-caste.[29] Much the

names that indicated their caste and religion.'
26 Siddharth Varadarajan. 2006. 'Caste matters in the Indian media', *The Hindu*, June 3.
27 Sohail Hashmi. 2011. 'Corruption has its Caste in the Judiciary: All India Confederation of SC/ST Organisations', Kafila.org, April 7.
28 Gail Omvedt. 2008. *Seeking Begumpura: The Social Vision of Anticaste Intellectuals.* Navayana.
29 Deeptha Achar and Deepa Sreenivas. 2010. 'Storybooks for a Plural World', *Himal Southasian*, May.

same is true of sitcoms, soap operas, and commercials on TV.[30] Dalits are invisible from all popular culture that gets any airtime. Even the Indian army refuses to mirror the social composition of the Indian republic and has largely kept out Muslims from its ranks.[31] There is no comparable Indian counterpart of the American Civil Liberties Union (ACLU). Or a Dalit history month on public TV, or exhibits in museums, that seek to educate the upper castes about a long and dark chapter of their past (and present[32]). Unless a sizable proportion of elites, benumbed by privilege, open their eyes and learn to see both within and without, can there be much hope for relief from our inherited inequalities?

---

30 Aakar Patel. 2014. 'Caste and conservatism in our TV serials', *Livemint*, September 27.

31 Omar Khalidi. 2009. *Khaki and Ethnic Violence in India*. Three Essays Collective.

32 'Caste Discrimination Against Dalits', a report prepared by Center for Human Rights and Global Justice and Human Rights Watch, 2007.

The Moral Universe of the *Bhagavad Gita*[1]

Part 1

In mid-first millennium BCE, a great spiritual awakening was underway in areas around the middle Ganga. People were moving away from the old Vedic religion—which revolved around rituals, animal sacrifices, and nature gods—to more abstract, inner-directed, and contemplative ideas. They now asked about the nature of the self and consciousness, thought and perception. They asked if virtue and vice were absolute or mere social conventions. Personal spiritual quests, aided by meditation and renunciation of material gain, had slowly gathered pace. From this churn arose new ideas like karma and dharma, non-dualism, and the unity of an individual's soul (*atman*) with the universal soul (*Brahman*)—all pivotal ideas in Brahminical Hinduism.

Some of these innovations in thought soon made their way into the texts we now know as the *Upanishads*, setting

---

1   All *Gita* quotes in this essay come from *The Bhagavad Gita: Translated with a General Introduction by Eknath Easwaran*. Penguin Books India, 1996. An earlier version of this essay appeared in two installments on 3 Quarks Daily on Dec 5, 2011 and Jan 2, 2012.

them qualitatively apart from the earlier *Vedas*. All of this occurred in the context of great sociopolitical and economic changes, marked by the rise of cities, trade and commerce, social mobility, public debates, new institutions of state, and even some early republics. This was also the world of the Buddha, Mahavira, and Carvaka.

The Great War of Yore

By this time, versions of a *Mahabharata* story had been circulating for centuries. Perhaps inspired by a war that took place c. 950 BCE around modern Delhi (the date is tentative), the story, through oral transmission, took on a life of its own. In *The Hindus: An Alternative History* (2009), Wendy Doniger writes that the earliest bards who told the *Mahabharata* story came from a caste of charioteers, who served as drivers, confidantes, and bodyguards to the Kshatriya warrior-castes. While on military campaigns, they recited stories around campfires. (No wonder God is a charioteer in the epic! Even Karna is raised by a charioteer.) In later ages and in times of peace, many bards took their performance art to lay audiences in villages and folk festivals. The story also came to be recited during royal sacrifices, where the Brahmins gradually took over its delivery and evolution, eventually writing it down in Sanskrit. Its 'final form' dates from 300 BCE-300 CE and ranges from 75K to 100K verses, seven to ten times the *Iliad* and the *Odyssey* combined.

The *Mahabharata*, writes Doniger, 'is so extremely fluid that there is no single *Mahabharata*; there are hundreds of *Mahabharatas*, hundreds of different manuscripts and innumerable oral versions (one reason why it is impossible to make an accurate calculation of the number of its verses). The *Mahabharata* is not contained in a text; the story is there to be picked up and found, salvaged as anonymous treasure from the ocean of story.'[2] While these versions share the same narrative core—the struggle between two branches of a royal family, the Pandavas and the Kauravas, for the control of the Kuru capital, Hastinapura, culminating in a great civil war—around it 'are piled high many volumes of lore and doctrine contributed by Indian thinkers and storytellers over centuries', writes Sheldon Pollock, author of *The Language of the Gods in the World of Men*. Frustrated by this situation, scholars at the Bhandarkar Oriental Research Institute, Pune, collated 1259 manuscripts from 1919-66 to produce a critical edition of the *Mahabharata* with 89K verses; it is this version that most scholars reference today.

The *Mahabharata* has been variously read as 'history, poetry, moral law, and scripture', though its central problematic, writes Pollock, is about power. 'The dilemma of power—in the starkest terms, the need to destroy in order to preserve, to kill in order to live—becomes most poignant when those whom one must kill are one's own kin. That is why the *Mahabharata* is the most harrowing of all premodern political narratives in the world: the *Iliad*, like the *Ramayana*, is about a war far from home, the *Odyssey* about a post-war journey home, and the *Aeneid* about a war for a home. The *Mahabharata* is about a war fought at home', one in which both sides end up losing (to be precise, one side scores a pyrrhic victory).[3] Having read all of these epics, I think another point of departure for the *Mahabharata* is that the heroes in the other epics are much less reflective; they live by a received heroic code and are not too motivated as individuals to seek self-knowledge or worry about the right thing to do. Which other epic has a hero as introspective and truth-loving as Yu-

2 Wendy Doniger. 2009. *The Hindus: An Alternative History.* Penguin, p. 263.
3 Sheldon Pollock. 2006. *The Language of the Gods in the World of Men: Sanskrit, Culture, and Power in Premodern India.* University of California Press, p. 225.

dhisthira, or as prone to ethical doubt as Arjuna, or as magnanimous as Karna?

What the *Mahabharata* does share with the Homeric epics is that it, too, has been reworked so heavily at different times that it is hard to extract reliable historical or sociological data from it. For instance, in 950 BCE, the estimated time of the war that inspired the epic, Kuru society was clan-based; chieftainship was based on both kinship networks and personal qualities; the extent of the Kuru domain, over whose control the war was fought, was a small region of the Ganga-Yamuna Doab. But the bards later injected kings into the epic who went beyond clan chieftains; these kings ruled over bigger territories and practiced heredity succession. The bards even magnified the war to apparently include all of the peoples they knew of. John Keay, author of *India: A History*, notes that the epic's royal palaces too were upgraded to those of later times, with 'pillared pavilions and marble halls, their interiors opulently furnished', polished and shiny floors, untold wealth, and so on—descriptions that legitimized 'the grandiose ambitions of later empire builders.' That said, one aspect of the epic that likely goes way back is its view of the forest-dwelling clans of hunter-gatherers; the epic's heroes encounter them in exile as *rakshasas*, or demons, some hostile and some who turn into allies—depictions that seem in line with 'the presumed pattern of Aryan colonization and settlement'.

Clearly, lots of people contributed to the *Mahabharata*. Accepting Vyasa as its author has more to do with our need to personalize storytelling. Doniger writes that 'non-Brahmins, people of low caste, were originally in charge of the care and feeding of the two great Sanskrit poems [the other being the *Ramayana*], which Brahmins took over only sometime later, one of many instances of the contributions of low-caste people to Sanskrit literature.' The basis of caste was more fluid earlier, ranging from heredity to personal character, occupation, and even choice. Vyasa, himself a character in the story as the son of a ferryman's daughter, is a half-caste. All this might help explain the polyphony and plurality of views that have survived in the *Mahabharata*—in its range of moral dilemmas, ideas of duty, flaws of character, conflicts of virtues and values—and why it continues to have such popular appeal in India. As Doniger writes, the *Mahabharata* remains a contested text, 'a brilliantly orchestrated hybrid narrative with no single party line on any subject.'

The Celestial Song of God

The *Bhagavad Gita* ('The God's Song'), widely regarded as the philosophical core of the *Mahabharata*, was composed much later under the realities of a new age. It was merged into the epic's later drafts, perhaps as late as first century CE. This means that the philosophy it espouses is often not in accord with the moral ambiguities of the larger epic. Presented as a Q&A style exchange between Lord Krishna and the warrior-prince Arjuna, the *Gita* channels certain ideas from the Upanishads and the newly ascendant Bhagavata sect (whose devotionalism, notably, is not prominent elsewhere in the *Mahabharata*). It attempts to render esoteric philosophy more accessible by making it weigh in on concrete dilemmas of war and peace. In doing so, it also strives to privilege certain ideas and values.

In the opening scene of the *Gita*, Arjuna—repulsed by the thought of killing his kin and elders—suffers an emotional meltdown in the middle of the battlefield, right before the start of the Great War between the Pandavas and the Kauravas. Despite his relatively righteous cause, he cannot see enough moral justification for the war and refuses to fight. 'I do not see that any good can come from killing our relations in battle.' (Some have compared this to Ashoka's turning away from war, which likely preceded the composition of the

Gita and may have inspired this framing.) The powerful immediacy of Arjuna's crisis commands our attention. In about 700 verses that follow—using a dazzling array of ideas and tactics, many of which inspire people even today—Krishna explains to Arjuna why he must fight. Arjuna's questions are large indeed: How do I know where my duty lies? How can I see the reality that lies beyond my worldly illusions? How can the restless mind attain lasting peace?

The *Gita* ends with Arjuna regaining his resolve to fight and overcoming his ethical concerns about the war. Eighteen days later, the war ends catastrophically; nearly everyone is killed. If you knew this but haven't read the *Gita*, you might suspect Krishna's 'wisdom' and find more instinctive sympathy with Arjuna's initial doubts about the war. Indeed, the arguments that Krishna employs to persuade Arjuna to fight often seem cold, too distant, manipulative, and even warmongering—unlike the rest of the *Mahabharata* which comes across as decidedly anti-war. Why then have so many thinkers waxed eloquent about the wisdom of the *Gita*, including Emerson, Thoreau, Gandhi, Nehru, Vivekananda, Radhakrishnan, Huxley, and Hesse? The *Gita* in fact occupies a place more exalted that most other religious texts in the world. Most Hindus, even today, accord it the cultural cachet of a work whose philosophical depth and profundity is taken for granted. What then is so great about the *Gita*?

As with other ancient religious texts—perhaps more so than many others—one can weave a path through the *Gita* (while willfully avoiding others) that can make it seem deep, inspiring, and even wise. It has some soaring verses that hit just the right universal notes. They emphasize the equal spiritual status of all seekers of truth. They exhort everyone to see the journey as the reward, not the destination. They disparage priestly rituals, and privilege self-awareness as a means of penetrating our veils of illusion—also defining higher and lower states of self-awareness and attributes thereof. Various verses downgrade selfish desire, pride, lust, greed, and the pursuit of power and sensual pleasure. Modern cosmologists may find charming the advice to 'Seek That, the First Cause, from which the universe came long ago.'

While not so novel in light of other South Asian philosophies of the day, especially Buddhism, such ideas would enhance any world religion. But they are not the whole story; the *Gita* in fact says a lot more. It promotes a specific ethical and metaphysical worldview, as it tries to answer the age-old question: how to live? To properly evaluate the *Gita*, *this worldview is what we should look at*, not isolated verses taken out of context—many of which are flatly contradicted by other verses. What then are the dominant ethics of the *Gita*? What is the picture of reality that it promotes? Is the *Gita* as good a guide to everyday life (i.e., to our 'inner battlefield') as so many claim it is?

What Song Do the Hindus Hear?

Many Hindus, including Mahatma Gandhi, have done highly selective and allegorical readings of the *Gita*. Gandhi even made it stand for peace and nonviolence. The message of the *Gita*, he wrote, is that spiritual fulfillment comes from self-less work; we must cultivate non-attachment to the outcome of our action—which doesn't mean indifference to the outcome, only the lack of hankering after and brooding over it. If one follows this 'central teaching of the *Gita*,' he added without explaining why, 'one is bound to follow truth and ahimsa [nonviolence]'. Gandhi translated the *Gita* from Sanskrit to Gujarati; in his introduction, he writes, 'Krishna of the *Gita* is perfection and right knowledge personified.' Shortly after though, he concedes that the *Gita*'s stance seems opposed to ahimsa, but then offers a painfully convoluted apology for it, citing different standards back then and calling for poetic license—going as far as saying that we don't need to probe the mind of the author too much! This suggests that he had at least struggled with the *Gita*.[4]

Gandhi's case reminds us that what people take away from a scriptural text is inseparable from who they are and what they bring to it. Which makes me wonder about Swami Vivekananda who seems to have betrayed no struggle with the *Gita*, let alone the need for an apologia. Instead, with an almost thuggish glee, he coldly rubbished Arjuna's doubt, calling it a case of fear, jitters, and unmanliness that Krishna promptly fixes by awakening his latent power.[5] Radhakrishnan, beneath his scholarly veneer, is not much better; to him the pursuit of duty for duty's sake is the unequivocal call of reason, and Krishna is 'the voice of God echoing in every man' (why not also the voice of Arjuna?).[6]

Until a couple of centuries ago, only a tiny minority of Indians—mostly Brahmins attached to institutions, the kind Al-Beruni must have interacted with in the 11th century—revered the *Gita*. This changed after modern European scholars, under the auspices of the Honorable East India Company, began investigating Hinduism, mainly because a sound knowledge of Indian history, religions, and customs would help in governing the locals (an impetus that grew after the 1857 revolt), as well as help Christian missionaries identify vulnerabilities in the local religious edifice so they could device their strategies. These scholars, such as William Jones, James Mill, and Max Müller, began researching the past, translating ancient scriptures, and theorizing about

4 Mahatma Gandhi. 2012. *Bhagavad Gita: According to Gandhi*. Orient Publishing.

5 *The Complete Works of Swami Vivekananda*, Volume 4; *Lectures and Discourses: Thoughts on the Gita*.

6 S. Radhakrishnan. 1911. 'The Ethics of the Bhagavadgita and Kant'. *International Journal of Ethics*, Vol. 21, No. 4 (July), pp. 465-475.

'Hinduism' as a coherent religion they could relate to (Mill even wrote an influential history of India without ever setting foot on the Subcontinent). Owing to their preconceived ideas of religion, class biases, reliance on elite Brahmins as native informants, focus on texts, and limited exposure to folk beliefs and lived practices, they began to elevate the *Gita* as the 'Hindu Bible'.[7] Not only were they drawn to 'the monism of the *Upanishads*', writes Doniger in *On Hinduism*:

> Some Protestants within the British Raj tried to recast Hinduism as a monotheism, with a *Bible*: the *Bhagavad Gita* [which] had never had anything remotely approaching canonical status before this, though it had always been an important text. Other texts—Sanskrit texts like the *Upanishads* and vernacular texts such as the Hindi and Tamil version[s] of the *Ramayana*, and, **most of all, oral traditions**—were what most Hindus actually used in their worship. The British exclusionary focus on the *Gita*, and on Krishna/Vishnu, amounted to mistaking kathenotheistic polytheism for monistic monotheism' [emphasis added].[8]

In *Castes of Mind*, historian and anthropologist Nicholas B. Dirks has argued that Müller, who left a strong imprint on later scholarship and even on Gandhi, believed 'that textual authority should have pride of place in official knowledge about India.' According to Dirks, Müller held that 'Indian problems were the result of degradation and corruption from the Vedic ideal.' Dirks adds that many early- and mid-19th century Orientalists, led by their own dubious reasons to create a particular view of Indian society, and with little knowledge of the social and religious lives of ordinary Indians (un-

---

7   Historian RS Sharma writes in *Rethinking India's Past* (p. 87): 'Even European writers gave their attention mainly to the study of the upper classes of Hindu society … It is difficult to explain these writers' lack of interest in the fortunes of the lower orders unless we suppose that their vision was circumscribed by the dominant class outlook of their age.'

8   Wendy Doniger. 2013. *On Hinduism*. Aleph Book Company. Kindle Edition, Locations 590-597.

like that of the elites), also accorded to the *Laws of Manu*
(translated by Jones) an 'unprecedented status', a 'canonic importance', and a 'significance it could never have had before'.
They also generalized heavily—that Indians lacked a sense of
history, took despotic rule as the norm, had no experience
of political unity, felt no sense of nationhood, lacked any impulse for self-governance, and were too preoccupied with the
next world to pay any attention to this one. Was there any
doubt that the Indians needed the resolute sobriety of British
rule?

This scholarship both influenced and upset a class of
elite Bengali Brahmins like Ram Mohan Roy of the Brahmo
Samaj, who came to be called 'reformist' and 'progressive'.
These elites, schooled in western education and the English
language, took up the work of forging a new 'Hinduism' they
could be proud of. Not surprisingly, they leaned towards a
monotheistic framework based on a 'classical Hinduism'
and elevated a textual canon—which only a tiny minority of
Hindus had ever read or even heard—with a limited set of
male gods and rituals over the 'degenerate polytheism' of folk
religion. While they challenged many European prejudices
and pointed out errors, they also fostered an inflated, often
mythologized, story of ancient India that began to shape the
consciousness of a new elite and provided ideological bal-
last for a nascent Hindu nationalism. The Brahmo Samaj and
other 'progressive' elites saw caste, idolatry, and Sati as aber-
rant practices. Partly in order to recruit the authority of the
scriptures in their fight against such practices—but also out
of their regard for these scriptures and defensiveness at smug
European critiques of Hindu degeneracy—they expended
considerable energy on selective readings and establishing
the loftiness of the Vedic corpus, the 'Hindoo religion', its
'tolerance', and 'the pure spirit of its dictates'. As Christophe
Jaffrelot writes, 'Reformists, therefore, became revivalists by

pretending that, in emulating the West, they were only restoring to pristine purity their own traditions via eliminat-
ing later accretions.'[9] This was the fountainhead of what later
came to be called Hindutva and took on a life of its own in
the closing decades of the 20th century. Ironically, for all their
reformist idealism on caste, even the Brahmo Samaj later
became 'an exclusive and largely endogamous community
within Hinduism.'[10]

This helps explain why the *Gita*, as well as other scriptures, have attracted such little critical attention in modern
India—I mean the kind that sacred books of many world religions have. In approaching the text, too few Indians have
cut through the fog of reverence that surrounds it. Among
them was the historian DD Kosambi (1907-66), who wasn't
too impressed by the *Gita*. In *Myth and Reality* (1962), he observed that a 'slippery opportunism characterizes the whole
book.'[11] BR Ambedkar (1891-1956) saw it as Brahmanism's
response to the rising fortunes of Buddhism. In his essay,
Krishna and His Gita, Ambedkar wrote, 'The philosophic
defense offered by the Bhagavad *Gita* of the Kshatriya's duty
to kill is, to say the least, puerile.'[12] The journalist and secular humanist VR Narla (1908-85) called its moral perspective 'retrograde'. In *The Truth About the Gita*, Narla argued
that the book condones violence and wholesale slaughter;
Krishna was Machiavellian, who employed trickery, deceit,
falsehood, intimidation, and blackmail to get Arjuna to over-

9   Christophe Jaffrelot. 2013. *Hindu Nationalism: A Reader*. Perma-
    nent Black. Kindle Edition, p. 7.
10 Susan Bayly. 1999. *Caste, Society and Politics in India: from the Eigh-
    teenth Century to the Modern Age*. Cambridge University Press, p.
    148.
11 DD Kosambi. 1962. *Myth and Reality*. Popular Prakashan, p. 17.
12 BR Ambedkar. 2002. 'Krishna and his Gita'. From *The Essential
    Writings of BR Ambedkar*. Edited by Valerian Rodrigues. Oxford
    India Paperbacks, pp. 193-204.

come his moral qualms.[13] More recently, in *Who Wrote the Bhagvadgita*, Meghnad Desai, economist and politician, declared the text 'unsuitable to modern India' whose Constitution commits it to 'a world of social equity and democratic freedoms. The message of the *Gita* is casteist and misogynist and as such profoundly in opposition to the spirit of modern India.' He suggests 'that some of the many hypocrisies we observe in Indian life today may have their origins in the way the message of the *Gita* can be read.'[14]

The *Gita*, written by mere mortals in a political setting but presented as the voice of God, strives to imbue the reader with a host of ideas, beliefs, and values. Classics are ultimately defined by their ability to survive criticism. Critiques of the *Gita*, too, are necessary in every age, if only to know where we stand in relation to this pillar of cultural thought in modern Hinduism. Such critiques are essentially a project of self-definition, of self-knowledge. My own engagement with the *Gita* has persuaded me that it is an overrated text with a deplorable morality at its core, which should be confronted—not explained away or swept under the holy mat (admittedly, this is not as bad as sincerely trying to follow the morality of the *Gita* today). Notably, its reflexive admirers even abound among the modern, educated Hindu upper crust, including those who live in the West.

Part 2 of this essay probes the *Gita* more closely and also revives a critique of it that existed over two millennia ago, in the thought of the Buddha and then Nagarjuna. I hope that this line of inquiry will also disarm those Hindu religionists who tend to be ultra-sensitive about critiques of their sacred books from Western perspectives (some of which may well harbor Eurocentric biases).

---

13 VR Narla. 2010. *The Truth about the Gita*. Prometheus Books.
14 Meghnad Desai. 2015. *Who Wrote the Bhagvadgita*. Element.

Part 2

The *Bhagavad Gita*, less than one percent of the sprawling *Mahabharata*, contains 700 verses in 18 chapters. It opens with Arjuna's crisis on the battlefield, right before the start of the Great War. Turning to his friend and charioteer, Arjuna cries out,

> O Krishna, I see my own relations here anxious to fight, and my limbs grow weak; my mouth is dry, my body shakes, and my hair is standing on end. My skin burns, and the bow Gandiva has slipped from my hand; my mind seems to be whirling.

Arjuna is one of the bravest warriors alive and this visceral physical response, it is amply clear, is not due to performance anxiety, or fear of injury or death. Rather, it arises from Arjuna's grave doubts over whether he is doing the right thing. He and his Pandava brothers wanted a minimally fair share of their material inheritance, but the devious, stubborn, and unjust Kauravas rebuffed them repeatedly. Though his cause is righteous enough, Arjuna now feels that the ends do not justify the means. He continues,

> O Krishna, I have no desire for victory, or for a kingdom or pleasures. Of what use is a kingdom or pleasure or even life, if those for whose sake we desire these things—teachers, fathers, sons, grandfathers, uncles, in-laws, grandsons and others with family ties—are engaging in this battle, renouncing their wealth and their lives? Even if they were to kill me, I would not want to kill them, not even to become ruler of the three worlds. How much less for the earth alone? … We are prepared to kill our own relations out of greed for the pleasures of a kingdom. Better for me if the [Kauravas] were to attack me in battle and kill me unarmed and unresisting.

Who among us can fail to be moved by Arjuna's anguish? Hopelessly confused, Arjuna pleads with Lord Krishna to show him the way. Krishna obliges, taking on the role of a teacher to help Arjuna figure out the right course of action, which Krishna believes is to fight this war. The wisdom of the *Gita*—and the claim that it remains a relevant guide to our inner battlefield—is inseparable from Krishna's advice to Arjuna. So, to evaluate the *Gita*, we need to evaluate the arguments Krishna uses to persuade Arjuna to fight. How good are these arguments?

I am aware that my reading of the *Gita*—like every other reading of it—is subjective and selective; I know that there are other ways of reading it. I have approached the *Gita* as expository literature, using the same yardsticks of truth and beauty that I take to other literary texts. I agree with Eknath Easwaran, an admirer and well-known translator of the *Gita*, when he says, 'To understand the *Gita*, it is important to look beneath the surface of its injunctions and see the mental state involved.' I have tried to do the same. I know that the *Gita* is not 'mere literature' to millions of Hindus, including many of my family and friends. It is also sacred scripture, a guide to practical wisdom, a source of personal and social identity, cultural and national pride, and more. My intention is not to offend as an end in itself, but this book review will likely unsettle many; a few will respond in angry and defensive ways. May they find in the *Gita* the wisdom to forgive my indiscretions.

Get Up and Fight!

Imagine the scene. Having charioted Arjuna into the war zone with two vast armies arrayed against each other, Krishna watches Arjuna's meltdown. Baffled by it, Krishna proceeds to shame Arjuna by calling his meltdown a 'weakness in a time of crisis', which is 'mean and unworthy' of him. He urges Arjuna to 'arise with a brave heart and destroy his enemy.' Refusing to fight, Krishna warns, will lead to loss of honor, which is worse than death. Arjuna will lose the respect of others and be ridiculed by his enemies, who will taunt him and call him a coward. 'What could be more painful than this?'

Krishna continues, 'Considering your dharma, you should not vacillate. For a warrior, nothing is higher than a war against evil'. Such a war should delight Arjuna, for it will guarantee him a place in heaven. If Arjuna dies in battle, he will attain heaven; if he wins, he will enjoy the earth. So what's his bloody problem? A red flag for me here is the fact that Krishna takes Arjuna's duty for granted, avoiding the thorniest of all problems with duty: how does one know what duty is? Later in the *Gita*, Krishna reveals how he thinks about it: one's duty depends on one's place in the caste hierarchy, which is 'based on [one's] nature.' 'By fulfilling the obligations one is born with, a person never comes to grief. No one should abandon duties because he sees defects in them' and 'by devotion to one's own particular duty, everyone can attain perfection.'

But Arjuna remains unmoved as Krishna tries to shame him, hold up rewards, and remind him of his duty. Arjuna simply cannot imagine fighting elders he reveres, like Bhishma and Drona. He is not sure where his duty lies. Doesn't his duty as a warrior conflict with his duty to not slaughter his kin and elders? Isn't there a point when the means of upholding dharma risk pushing one into adharma? Arjuna would rather spend his life 'begging than to kill these great and worthy souls.' His will paralyzed, he complains of 'a sorrow that saps all his vitality.' Krishna, realizing that Arjuna's crisis is pretty serious, shifts his strategy. He wheels in some heavy-duty philosophy into his arguments.

Krishna could have argued that this is a 'just war', that Arjuna's relatives are aligned with an evil large enough to justify killing them—but he does not. Both of them indicate that the cause they are fighting for is to obtain for the Pandavas their share of the kingdom. If a larger cause is at stake—

such as restoring righteousness on earth—Krishna neither elaborates one, nor invokes it to make a case for 'just war' in the *Gita*, preferring other arguments. So rather than offer up hypothetical reasons or apologia on behalf of Krishna, we should judge the *Gita* in light of the arguments for war that he does actually make in it, especially the ones he repeatedly makes—which is what I intend to focus on in this essay.

The Metaphysics of Detachment

The *Gita*'s core metaphysics is based on the *Upanishads*, which represent, in my view, a major milestone in the history of abstract thought and a great leap in conceiving our relationship to nature—but not quite of an advance in terms of ethical philosophy. At the risk of oversimplification, I'll summarize the metaphysics of the *Upanishads* by saying that they speak of a formless and all-pervasive vital force, or *Brahman*, which is the Ultimate Reality beneath the world of shifting appearances. Our own life force, the Self, or *atman*, is but one manifestation of *Brahman*, and it has the same nature as the *atman* of other beings, such as a dog's. *Atman* is immortal; after the death of a body it migrates to inhabit another body. Grasping the true nature of *atman* and its essential unity with *Brahman* is what enables one to attain *Moksha*, or release from the endless cycle of rebirth—a preeminent individual pursuit. To attain *Moksha*, one must penetrate his or her veils of illusion and realize the truth of *Brahman*—a bracing view of reality as it might appear to the 'cosmic eye'. In this view, our dualist conceptions of the world fall away, revealing the deeply interwoven strands of the phenomenal world (some dualist ideas based on *samkhya* metaphysics also appear in the *Gita*). As the *Isha Upanishad* relates, 'He who sees everywhere the Self in all existences and all existences in the Self, shrinks not thereafter from aught.'[15] Nor are humans at the

---

15 *Isha Upanishad*, Translated and with a commentary by Sri Aurob-

center of life or creation; in fact, particular human lives and concerns are seen as entirely insignificant in cosmic terms.

Krishna interprets this metaphysics to support a tangible objective, namely, persuading Arjuna to fight. Krishna's is not the only possible interpretation, nor the most sensible one. Indeed, he belongs in the long line of shrewd characters who have bent metaphysics to their own ends. For instance, consider this interpretation: Krishna tells Arjuna that his sorrow is misguided. Those who grasp the true nature of reality, he says, 'grieve neither for the living nor for the dead. There has never been a time when you and I and the kings gathered here have not existed, nor will there be a time when they will cease to exist. ... The body is mortal, but he who dwells in the body is immortal and immeasurable. Therefore, Arjuna, fight in this battle.' It is out of ignorance of the true nature of reality, he says, that we call one man a slayer, another man slain. 'There is neither slayer nor slain. You were never born; you will never die.' Krishna's sleight-of-hand here lies in equating the people we care about with their *atmans*, and since *atman* is immortal, it matters not if their bodies are destroyed. 'There could hardly be a better example of forked-tongue speciousness,' wrote P. Lal (1929-2010), professor of literature and Indian Studies and translator of the entire *Mahabharata* into English, in the introduction to his translation of the *Gita* (1965).[16]

Arjuna is still not sold, so Krishna presses on. O Arjuna, he says, 'even if you believe the Self to be subject to birth and death, you should not grieve. Death is inevitable for the living ... you should not sorrow.' Every creature is unmanifested at first, is then manifested, and in time, is unmanifested again, so 'what is there to lament in this?' Krishna's point is

indo between 1900-14. Vol. 17, *The Complete Works of Sri Aurobindo*. Sri Aurobindo Ashram Press, Pondicherry, p. 7.

16 P. Lal. 1986. *The Mahabharata Of Vyasa (English and Sanskrit Edition)*. Vikas Publishing House.

that if Arjuna's arrow is what 'unmanifests' his uncle from earthly life, there is nothing wrong in it because it is all part of a cyclical process. Ambedkar called this line of reasoning 'an unheard-of defense of murder', adding that if Krishna was a lawyer today and pleaded such a defense for a client, there is 'not the slightest doubt that he would be sent to the lunatic asylum'.

The Path of Selfless Action

The dialog continues. Krishna enjoins Arjuna to 'seek refuge in the attitude of detachment ... those who are motivated only by the desire for the fruits of action are miserable, for they are constantly anxious about the results of what they do.' But in those who are detached, 'all vain anxiety is left behind. There is no cause for worry, whether things go well or ill ... thus they attain a state beyond all evil' and attain Moksha. Several times he instructs Arjuna to 'Act selflessly, without any thought of personal profit.' This is to many, including Gandhi, the central teaching of the *Gita*.

On the face of it, this seems reasonable. What can be wrong with performing one's duty without selfish desire and attachment? Self-control over one's ego and passions are likely even good for one's moral conduct. A thick skin against how others perceive our actions can sometimes be helpful. But a major problem lurks here. Krishna frequently talks about the duty that one is born into. 'The distinctions of caste, guna, and karma have come from me,' he says. 'The responsibilities to which a brahmin is born, based on his nature, are self-control, tranquility, purity of heart, patience, humility, learning, austerity, wisdom, and faith,' whereas 'the proper work of the shudra is service.' The problem is that Krishna never talks about the use of reason to figure out one's duty—as the Buddha did—or to modify it in light of the potential and actual consequences of one's action.

Without this corrective, the injunction to do one's duty with total detachment serves only to bolster the doer's equanimity, whatever the outcome. It becomes all about keeping the doer's peace of mind, not about his impact on others. Rather than acknowledge that our worldly acts carry an ineliminable moral risk, the *Gita* says that this risk can be eliminated through a personal attitude adjustment. In this sense, the *Gita*'s idea of detached duty is less an ethical precept, more a self-help precept. As Easwaran writes: 'Nishkama karma [selfless action] is not 'good works' or philanthropic activity; [the latter] may benefit others, but not necessarily benefit the doer.' And the *Gita*'s focus is relentlessly on the doer's attitude while he dispenses his dharmic duty, not on what he actually does to others and its human impact. Krishna is thus able to ask Arjuna to perform 'all actions for my sake, completely absorbed in the Self, and without expectations, fight!' In *The Idea of Justice*, Amartya Sen too finds this problematic: 'Krishna argues that Arjuna must do his duty, come what may, and in this case he has a duty to fight, no matter what results from it ... Why should we want only to 'fare forward' and not also 'fare well'? Can a belief in a consequence-independent duty to fight for a just cause convincingly override one's reasons for not wanting to kill people, including those for whom one has affection?'[17]

Krishna further elaborates what selfless action looks like and how meditation can help. 'Those who cannot renounce attachment to the results of their work are far from the path', he says. Those who conquer their senses, climb 'to the summit of human consciousness. To such people a clod of dirt, a stone, and gold are the same. They are equally disposed to family, enemies, and friends, to those who support them and those who are hostile, to the good and the evil alike. Because

---

17 Amartya Sen. 2011. *The Idea of Justice*. Harvard University Press, pp. 209-211.

they are impartial, they rise to great heights.' They can control their turbulent mind 'through regular practice and detachment' to discover inner peace and joy by attaining union with Brahman.

Again, this stance is morally dubious and reflects the anti-humanistic sensibility that pervades the *Gita*. It may be good for achieving oneness with Ultimate Reality (whatever that is), but it is bad for moral life—it rejects the very idea that some actions have greater moral worth than others. It denies that some human bonds are more precious than others, which is part of what makes us human. This is the kind of detachment that can make moral villains out of men. It is a suitably desensitizing stance that can get a warrior to kill and feel no remorse, or to make us oblivious to each other's human plight, as we pursue our given ideas of duty while upholding incoherent ideals like Brahman. As VR Narla put it, 'while action without seeking some personal gain can be noble, action without any care for its evil consequences to other men [is] reprehensible, even diabolical.'

After all this talk, Arjuna longs to see a vision of Brahman. Krishna obliges and gives him a dazzling and ecstatic glimpse into cosmic reality, including his 'radiant, universal form, without beginning or end'. While this is a brilliantly imaginative vision in many ways, Krishna unfortunately spoils it by infusing it with dubious morality. 'I am time, the destroyer of all,' Krishna tells Arjuna, 'Even without your participation, all the warriors gathered here will die. Therefore, arise, Arjuna; conquer your enemies and enjoy the glory of sovereignty. I have already slain all these warriors; you will only be my instrument.' The war hasn't even begun and Krishna says, 'Bhishma, Drona, Jayadrata, Karna, and many others are already slain. Kill those whom I have killed. Do not hesitate. Fight in this battle and you will conquer your enemies.' How comforting, to have the Lord of the Universe (or Ultimate Reality personified) issue a moral blank cheque to a man disinclined to slaughter his relatives!

The Path of Devotion

Krishna, now back in human form, tries another tack: Trust me! 'Fill your mind with me; love me; serve me; worship me always,' he urges Arjuna. In return, Krishna will take care of him. 'You are dear to me,' says Krishna. 'Abandon all supports and look to me for protection. I shall purify you from the sins of the past; do not grieve.' This is similar to the personal god in the mystical strains of many religions (e.g., Bhakti, Sufi), in which the mystic finds his rationality inadequate in knowing God and his design. Love and devotion—even rapturous ecstasy—help bridge the gulf the believer feels between himself and God. 'By loving me he comes to know me truly,' adds Krishna, 'then he knows my glory and enters into my boundless being. All his acts are performed in my service, and through my grace he wins eternal life.' But Krishna's motives here are again dubious. He wants Arjuna to put all his faith and devotion in him and fight this war; in return, Krishna will ensure that no harm or anxiety befall him. The ostensible morality of the *Gita*, wrote DD Kosambi, is to 'Kill your brother if duty calls, without passion; as long as you have faith in Me, all sins are forgiven.'[18]

'Many of the answers given by Krishna appear to be evasive and occasionally sophistic,' wrote Lal. 'Unable to satisfy a worried warrior's stricken conscience with rational arguments, Krishna opts for the unusual—he stuns Arjuna with a glorious revelation of psychedelic intensity. He succeeds; [thereafter] Arjuna accepts whatever Krishna has to offer. Brain is overpowered by bhakti—but is it ethical to silence logic with magic?' Arjuna, wrote Lal, is a 'humanist hero who has risen above the demands of military caste and conven-

18 DD Kosambi. 1962. *Myth and Reality*. Popular Prakashan, p. 18.

tion-ridden community. His plight on the field of Kuruk-shetra is not an abstract, condemnable intellectual perplexity that can be juggled away by 'Cosmic Multi-Revelation.' It is a painful and honest problem that Krishna should have faced on its own terms, painfully and honestly, and did not. Or so the modern critical mind thinks.'[19]

Near the end of the *Gita*, Krishna ominously warns Arjuna: 'If you egotistically say, 'I will not fight this battle,' your resolve will be useless; your own nature will drive you into it.' Then almost immediately, he begins his closing remarks and makes a seemingly expansive gesture, 'I give you these precious words of wisdom; reflect on them and then do as you choose.' It is the perfect opening to let Arjuna, without giving him a real choice, feel as if he is making his own decision. Arjuna promptly succumbs, a sad ending to the *Gita*. 'You have dispelled my doubts and delusions and I understand through your grace,' Arjuna says. 'My faith is firm now, and I will do your will.' At the end of the *Mahabharata*, nearly everyone on both sides is killed. The epic, writes Sen, 'ends largely as a tragedy, with a lamentation about death and carnage, and there is anguish and grief ... It is hard not to see in this something of a vindication of Arjuna's profound doubts.'[20]

Not the Best of Its Age

How do the metaphysical and moral ideas in the *Gita* stack up against other contenders in its day, for example, the teachings of the Buddha and the Carvaka? Was the smart money back then on the *Gita*? These questions can provide us another data point alongside critiques based on modern standards.

---

19   P. Lal. 1965. *The Bhagavadgita*. Orient Paperbacks.
20   Amartya Sen. 2011. *The Idea of Justice*. Harvard University Press, pp. 209-211.

Of course, as I noted in Part 1, there are a few morally good and many morally neutral injunctions in the *Gita*. Krishna occasionally urges the spiritual aspirant to do his work 'with the welfare of others always in mind ... guided by compassion.' He adds that 'when a person responds to the joys and sorrows of others as if they were his own, he has attained the highest state of spiritual union.' However, such emphasis on others is conspicuous by its presence in the *Gita*, which otherwise obsesses over given duties, detached action, evenness of mind, avoiding certain passions (greed, anger, lust, etc.), piercing one's illusions to find Ultimate Reality, and (for folks too simple to relate to *Brahman*) a total devotion to God. Further, Krishna seems not to notice any conflict between his morally good advice—for instance, to not 'harm any living creature, but be compassionate and gentle; show good will to all'—with goading Arjuna to war and detached action. It is almost as if the authors of the *Gita* felt compelled to acknowledge the 'compassion meme' of Buddhism (then growing at the expense of Hinduism) without thinking it through—the *Gita* neither articulates the basis for this compassion, nor reconciles it with Krishna's advocacy.

That said, these empathic verses do leave the door open for a selective reading that is more charitable to *karma-yoga*, or the path of action. But it still remains a far cry from the Buddha's central emphasis on compassion based on an active empathy with sentient beings, for they too suffer like us. He also advocated a far more egalitarian social ethics than the one implicit in the *Gita*. As historian Romila Thapar put it, 'Had the Buddha been the charioteer the message would have been different.' Going by the *Dhammapada*, he might have said: 'They are not following dharma who resort to violence to achieve their purpose. But those who lead others through nonviolent means, knowing right and wrong, may be called guardians of the dharma.' My goal here is not to score cheap

points for the Buddha, or for Buddhism over Hinduism—I
have no interest in doing so here, and this essay should not
be read as such—Hinduism, as a living religion, is not what
is written in an old poem; nor is Buddhism the same as the
words of a teacher. My goal here is to evaluate the quality of
ideas in the *Gita* in light of other ideas that were on offer to
discerning people back then. For instance, here is how the
Buddha approached dharmic duties and spiritual paths:

> It is proper to doubt. Do not be led by Holy Scriptures, or by
> mere logic or inference, or by appearances, or by the author-
> ity of religious teachers. But when you realize that something
> is unwholesome and bad for you, give it up. And when you
> realize that something is wholesome and good for you, do it.
> ... Be prepared to let go of even the most profound insight or
> the most wholesome teaching. Be a lamp to yourself. Be your
> own confidence.

Such ideas are alien to the sensibility of the *Gita*. Krishna
instead wants all aspirants to 'realize the truth of the scriptures' and set their hearts on him and worship him 'with
unfailing devotion and faith'. Those who listen to him 'with
faith, free from doubts, will find a happier world'. The *Gita*'s
Krishna wants us to live free from doubt, 'in accordance with
these divine laws without complaining, firmly established in
faith'. Those who claim, 'There is no God,' are 'demonic' (an
extremist position; two of the six schools of Hinduism embraced atheism back then). Nor are humans to be relied on to
make up their own dharma. 'Whenever dharma declines and
the purpose of life is forgotten,' says Krishna, 'I manifest myself on earth. I am born in every age to protect the good, to
destroy evil, and to re-establish dharma.' Contrast this with
the views of the Carvaka, a skeptic of the materialist school
named after him, who had proclaimed centuries earlier that
good and evil are mere social conventions; the soul is only
the body qualified by intelligence—it has no existence apart
from the body. Only this world exists, there is no beyond. The

Carvaka held that the *Vedas* are a cheat; they serve to make men submissive through fear and rituals. Nature is indifferent to good and evil, and history does not bear witness to Divine Providence. Such qualitatively different worldviews coexisted with the one in the *Gita*.

Krishna frequently insists that a mind established in *Brahman* is free from delusion. One then lives 'in peace, alike in cold and heat, pleasure and pain, praise and blame'. That *Brahman* itself is a grand delusion was something the Buddha realized centuries earlier, arguing instead that there is no objective, mind-independent reality that is accessible to us. In the second century CE, Nagarjuna explained why 'reality' inevitably depends on the cognitive structure of our mind, rather than on anything we can identify as fundamental, innate, or essential attributes of reality itself. In other words, it is incoherent to speak of a firm foundation beneath the world of appearances, which the mind perceives through its conceptual categories. Nor is there a stable and unchanging Self. As our illusions fall away, we begin to see ourselves as contingent beings, inextricable from a reality that we shape and which in turn shapes us, rather than as beings able to detach ourselves to contemplate reality as it truly is (the so-called 'view from nowhere'—much like the absurd, if poetic, *Brahman*).

Finally, the Upanishadic obsession with an abstract Self, the *atman*, and its unity with *Brahman*, seems amoral at best—and arguably worse—given its silence about the implication of such metaphysics for the individual's earthly state or his ethical behavior. Kabir, the radical Bhakti poet, criticized this disjunction in simple terms, 'If you can't see what's before your eyes, you're as good as blind.' Is it any surprise, then, that caste hierarchy and its prejudices—not to mention Krishna's deceitful advice in the *Gita*—would turn out to be perfectly compatible with such a rarefied metaphysics?

The Context of the Mahabharata

The *Gita* adapted certain philosophical ideas that were surely revolutionary when they first arose and challenged the ritualistic Vedic religion. However, a few centuries later, in light of the contending intellectual and moral ideas of its day, it had assumed the role of a highly conservative tract, aligning itself with orthodoxy, authority, and hierarchy. Whereas I see the *Mahabharata* as great literature: many-layered, open-ended, and replete with the pleasures of a complex story, which also happens to have a decidedly anti-war sensibility. The *Gita*, as I noted in Part 1, was composed much later under the realities of a new age. It 'is not an integral part of the *Mahabharata*,' writes Easwaran. 'It is essentially an *Upanishad*, and my conjecture is that it was set down by an inspired seer and inserted into the epic [later].' To the extent it can be admired as a standalone text (a commonplace treatment, as standalone commentaries on it abound; these days some even advocate making it the first 'National Book' of India[21]), it can be critiqued as one too.

A common defensive response to a critique like this is to say that the *Gita* needs to be read in the context of the *Mahabharata*. If one reads the *Mahabharata* closely, some say, it will become evident that the Kauravas' bad behavior made the war unavoidable and eminently justified. That is, it was a 'just war'. Perhaps, but that's not the point. The point is about the quality of the arguments Krishna actually uses to persuade Arjuna to fight. If the best moral justifications for the war purportedly exist outside the *Gita*, and some of the worst inside it, what have we left? What then makes the *Gita* so great?

Besides, it can be persuasively argued that the case for 'just war' is not clear even in the *Mahabharata*. It's debat-

---

21 'Declare *Bhagavad Gita* as national book, demands BJP', *Hindustan Times*, Dec 20, 2011.

able—and not black and white—which is exactly what makes the *Mahabharata* great. Let us consider some specific examples. For starters, the normal rules of royal succession did not apply to the situation at hand: Dhritarashtra is blind, so his younger brother, Pandu, is made the king. But then Pandu lands a curse and retreats to the forest with his two wives, leaving Dhritarashtra to rule instead. Yudhisthira is indeed the eldest son in the family but Pandu, due to the curse, didn't father him or the other four Pandavas. Rather, Pandu's two wives manage to find some 'divine' lovers in the forest (!), raising legitimate questions about the lineage of the Pandavas—do they even belong to the 'royal' Kuru clan? Nor did Pandu rule anytime during Yudhisthira's life. On the other hand, Duryodhana is *the first son of the reigning and elder brother Dhritarashtra*, who in his heart wants his son to be the king. So, doesn't Duryodhana, a warrior as skilled as any and an able administrator, have a claim to succession as well? I mean a good case can be made, right?

Meanwhile, Duryodhana gets ambitious and wants the entire kingdom for the Kauravas, not just the better half of the Kuru kingdom that he stands to inherit. He loathes the Pandavas, partly because he saw them as uppity and mean to him in their youth, as young princes are wont to be. So, as an adult, Duryodhana is scheming and vicious to the Pandavas. But he can be kind to others, such as to the low-caste Karna. 'Birth is obscure,' he says, 'and men are like rivers whose origins are often unknown.' So, while the Kauravas are not all-bad (it's worth noting that the elders, respected by both sides, end up supporting them, however reluctantly), the Pandavas are not all-good. They spurn and insult Karna based on his caste; Arjuna's pride leads to Eklavya chopping off his thumb—and his hopes and livelihood. Draupadi taunts Duryodhana and his father's blindness. And why does Yudhisthira get so little flak for gambling and losing everything *twice*, including his half of the Kuru kingdom (after being forgiven the first time, he is foolish enough to play again), even wagering his own wife's body? What kind of a man does that? Can we trust his judgment again with a kingdom? (And this when his real father is none other than the Lord of Judgment, Dharma.)

Is it any less morally bizarre that while Krishna, in the *Gita*, goads Arjuna to fight the supposedly evil Kauravas, he has asked his own Yadava army to fight on the Kaurava side—apparently because he wants to be officially neutral! Countless foot soldiers get killed as a result—pawns in the dharmic imperatives of big men, which we are so eager to applaud. The Pandavas, too, break the protocols of war and we rationalize it. Why? Further, was it, or was it not, in the public interest to continue the 13 years of Kaurava rule? These are all legitimate readings, befitting great literature.

So, in the context of the entire *Mahabharata*, the *Gita* can be read as a Brahminical insert catering to the need to justify the war and expound some Upanishadic ideas en route, where Krishna nevertheless comes off looking terribly disingenuous. He combines blatant anti-humanism with his authority and magical powers to brainwash Arjuna. Indeed, during the war, Krishna himself often does not do what he preaches in the *Gita*, though the gaps vary across the many extant versions of the epic. What do we make of the fact that while advocating detachment from the war's outcome in the *Gita*, he repeatedly plays foul and dispenses murderous advice (as in the killing of Karna, in asking Yudhisthira to lie to Dronacharya about Ashwathama, in defending Bhima's killing of Duryodhana, and so on)?

Epilogue

People in every time and place have succumbed to simple narratives of good and evil. They are even more easily blinded by their instinct to defend the side 'God' is on, not just the God of the *Gita* but also in other religious texts. They go to absurd lengths to defend 'his words and deeds'. These may be commonplace observations about a very human weakness but the question remains: Given all the bad faith reasoning and the starkly instrumental view of human life in the *Gita*, which many saw through even in ancient times, what makes the *Gita* a work of wisdom? Why not get the *Gita* off its exalted pedestal in our minds and let it be an uncelebrated episode in the *Mahabharata*—an artful plot element in an epic work of literature?

Without drastic overlooking and embellishing (in the manner of Gandhi), I consider the *Gita* a poor moral guide to our daily lives. Why do so many people resist this idea? Perhaps they have neither read the *Gita*, nor any contrarian critiques; or they are being reactionary patriots about 'their heritage'; or perhaps their faith in it is too strong. After all, which book deserves the sort of uncritical adoration that so many Hindus, especially among the highly educated members of the upper classes, have for the *Gita* today?

SECTION 3

The Intersections of Inequality

Delhi: The City of Rape?[1]

Delhi now lives in infamy as India's 'rape capital'. In December 2012, the gruesome and fatal gang rape of a young woman, named Nirbhaya ('fearless') by the media, unleashed intense media and public outrage across India. Angry middle-class men and women, breaking some of their taboos and silences around sexual crimes, marched in Delhi shouting 'Death to Rapists!' The parliament scrambled to enact tough new anti-rape laws.[2]

Many Delhiites have since grown fearful of their city's public spaces. Spotting an emotionally charged issue, opposition politicians promised to make Delhi safe for women. Campaigning for the Bharatiya Janata Party (BJP) in 2013, Narendra Modi told Delhiites, 'When you go out to vote, keep in mind 'Nirbhaya' who became a victim of rape.' The Aam Aadmi Party (AAP) convenor, Arvind Kejriwal, even promised private security guards with 'commando training'

---

1   An earlier version of this essay appeared on 3 Quarks Daily on Dec 15, 2014.
2   PTI, 'New anti-rape law comes into force', *The Times of India*, April 3, 2013.

in every neighborhood.[3] All this might suggest that a rape epidemic has broken out in Delhi's streets, alleys, and buses. Mainstream media outlets in India and abroad seem to agree.[4]

Anyone trying to analyze the issue must at least ask three questions: who are the rapists, where do they rape, and how common is rape in Delhi? The 2014 Delhi Police data[5] on rape is a great place to start, not the least because it challenges the conventional wisdom of Delhiites and their media and politicians. It shows that, as in other countries[6] and consistent with previous years in Delhi, men known to the victims commit the vast majority of rapes—96 percent in Delhi. These men include friends, neighbors, 'relatives such as brother-in-law, uncle, husband or ex-husband and even father.' More than 80 percent of them rape inside the victim's home or their own.[7] *Strangers commit only 4 percent of rapes*, which are also likelier to be reported. Yet so many people fixate on this latter scenario and take it as proof that Delhi is unsafe for women to go out by themselves.

The hard truth is that sexual predators are not so much 'out there' in the faceless crowd as among the familiar ones. 'Statistically speaking', journalist Cordelia Jenkins wrote in August 2013, 'the problem [of rape in Delhi] is not on the streets at all, but in the home; the greatest threat to most women is not from strangers but from their own families,

3   'AAP proposes 'citizen security force' for women's safety', *News 18*, April 21, 2013.
4   *Time Magazine* listed 'India's Rape epidemic' amongst the top 10 world stories of 2013.
5   Mohammed Iqbal. 2014. 'Majority of rape accused are known to victims', *The Hindu*, November 19.
6   'Myths vs. Realities', *Rape Crisis England & Wales*, 2016. http://rapecrisis.org.uk/mythsvsrealities.php
7   IANS. 2014. 'Girls below 18 victims in most Delhi rapes: Study', *India Today*, July 14.

neighbours and friends.'[8] According to Ranjana Kumari, director of the Centre for Social Research, a women's rights organization in Delhi, 'This data compels us to look at what is happening in and around our homes and workplaces.'[9] In other words, we ought to worry about rape less when women enter public spaces on their own, and more when they return home or hang out with friends. Why do so few Indians—men and women, including policy makers and public figures—seem to realize this? Some feminists have argued that this blend of pious concern with plain denial is the modus operandi of patriarchy itself.[10]

* * *

So how common is rape in Delhi? The reported incidence, which drives the media and public fear and perception of this crime, is far lower than in every one of the 76 American cities in a 2009 report from the US Department of Justice (DoJ). Delhi in 2012 reported 4 rapes per 100K population[11] vs. 107 in Minneapolis, 88 in Cleveland, 58 in Philadelphia, 43 in Boston, 36 in Houston, and so on.[12] In 2009, the national US average was 29 rapes per 100K population, which is 33 percent less than the rate in the early 1990s (all violent crime in the US has dropped in recent decades).[13]

---

8 Cordelia Jenkins. 2013. 'Freedom from Assault | Fear and loathing in New Delhi', *Mint*, Aug 10.

9 Nita Bhalla. 2015. 'Almost 90 percent of India's rapes committed by people known to victim', *Reuters India*, Aug 21.

10 Whisnant, Rebecca, 'Feminist Perspectives on Rape'. Edward N. Zalta (ed.), *The Stanford Encyclopedia of Philosophy* (Fall 2013).

11 'Data busts some myths on sexual violence', *The Hindu*, September 3, 2013. See under 'Urban Spaces', the infographic 'Incidence of crimes against women during 2012', which is normalized per 100K women whereas the US statistics use per 100K population.

12 Sally Kohn. 2013. 'Is India the Rape Capital of the World?', *More. com*, April 10.

13 FBI, 'Crime in the United States by Volume and Rate per 100K Inhabitants, 1990–2009'. https://www2.fbi.gov/ucr/cius2009/data/

Western European capitals are better on average than US cities but not by much. Even in terms of other violent crimes like robbery and murder, Delhi is better than most of these 76 US cities. This year in Delhi, the second largest city in the world with 25 million people,[14] strangers committed about 8 rapes per month.[15] In London, a third as populous as Delhi, strangers committed about 36 rapes per month—a rate 13X Delhi's.[16] Every rape is one too many, but by comparison Delhi seems significantly safer for women. Other Indian metros are even safer than Delhi. Could this really be true?

Although the media and public outrage is clearly based on the reported cases of rape, many still ask when comparative data is trotted out: but isn't rape significantly under-reported in India? Yes, as in every country, under-reporting happens in India too, and surely more so than in the US (especially when rapists are known to the victim, and partly because marital rape is not recognized as rape in India). Various studies have estimated the extent of under-reporting but they vary a lot because estimating actual incidence is tricky.[17] Most estimates of under-reporting range from 60-80 percent for US cities, and up to 90 percent for Delhi.[18] Taking an even

---

table_01.html

14 PTI. 2014. Delhi is world's second most populous city in 2014 after Tokyo: UN report, *Hindustan Times*, July 12.

15 'Majority of rape accused are known to victims', *The Hindu*, November 19, 2014.

16 London rape statistics are available on the Metropolitan Police site. Data can be adjusted based on UK government data that reveals 90 percent of rapists were known to the victim. http://www.met.police.uk/crimefigures/

17 Carl Bialik. 2013. 'Statistics Shed Little Light on Rape Rates', *The Wall Street Journal*, August 30.

18 See the following studies and reports: (1) 'The Criminal Justice System: Statistics', RAINN (Rape, Abuse & Incest National Network), 2012-15; (2) Alexandra Raphel. 2014. 'Estimating the incidence of rape and sexual assault: The problem of under-reporting', *Journalist's Resource*, April 21; (3) Xiaofan Pan. 2012. 'Holding Campuses

more pessimistic case of 95 percent under-reporting in Delhi (only 1 in 20 reports) and the optimistic case for US cities (1 in 3 reports), the actual number of rapes in Delhi becomes 20X more than reported, and in US cities 3X more than reported. If we do the math, Delhi still registers a lower incidence of rape than most of the 76 US cities in the DoJ list. Indeed, why aren't the Americans anywhere near as fearful of rape in their public spaces as Indians are in theirs? Could this partly be because a raped woman has a lot more to lose in India's caste patriarchal society, which frequently blames and shames women for their own rape, than in the US?[19]

The statistical comparisons above are validated by other sources, such as UN Office on Drugs and Crime (UNODC) and UN Women, the UN organization dedicated to gender equality and the empowerment of women. Bypassing data reported by governments, UN Women 'compiled the rates of unreported partner and non-partner sexual violence across 99 countries [based on] large-size household surveys.' According to journalist Rukmini S. in *The Hindu*, 'Both sets of statistics together place India towards the middle to lower end of the global scale of sexual violence. Yet, for the last two years, the rhetoric around rape in India has not reflected this … this statistically faulty focus on rape has led to both a mis-

Accountable in Reporting Sexual Assault', *National Women's Health Network*; (4) Rukmini S. 2013. 'NGO surveys test official data on crime against women', *The Hindu*, September 9; (5) Samanth Subramanian. 2013. 'India tries to define rape', *The National*, January 6; (6) Jasmine Bala. 2013. 'Behind the Curtain: On Unreported Rapes in India', *Girls' Globe*, March 9; (7) Tom Wright. 2013. 'Are Women Safer in India or the U.S.?', *The Wall Street Journal*, January 2; (8) 'Estimates of Unreported Rapes' in Wikipedia article on 'Rape in India' (as on December 2014).
19 For an example from UP, see Divya Arya. 2016. 'The WhatsApp Suicide', *BBC Magazine*, October 29.

diagnosis and a worsening of India's real problem when it comes to women: [little] autonomy.'[20]

Indians who invoke comparative statistics in discussions of rape are sometimes accused of whataboutery or a toxic nationalism in trying to show that India is 'not that bad'. As even a cursory look at social media commentary shows, this accusation is often true and justified. But should this accusation absolve the accusers from the need to reflect on comparative data? On so many social indicators, cross-country comparisons are natural and instructive—why not on rape? Comparisons, for instance, reveal just how bad the rates of incarceration or gun violence are in the United States. They can help us calibrate our concerns about child and maternal mortality in India. Comparative data on press freedom or state executions gives us an objective basis by which to call China politically repressive, and so on. They reveal, too, that human cultures vary a lot in the particular forms and relative mix of inhumanities and kindnesses they dole out to their members, including women. So international comparisons can be quite illuminating.

What makes the picture more complex is that a significant number of alleged rapes in India—about 40 percent of all cases tried by Delhi's courts in 2013—involve consensual sex or elopement in which rape charges are filed by the girl's irate parents. Many of these involve inter-caste or inter-religion couples who intend to marry and whose suffering in fact comes at the hands of their parents, including 'beatings, confinement, threats, being forced to undergo medical examinations, being forced to undergo abortions' and more. Another big chunk of alleged rapes—25 percent of all cases tried by Delhi's courts in 2013—involve 'breach of promise to marry.'[21]

---

20 Rukmini S. 2014. 'Rape, rhetoric and reality', *The Hindu*, December 19.

21 Rukmini S. 2015. 'The many shades of rape cases in Delhi', *The*

Whatever the actual number, it is useful to remember that strangers account for only a tiny fraction of rapes in Delhi. This is also true for most cities across the world, give or take a few percentage points. A common pitfall of our psychology is that a traumatic public event can fuel huge misconceptions. If we repeatedly hear about something we see as a threat or social malady, it grows much larger in our minds. Highly unlikely events often worry us more than common dangers, and our emotions about an event can skew our assessment of its frequency. For instance, post-9/11 media coverage led Americans to grossly inflate the threat of terrorism in their daily lives. Polls show that the British fear their teens to be getting pregnant at a rate 25X higher than actual. The extensive media coverage of every plane crash raises our anxiety about air travel even though it is many orders of magnitude safer than traveling by road.[22] When a recent poll asked people about the percentage of Muslims in their country, Americans estimated 15 percent, whereas the actual number is 1 percent.[23] Fear induced by 24x7 news cycles plays havoc with our estimation of risk. On perceived risk vs. actual risk, American security expert Steve Schneier wrote:[24]

> [People] overestimate risks that are being talked about and remain an object of public scrutiny. News, by definition, is about anomalies. Endless numbers of automobile crashes hardly make news like one airplane crash does. The West Nile virus outbreak in 2002 killed very few people, but it worried many more because it was in the news day after day. AIDS kills about 3 million people per year worldwide—about three times as many people each day as died in the terrorist attacks of 9/11. If a lunatic goes back to the office after being fired

Hindu, April 10.

22 Aurelio Locsin. 'Is Air Travel Safer Than Car Travel?', *USA Today.*
23 Carol Kuruvilla. 2014. 'Americans Think The Country's Muslim Population Is Much Bigger Than It Really Is', *The Huffington Post,* November 2.
24 Steve Schneier. 2013. *Beyond Fear: Thinking Sensibly about Security in an Uncertain World.* Copernicus Books.

and kills his boss and two coworkers, it's national news for days. If the same lunatic shoots his ex-wife and two kids instead, it's local news ... maybe not even the lead story.

In other words, our perceptions on social issues can easily get detached from facts and reality, more so perhaps with a market-led corporate media that promotes the sensational while representing the views and interests of privileged groups.[25] Even academicians routinely fall for it. Two weeks after the Nirbhaya incident, a historian at Delhi's Center for the Study of Developing Societies imagined a war zone around her when she wrote on a public page on social media: 'I don't see how India is any better than the DRC' (Democratic Republic of Congo, which has been in the throes of a brutal civil war for years).[26] It may well be that such hyperbole and temporary over-reaction can help break down societal apathy and bring a long neglected issue to the fore, but what if it also promotes unreflective fears among women and in the voting majority?[27]

* * *

The Indian media now talks a lot about rape. As economist and philosopher Amartya Sen has written, Indian newspapers, 'smarting from intense criticism of the negligence in their coverage, rapidly reinvented themselves as rape-reporting journals'. But he wonders 'whether the ongoing news re-

---

25 'Perceptions are not reality: The top 10 we get wrong', Ipsos MORI, July 9, 2013.
26 Jo Adetunji. 2011. 'Forty-eight women raped every hour in Congo, study finds', *The Guardian*, May 12.
27 This includes fears that raise public appetite for draconian but unwise measures. For instance, in December 2015, led by public outrage over the 2012 'Nirbhaya' case—and flouting the recommendations by the Justice Verma Committee and other experts—the Indian Parliament amended the age for rape and murder trials to 16 (until then the age limit was 18). Maseeh Rahman. 2015. 'India amends law to allow 16-year-olds to be tried as adults for serious crimes', *The Guardian*, December 22.

porting is well aimed and as helpful for public discussion as it could be.'[28] Among its positives are that it has helped pass new laws that were long overdue—criminalizing stalking and voyeurism, for instance—and it has created a lot more discussion around sexism, sexual harassment, and misogyny. In effect, the issue of rape has created more space for the discussion and analysis of a range of issues faced by women that do not otherwise get much attention. It has also helped improve response mechanisms to crimes against women— a third more victims reported rape in 2013, thanks to new helplines, women cops, penalties for cops if they refuse to register a case, etc.

But this media coverage, especially by TV news channels, has also been skewed and misleading. One of its downsides has been that most people not only continue to conflate the 4 percent of 'stranger rapes' with the whole problem of rape, they imagine its incidence to be much higher than it is. As a result, people have ended up with a heightened sense of fear for women being raped when they venture out by themselves—above and beyond their longstanding dread of women being catcalled, ogled, stalked, or groped in public transportation.[29] As many middle-aged women residents testify, the latter are the primary threats that women have long faced in Delhi's public spaces; they continue to fuel a legitimate sense of insecurity and make women feel they are not as free to loiter as men are, especially in certain areas and during late hours.[30] In the backdrop of such threats, a

---

28 Amartya Sen. 2013. 'India's Women: The Mixed Truth', *New York Review of Books*, October 10.

29 See, for example, *Mera Apna Sheher* (My Own City). 2011. A documentary film by Sameera Jain, available on YouTube.com. It focuses on the unpleasant 'experience of a gendered urban landscape' in Delhi.

30 Shilpa Phadke, Sameera Khan, Shilpa Ranade. 2011. *Why Loiter?: Women And Risk On Mumbai Streets*. Penguin Books. This book argues 'that only by celebrating loitering, a radical act for most Indian

highly disproportionate focus on 'stranger rapes' unreasonably heightens that sense of insecurity. It has helped push the already low participation of women in the workforce to among the lowest in the world.[31]

This is not to minimize the problems of women in Delhi or elsewhere in India. Groping and other harassment are serious issues that need to be dealt with, but it does not help to conflate them with rape. Delhi's public spaces today are unsafe not because the incidence of rape is much higher now but due to the other longstanding threats. Indian women also struggle with a great many other problems different from, or more severe than, those faced by women in the West, such as female foeticide and infanticide, child marriage, maternal mortality, dowry and related killings, sex trafficking, feudal claims on their bodies, and a host of nutritional, educational, economic, medical, workplace, and other patriarchal and casteist discrimination.[32] The gender wage gap remains large. The cops and the courts are not sensitive and responsive enough to gender crimes, more so against women from marginalized communities of Dalits, Adivasis, and Muslims.[33] The mainstream media too, given the class/caste of its owners and employees, reflexively echoes and normalizes

women, can a truly equal, global city be created?'

31 Harry Stevens. 2016. 'Indian women are rapidly leaving the workforce', *Hindustan Times*, June 29.
32 See the following articles and reports: (1) Amartya Sen. 2013. 'India's Women: The Mixed Truth', *New York Review of Books*, October 10; (2) Lois Parshley. 2013. 'Inside India's Perna Caste, Where Women Are Routinely Prostituted by Their In-Laws', *Pacific Standard*, June 17; (3) 'The plight of women in India', *CNN Video*, January 9. https://www.youtube.com/watch?v=XtHgTf67hzc; (4) 'Child Undernutrition in India: A Gender Issue', *UNICEF India*; (5) Saritha Rai. 2015. 'The Fifth Metro: Given by women, received by men', *Indian Express*, March 16.
33 'Dalit Women (We are not untouchable - End caste discrimination now)', ISDNVideo on YouTube, June 7, 2012. https://www.youtube.com/watch?v=NUaFQeUIclo

the viewpoints of the urban middle- and upper-class/caste minority. In a plural society, tolerating biases in individuals may well be prudent, but can the same be said for tolerating biases in our primary civic institutions?

Not only does the outrage of the media elites varies by the social class of the victim and the rapist[34] but most people don't ever seem to ask, as feminist author Urvashi Butalia did, 'When we demand the death penalty, do we mean therefore that we should kill large numbers of uncles, fathers, brothers, husbands, neighbours? How many of us would even report cases of rape then?'[35] Even without the higher risk of retaliation against victims, the truth is that capital punishment is not the answer because there is no evidence that it deters criminals, nor can it be administered fairly in a deeply hierarchical society.[36]

Meanwhile, the same political parties (including AAP, Congress, and BJP) that make populist promises to protect women—via CCTV cameras on every street, marshals in every bus, guards with 'commando training' in every neighborhood[37]—greatly under-represent women in their leadership ranks. In the 2014 General Election, they again allocated few seats to women candidates (BJP: 9 percent, Congress: 13

---

34 Madhuri Xalxo. 2012. 'Delhi Protests and the Caste Hindu Paradigm: Of Sacred and Paraded Bodies', *Round Table India*, December 27.

35 Urvashi Butalia. 2012. 'Let's ask how we contribute to rape', *The Hindu*, December 26.

36 See the following: (1) David T. Johnson, Franklin E. Zimring. 2013. 'On Rape and Capital Punishment', *EPW*, Vol. 48, Issue No. 04, January 26; (2) Michael L. Radalet, Traci L. Lacock. 2009. 'Do Executions Lower Homicide Rates? The Views of Leading Criminologists', *The Journal of Criminal Law and Criminology*, Vol. 99, No. 2; (3) David A. Love. 2012. 'The racial bias of the US death penalty', *The Guardian*, January 3.

37 'Women Dialogue: 10-point agenda for women of Delhi unveiled', Aam Aadmi Party, November 26, 2014.

percent, AAP: 14 percent).[38] No wonder only 11 percent of
legislators in India are women (2014), far below the global
average of 22 percent, 23 percent in China and Sub-Saharan
Africa, and 42 percent in the Nordic countries.[39]

* * *

A major obstacle to a more progressive discourse on rape is
the caste patriarchy of Delhi's mainstream media and politicians, including the liberals. Rather than focusing more on
the home front where most of the problem lies, the dominant narrative inflates the fear of 'stranger rape' and focuses
on 'protecting' women from unwashed strangers, especially
when the victims come from privileged classes.[40] Such rapes
receive the highest coverage and tend to be presented as an
assault on the social collective—'Delhi shamed again', pro-
claim the headlines. This feeds on caste patriarchy's per-
sona of some women—especially middle- and upper-class
women—as passive, dependent, demure, chaste, flower-like
beings, whose sexual violation is seen as more tragic than
that of other women (such as of Suzette Jordan,[41] prostitutes,

---

38 'Lok Sabha elections 2014: Parties give women contenders a miss!',
   DNA, May 13, 2014.
39 According to data compiled by the Inter-Parliamentary Union on
   the basis of information provided by National Parliaments. http://
   www.ipu.org/wmn-e/world.htm
40 For examples, see the following: (1) Shubhomoy Sikdar. 2014. 'AAP
   bats for women's safety, issues', *The Hindu*, November 21; (2) Nita
   Bhalla. 2014. 'Modi says India is shamed by rape in Independence
   Day speech', *Reuters*, August 15; (3) Raj Shekar. 2014. 'Delhi cab-
   bie rapes executive returning from party', *The Times of India*, December 7; (4) Namit Arora. 2012. 'Of Sacred and Paraded Bodies',
   Shunya's Notes, December 31; (5) Shakti Mills gang rape (2013).
   Wikipedia. https://en.wikipedia.org/wiki/Shakti_Mills_gang_rape;
   (6) 'Concern in LS Over Rising Rape Incidents', *Outlook India*,
   December 10, 2014; (7) 'Delhi shame: Woman executive raped by
   Uber cab driver', *Hindustan Times*, December 7, 2014.
41 Flavia Agnes. 2015. 'Why India loves Nirbhaya, hates Suzette', *The
   Asian Age*, March 19.

Dalits, and other working-class women).[42] As activist Kavita Krishnan has written, 'Protection also implies that not all women are worthy of it. Women who fail the test of patriarchal morality; women whose caste and class identity does not spell sexual 'respectability,' fall outside the embrace of protection.' According to Krishnan, 'The only useful movement against sexual violence can be one that brings the problem home, right into the comfort zone, that challenges rather than reassures patriarchy, that exposes the violence found in the 'normal' rather than locating violence in the far-away and exotic'—or in the fraction of rapes committed by strangers, especially the most morbid and 'sensational'.[43]

'The woman's body is the terrain on which patriarchy is erected,' wrote American author Adrienne Rich. Patriarchy's origins lie in the prehistoric shift away from hunting-gathering to settled agriculture and domestication of animals. Women, who gathered a significant part of the group's overall food intake, were also the early agriculturalists and held considerable power;[44] matrilineality was common. But with growing claims to ownership of fertile land, the rise of heavy plows pulled by oxen, and more organized urban life in river valley civilizations, men gained more power as farmers, warriors, protectors of land and wealth, rulers, and long-distance traders. Societies began forsaking the gender egalitarianism of hunter-gatherers, a trend that was later sanctified by the

---

42 Some have argued that even the December 2012 'Nirbhaya' case in Delhi received much greater attention (say, versus the infamous Khairlanji case and others in nearby Haryana villages that had Dalit victims) partly because the media withheld the victim's identity and presented her from the start as a casteless 'daughter of the nation', as a young urban middle-class student of a modern profession.
43 Kavita Krishnan. 2013. 'The Anti-Rape Movement—The Political Vision of 'Naari Mukti/Sabki Mukti'', Kafila, December 15.
44 Hannah Devlin. 2015. 'Early men and women were equal, say scientists', The Guardian, May 14.

major religions of the Axial age.[45] Over time, male ownership of property and its rightful propagation meant strict
control over women's sexuality, and even the tendency to regard a woman as her husband's property.

In patriarchy, the female is not only seen as property—
first her father's, then husband's—her sexual sanctity and
propriety become central to these men's *izzat*, or dignity and
honor. Men think of settling feuds by 'sullying' each other's
women. Marital rape too seems incoherent when the wife is
seen as the husband's property. Caste patriarchy, above and
beyond the inequities inherent in all patriarchies,[46] imposes
graded notions of sexual purity and violability on the female
body, greatly amplifying the fear, distress, and shame of being
raped by the 'inferior Other'.[47] As historian Uma Chakravarti
pointed out, 'Under Brahmanical patriarchy women of the
upper castes are regarded as gateways—literally points of entry into the caste system. Lower caste males whose sexuality
is a threat to upper-caste purity of blood has to be *institution-
ally* prevented from having sexual access to women of the
higher castes, so such women have to be carefully guarded.'[48]
Preservation of caste has long required strict control over
women's sexuality, giving rise to the custom of child marriage and prohibition on marriage, including of widows,
to lower caste men.[49] 'Women's cooperation in the system,'

45 Margaret Ehrenberg. 1989. *Women in Prehistory*, University of
   Oklahoma Press; also see article titled 'Women in Patriarchal Societies: The Origins of Civilizations', *International World History
   Project*, 1992.
46 Robert Jensen. 2014. 'Rape, rape culture and the problem of patriarchy', *Waging Nonviolence*, April 29.
47 Jackie and Rebecca. 2012. 'Patriarchal Control of the Body: Sexuality and the Purity Myth', *The Purity Problem*, November 7.
48 Uma Chakravarti. 2003. *Gendering Caste: Through a Feminist Lens*.
   Stree, p. 35.
49 Sule Tomkinson. 2009. 'Childhood to Womanhood – Child Brides
   and the Inefficiency of the Indian State', *Australian Journal of Gender and Law*.

Chakravarti wrote, 'was secured by various means: ideology, economic dependency on the male head of the family, class privileges and veneration bestowed upon conforming and dependent women of the upper classes, and, finally, the use of force when required.'[50]

Only in a society saturated with caste patriarchy do certain rapes by strangers, and not other rapes and other violence against women, generate calls for killing the offenders. In extreme cases, as with Sikh women during Partition, women may even choose preemptive suicide—or fathers and husbands might kill them in the name of preserving 'honor'—rather than risk defilement by the 'inferior Other' and live with its stigma and social ostracism.[51] Both fear of rape and 'protection talk' have long been patriarchy's instruments to control women's mobility, choices, and behavior by increasing their fear of 'bad men' and their subordination to 'good men'. Obsessive fear of this sort, fueled by 'fear of fear itself', has in fact reduced women's participation in Delhi's workforce in recent years, increasing their subordination to men (it may well be that if women never left home, 'stranger rapes' would decline steeply from the current incidence of 4 percent to perhaps almost zero, but at what cost to women's freedom and empowerment?). Such fear even contributes to the urban upper-class flight towards gated communities.

In India, class and caste are writ large on the media's imagination of 'good' and 'bad' men. Sundry laborers and semi-literate migrants from the provinces are 'bad'. Novelist Lavanya Sankaran described them as 'feral men, untethered from

---

50 Uma Chakravarti. 2006. *Beyond the Kings and Brahmanas of 'Ancient' India*. Tulika Books; from the chapter titled 'Conceptualizing Brahminical Patriarchy in Early India', p. 140.

51 For a flavor, see David Lester. 2010. 'Suicide and the Partition of India: A Need for Further Investigation', *Suicidology Online*: 1:2-4; also see the documentary 'Partition: The Day India Burned', *BBC*, 2007.

their distant villages ... newly exposed to the smart young women of the cities, with their glistening jobs and clothes and casual independence'.[52] But since rapes largely happen among social familiars, it's not so much the unknown 'they' who are raping 'our' girls and women. With her thoughtless fear mongering—akin to some White folks' projection of Black men as lechers and dangers for wholesome White women—Sankaran too shows herself to be in thrall of a caste patriarchy that would keep women passive and sheltered, rather than support them as they venture out and negotiate equality in every arena of public and private life.[53]

With so much at stake, the urgent need is for measures designed to reduce the public fear of sexual violence outdoors, and to get on with the slow, difficult, and necessary work on two obvious fronts: (1) changing minds through efforts like better gender and sex education in schools,[54] more public debate and cultural conversation on gender equality, deeper reflection on our obsession with 'stranger rape' versus our relative apathy to the more pervasive structural violence of female foeticide, child marriage, marital rape, and trafficking, and (2) using various means, such as affirmative action for women[55] and gender sensitivity training, to reform our civic institutions—the police, the courts, legislative bodies,

---

52 Lavanya Sankaran. 2013. 'The Good Men of India', New York Times, October 19.
53 See the following: (1) Rita Banerji. 2014. 'What Sanskrit Taught Me About Being an Indian Woman', The Huffington Post, December 13; (2) Mayank Jain. 2014. 'Indian women are loitering to make their cities safer', Scroll.in, December 18; (3) Aarefa Johari. 2014. 'The real problem with actress Shenaz Treasurywala's open letter on rape', Scroll.in, December 13.
54 For instance, as outlined in 'The India Womanifesto 2014', a 6-point plan for the freedom and safety, equality and flourishing of India's women and girls.
55 Such as the long pending Women's Reservation Bill that proposes to reserve 33 per cent of all seats in the Lok Sabha and in all state legislative assemblies for women.

and the media—so they are more efficient, responsive, and friendlier to a wider cross-section of women in India.

Additional References

Holly Henderson. 2013. 'Feminism, Foucault, and Rape: A Theory and Politics of Rape Prevention', *Berkeley Journal of Gender, Law & Justice*, Vol. 22, Issue 1, Article 7, September.

Sarah Ben-David and Ofra Schneider. 2005. 'Rape Perceptions, Gender Role Attitudes, and Victim-Perpetrator Acquaintance', *Sex Roles*, Vol. 53, Nos. 5/6, September.

'John Stoltenberg on manhood, male supremacy, and men as feminist allies', *Feminist Current*, September 9, 2013.

Justice Verma Committee Report. 2013 [which 'made recommendations on laws related to rape, sexual harassment, trafficking, child sexual abuse, medical examination of victims, police, electoral and educational reforms.']

Anumeha Yadav. 2014. 'The Khaps in our homes', *The Hindu*, December 11.

Geeta Charusivam. 2014. 'Rape Culture and Moral Policing', *YouTube*, April 21.

bell hooks, 'Understanding Patriarchy'. http://imaginenoborders.org/pdf/zines/UnderstandingPatriarchy.pdf

Decolonizing My Mind[1]

The modern era of European colonialism began in the Americas with bands of adventurers seeking El Dorado. Their early intrusions evolved into predatory monopolies like the East India Company and European states exerting direct control over the economic and political life of the colonies. The natives tended to not welcome and cooperate with the intruders, so alongside came great developments in the art of subjugating the natives, through military, political, and cultural means. In this essay, I'll look at some cultural means of controlling the natives, particularly through language, and its effect on the psyche of the colonized, using examples from Africa and India.

When it comes to colonial quests, military might is what breaches the metaphorical Gates of Damascus. Regime change follows. Thereafter, the most efficient and durable means of colonial control happens via culture. Culture holds the keys to how a group sees itself and knows its place in the world. As Ngugi wa Thiong'o—Kenyan novelist, profes-

1   An earlier version of this essay appeared on 3 Quarks Daily on Feburary 7, 2011.

sor, and author of *Decolonizing the Mind*—has pointed out, 'Economic and political control can never be complete or effective without mental control. To control a people's culture is to control their tools of self-definition in relationship to others.'[2]

When done right, the native comes to elevate and mimic his master's ways, to see his own culture as inferior, and to look down on his past as 'a wasteland of non-achievement'. He begins to defer to the colonizer's ideas on fundamental things like beauty, art, and politics. In time, writes Ngugi, he begins to understand himself and his culture through the eyes of the colonizer—using the latter's concepts, categories, and judgments. Before too long, he turns into a proxy for his master: colonialism with a native face.

How does the colonizer gain such control? The easiest method, explains Ngugi, is to actively spread his language among the natives, and to simultaneously denigrate the language of the natives as crude and unfit for proper education. It is amazing how much mileage this delivers. Simply make the colonizer's language the *lingua franca* of imperial administration, accord prestige and upward mobility to those who learn it in colonial schools, and before too long, there is a feeding frenzy among a native minority. This has been the way of the great colonialists of history, such as the Arabs in the 7-8th centuries, the British and the French in the 19th, and the Russians with the Baltic States in the 20th. Ngugi writes,

> For colonialism this involved two aspects of the same process: the destruction or the deliberate undervaluing of a people's culture, their art, dances, religions, history, geography, education, orature, and literature, and the conscious elevation of the language of the colonizer. The domination of a

---

2   Ngugi wa Thiong'o. 1986. *Decolonizing the Mind*. Heinemann, p. 16. All quotes in this article that are not otherwise attributed come from this book.

people's language by the language of the colonizing nations
was crucial to the domination of the mental universe of the
colonized. [p. 16]

Take colonial India. A great debate ensued in 1830s Brit-
ain on the choice of an official language of colonial administration and education. Making the winning case for English
over Sanskrit, Persian, and all other local languages, Thomas
B. Macaulay—a member of the Supreme Council of India—
observed that Indian languages 'contain neither literary nor
scientific information, and are, moreover, so poor and rude
that, until they are enriched from some other quarter, it will
not be easy to translate any valuable work into them.' He ad-
mitted that he did not know any Indian languages but insisted that he had nevertheless reached 'a correct estimate of
their value.' Referring to the Orientalists of his day, he said,
'I have never found one among them who could deny that a
single shelf of a good European library was worth the whole
native literature of India and Arabia.' Therefore, concluded
Macaulay, 'we have to educate a people who cannot at present be educated by means of their mother tongue. We must
teach them some foreign language.'[3]

Language is not a neutral vessel for conveying the ideas,
beliefs, and values that constitute culture. Nor is it a mere
tool for describing the world as it truly is—no language can
be said to describe the world as it truly is. To use a language—
any language—is to interpret the world in a particular way.
Shared ways of seeing, or culture, emerge through the shared

---

3   Thomas Babington Macaulay, 'On Empire and Education', 1833.
    The Orientalists held similar views about the Chinese language
    which they deemed incompatible with modern thought. In early
    19th century, German philosopher Hegel wrote that Chinese writ-
    ing, 'is at the outset a great hindrance to the development of the
    sciences.' Another tract in 1912 called the Chinese language, 'the
    most horrible that any sane man can be called upon to acquire. ...
    The Chinese language must go.' See Tom Mullaney. 2016. 'Chinese
    Is Not a Backward Language', *Foreign Policy*, May 12.

use of language. In other words, culture is organically inter-twined with language, evolving together to create a unique collective sensibility. No wonder language is so central to our identity and why so many political divisions have lin-guistic borders. Indeed, language profoundly shapes the way its incoming speakers think (this may be partly why it even makes sense to speak of an 'Anglophone culture'), an idea that now finds support among cognitive scientists. Bilingual folks think differently when they immerse themselves in dif-ferent languages.[4]

Colonial Languages and African Literature

In the late 19th and 20th century Africa, colonial regimes began mandating the exclusive use of European languages in missionary and state supported schools. The language of an African child's formal education soon became foreign, writes Ngugi. 'The language of books he read was foreign. The lan-guage of his conceptualization was foreign. Thought, in him, took the visible form of a foreign language.' In Kenya, Ngugi himself studied every subject in English at school but spoke Gikuyu at home—a language spoken by more people than speakers of Danish or Croatian. 'There was often not the slightest relationship between [English], and the world of his immediate environment in the family and the community.' Indeed, it was even worse:

> One of the most humiliating experiences was to be caught speaking [Gikuyu] in the vicinity of the school. The culprit was given corporal punishment — three to five strokes of the cane on bare buttocks — or was made to carry a metal plate around his neck with inscriptions such as I AM STUPID or I AM A DONKEY. Sometimes the culprits were fined money

---

4   Search online for three articles that relate experimental work in this area: 'Change languages, shift responses' by Maya Shwayder, and 'Lost in Translation', and 'How does language shape the way we think?' by Lera Boroditsky.

they could hardly afford. And how did the teachers catch the culprits? A button was initially given to one pupil who was supposed to hand it over to whoever was caught speaking his mother tongue. Whoever had the button at the end of the day would sing who had given it to him and the ensuing process would bring out all the culprits of the day. The children were turned into witch-hunters and in the process were being taught the lucrative value of being a traitor to one's immediate community. [p. 11]

Ngugi, born into a large peasant family, was baptized James Ngugi and educated in English, a language that evolved outside Africa, shaped by and organically intertwined with a very different cultural milieu. It had evolved to convey different ideas of self, individual, community, nature, time, beauty, loyalty, respect, kinship terms, humor, idioms, gender roles, animals, and so much else from a particular ontology. Moreover, it was alien to the language-world of Ngugi's daily life in Kenya—of the streets, boyhood fights, swear words, commerce, labor, family, love, food, festivals, geography, plants, and more. Not only that, his own language was 'associated in his impressionable mind with low status, humiliation, corporal punishment, slow-footed intelligence' and worse. Ngugi wrote that if the bullet was the means of physical subjugation, language was the means of spiritual subjugation of the African child, resulting 'in the dissociation of the sensibility of that child from his natural and social environment, what we might call colonial alienation.'

What then to make of literature written in European languages by Africans? What does it mean to write a realistic novel in which African peasants and factory workers speak English or French? Can a writer, his formal education entirely in English, capture in it the tenor and rhythms of ordinary African life? What tradition of the English language novel does the African writer look up to? Ngugi argues for classifying their work— including that of talented writers like Achebe, Soyinka, Armah, Ousmane, and others—not as

African literature but as Afro-European literature, i.e., 'literature written by Africans in European languages.'

After all, says Ngugi, such writers are products of a hybrid culture of a small African minority, one marked by 'colonial alienation'. Meanwhile, Europeans—unable to relate as easily to literature in native tongues (even in translation)—are instinctively drawn to European language works from Africa, which seem to them African flavors of their own language-worlds. Add the impact of modern economics, global media, publishing, and the scholarship industry in the West, and soon, a lot of people start equating European-language works with African literature (squeezing the life out of indigenous literary forms). Ngugi challenges this equation. African literature, he argues, can only be written in languages with long and organic roots in African culture. A colonial language largely external to it cannot adequately express the local ways of being—to believe that it can is to erroneously see language as a mere tool and vessel of culture, interchangeable with any other language.

So where did this viewpoint lead Ngugi? Though he wrote his early literary works in English, he now writes all his creative works only in Gikuyu and then translates them into English (he also continues to speak in English as before, not the least because he was forced into exile from Kenya). He made this switch in mid-career, soon after his great polemic, *Decolonizing the Mind*, came out in 1986. He recounts in it a story from his early career, when he attended the African Writers Conference in Kampala, which invited only authors writing in English. 'What is African Literature?' was a much-debated question at the conference, about which he wrote:

> The fact is that all of us who opted for European languages— the conference participants and the generation that followed them—accepted that fatalistic logic [of the unassailable position of English in our literature] to a greater or lesser degree. We were guided by it and the only question which preoccupied us was how best to make the borrowed tongues carry

the weight of our African experience by, for instance, making them 'prey' on African proverbs and other peculiarities of African speech and folklore. [p. 7]

English as a Language of Indian Literature

English also came to India through colonization. By the early 19th century, it had emerged as the new language of power and personal advancement. Among the first Indians to embrace it were the Bengali Brahmins of Calcutta. They, as well as other 'high caste and/or upper class Hindu men', as the scholar Alok K. Mukherjee has argued, took to English largely 'because English was a tool of power and domination—individually for them and collectively for the groups to which they belonged. It provided them ... the social, cultural, and economic capitals with which they maintained that domination.'[5] A British document from 1822, years before Macaulay's statement, mentions 'that many of the leading Hindoos [of Calcutta] were desirous of forming an establishment for the education of their children in a liberal manner, as practiced by Europeans of condition.'[6] Moreover, adds Mukherjee, 'The idea that English language and European knowledge was needed to revive Hindu society—or, more precisely, *aryadharma*—was a central consideration for the Indian proponents of English education in the nineteenth century'. So it wasn't as simple as the British imposing their language by diktat on India; their push was met by a reciprocal pull by a class of Indians. Some scholars have argued that

---

5 Alok K. Mukherjee, *This Gift of English: English Education and the Formation of Alternative Hegemonies in India.* Orient BlackSwan, 2009, p. 22-24. This is an excellent survey of the many forces that brought about the spread of English in colonial times and the class dynamics behind its unfolding in the early decades of the Indian republic.

6 *The Christian Observer, Vol. 20.* Hatchard and Company, 1822, p. 527.

the great prominence and prestige attained by this class of Indians not only helped spread Brahminism but also their new construct of 'Hinduism', an offshoot of which would later produce Hindutva. But that is a topic for another essay.

Ngugi's experience in Kenya will resonate with many Indians. I myself grew up in the Hindi belt, in the central Indian city of Gwalior. Though I went to an English medium school run by Carmelite nuns (of St. Teresa of Avila), I only spoke Hindi at home and in my neighborhood until I left home for college. In the classroom—except in the Hindi class—I too was required to speak only English. Failure to comply meant public embarrassment. Though English then had little relevance to my everyday life, I recall how parents in our neighborhood—of middle-class professionals in a textile factory—took pride in their children's English skills, but none ever for Hindi, which is what everyone spoke ('Hindi' is a catchall for a range of linguistic dialects, such as Hindustani, Awadhi, Bhojpuri, Garhwali, Haryanvi, etc., as well as Modern Standard Hindi, a recent innovation by the elites of North India, with its own hegemonic tendencies). English had become a class marker; one used it to distinguish oneself from the 'riff-raff'. Even today it is spoken by a small minority and floats atop a host of indigenous mother tongues.

By the time I went to school, English had already acquired enormous practical benefits. Like a goddess, it offered new visions to converts like me, opened new doors, gave me access to a more dominant culture and a global economy where English proficiency is an undeniable asset. The caste elites have understood this for generations and have used English as a tool to further entrench their power and dominance. The subaltern classes are only now using the same playbook to catch up, and understandably so!

But my point here is neither about the many practical benefits of English, nor to lament the course of history—who knows what an alternate history might have been? Rather it is to recall the politics surrounding the arrival and the spread of English in the colonies, to reflect on the reach and the world of the Indian writer in English, and—for the sake of a more complete accounting—to also consider the costs that our attitude to English, its parent culture and its speakers, continues to extract from us.

Moreover, following Ngugi on African writing in English, should we not also wonder whether Indian writing in English qualifies as Indian literature or as Indo-European literature (i.e., literature written by Indians in a European language), with Indian literature referring only to works in languages with long and pervasive roots in Indian cultures?

Some will shake their heads in disagreement and argue that English is already an Indian language. They will wonder why people keep casting doubts about its status again and again. They will cite its common use in the media, universities, billboards, signage, product labels, various application forms, social media, and so on.[7] In a way they would be right, but this is not the 'language of literature' that Ngugi alludes to. Let's explore whether English qualifies as an Indian language by looking at it in two distinct ways:

(a) As a language of opportunities and lingua franca:

English has spread in India for many of the same reasons it has spread in Malaysia, Denmark, and Argentina—it is the language of globalization, the Internet, and new economic opportunities. In India, it also serves as the lingua franca, albeit only for a small social class. But is this sufficient to make

---

7   Even the most critical public interest information, such as medical instructions on drugs and nutrition labels on packaged foods, appears almost entirely in English, shutting out the vast majority of Indians with little or no facility in it. For more on this, see Sahith Aula. 2014. 'The Problem With The English Language In India', *Forbes*, November 6.

English an Indian language? Perhaps it is. English, however, is also the lingua franca in Continental Europe. Most Dutch and Danes are quite proficient in English—on average more proficient than most educated, urban Indians. Yet do people call English a Dutch, Danish, or a Continental European language (it *is* considered a European language because the UK and Ireland are in Europe)? But just because the Dutch and the Danes do not call it that does not mean they would be wrong to do so. So, as a language of opportunity and as lingua franca, we could also call English an Indian language as long as we grant that English is no less qualified to be a Dutch, Danish, Continental European, Malaysian or Argentinian language (all regions where English language proficiency is actually higher than in India).[8]

(b) As a language of a people's literature:

Does English qualify as an Indian language in this capacity (this is also what Ngugi alludes to)? One answer is 'yes', since many Indians write in English with considerable flourish and creativity. However, this seems to me necessary but insufficient. Unlike other Indian languages, English is not rooted in any whole community, serving as a vehicle for the entire community's artistic and literary expression across all social groups, as well as its mundane and shared daily realm of myths, anxieties, humor, prejudices, greetings, folklore, songs, swear words, and so much else. A member of such a language community acquires all this through pervasive immersion in that language from birth, and even partakes of a linguistic heritage going back many generations. English in India simply cannot reach down to touch the more intimate, emotional reality and mythos of historical experience, which are incomparably expressed in mother tongues.

---

8   'English Proficiency Index: The world's largest ranking of countries by English skills', Third Edition, *Education First*, November 2013.

Doesn't a people's literature need that? More fundamentally, can a people's literature be written in a language other than the people's mother tongue? Could Tagore have written in English, and through his translated works, become the poet of the people of Bengal? In translation, he seems not to have made much of an impact on non-Bengali Indians.

In fact, those fluent in English today constitute only an elite social class spread thinly across India. According to a 2005 survey, they number no more than 3-5% of all Indians.[9] Another 15-20% have functional literarcy in English, barely able to express a few ideas in it. Even the perfectly fluent learned it as a second language in school, not through pervasive childhood use at home (this is now changing in a tiny upper class), and do not converse in it with their entire local community, i.e., with their maids, plumbers, and subzi-wallahs. Are there other national or people's languages elsewhere in the world that are similarly demarcated by social class, yet claim to produce national or people's literature in it?[10] In this sense, then, can we say that English is an Indian language, given there is no Indian community to which English is fundamentally and pervasively constitutive? I think the answer is 'no'.

In other words, English has not made sufficient inroads into Indian communities to qualify as a language of a people's literature. But this does not mean that such a thing can never happen. It can. It happened for the Indians in Trinidad, who were brought there as indentured laborers and gradu-

---

9   Samanth Subramanian. 2014. 'India After English?', *NY Review of Books Blog*, June.

10 If one cites Sanskrit in ancient India as an example here, that would be incorrect. While Sanskrit, say, from Panini to Gupta times, was indeed limited to a small social class, Sanskrit was closely related to the many Prakrit vernaculars spoken by the masses. Because most of these Prakrits were 'less refined' dialects of Sanskrit, they enabled linguistic continuity across social classes in ways that English doesn't.

ally lost their Indian tongues over 100-150 years. English is the language of VS Naipaul's island community in ways that English is not the language of any community in India today. So we can also argue that while many Indians today speak an increasingly global language that's useful and practical, serves as a lingua franca, opens new intellectual horizons, etc., it is not a language in which the great Indian novel can be written today. Instead, and for now, we should think of it as a language in which Indians are producing Indo-European literature. Until English, in a sizable Indian community, becomes the language in which folks across all social classes read, write, talk, think, and dream, can it be the literary language of anything more than a small and historically new and elite sub-culture, one that is 'linguistically alienated' from the larger communities it inhabits?

Hierarchy and Language

Such reflection also illuminates many contemporary trends in the Subcontinent. For instance, the deeply ingrained hierarchies of language and literary culture that Indian elites subscribe to even sixty years after independence. Oh, how we crave Anglo-American recognition for our writing on India and let it drive our sense of literary merit! If target markets and economics explained all, the Danes and the Dutch, quite proficient in English, would have similar attitudes. There is something else going on with the Indian literati—given how hierarchy bound we Indians are, it is as if we accord a higher caste to the British and subconsciously elevate and mimic their literary culture. It is one thing to admire and be inspired by other literary cultures—an entirely laudable thing—but our attitude is one of deference, lacking the self-confidence of equals.

I cited the Dutch and the Danes because they speak English yet were not colonized, and consequently do not suffer from 'colonial alienation'. They do not exhibit, as Indians do, the deference, insecurity, inferiority complex, and look-to-Britain-and-the-US-for-validation-and-yardsticks (that said, there are signs that indigenous yardsticks may be emerging). Unlike the former, the Indians accord a privileged status to English, turning it into a pivotal marker of a class hierarchy. It's true—we have arranged even languages into a hierarchy, with English sitting atop like the Brahmin and our attitude to indigenous languages Brahminical (with accents and dialects providing more ways of filling out the hierarchy). Writers and speakers of English are commonly seen as more sophisticated and are granted more respect and attention. If this is not mental colonization, what is? We are far from achieving intellectual independence. Nothing like a Booker prize, reviews, endorsements, and fat book deals in the Anglophone West to turn our heads. Indian novels that 'make it' abroad are then taken seriously in India—not vice-versa. Do we grant the same cachet to books that win Sahitya Akademi or Jnanpith awards? Or crave translations of our best non-English books? And we have not even considered the mental colonization in the terrain of popular culture, such as in our dominant ideals of beauty.

But wait, says a part of me. How can it be otherwise? The culture that brought us English and came to dominate us had greater power tied to its claim to greater knowledge. So long as this relationship holds in our minds, and we look up to that culture for our self-definition and direction, much else will remain too, including our writers' insecurities and our elites' colonial mindsets. I too am caught in its vortex. As an individual, perhaps the best approach to decolonizing my own mind is to be acutely aware of my predicament, interrogate my own linguistic and cultural hierarchies, and invite others to do the same.

This is certainly not to say that our literary artists ought to jettison English and return to native languages, as Ngugi did for his creative works (which he then translated from Gikuyu to English). For many, that ship has already sailed and there is no going back. Even if one could go back, it's not an unqualified 'better path' for all. Quite often, those who advocate this path are linguistic and cultural chauvinists best avoided like the plague.[11] On the contrary, this is to say that a key attribute of being modern is to try and understand how we came to be who we are, and to cultivate a truly modern, humanistic self—one that sees all humans as equal in status, participates in a creative, self-confident literary culture, and doesn't feverishly seek external validation or erect new hierarchies around language. No language in itself is a problem, our Brahminical approach to it is. To decolonize is to also begin to see the politics of received categories we so unselfconsciously use to understand and judge ourselves (this of course parallels the subalterns' relationship to their 'internal colonization' by Brahminical knowledge), and to explore ways of moving beyond and seeing things afresh. Where else should this start if not with our literary and cultural elites who have the fewest excuses and the longest exposure to modernity?

11 See Ashutosh Bhardwaj. 2016. 'Scrap English requirement, references that insult India: RSS education wing to HRD', *Indian Express*, October 21.

What Do We Deserve?[1]

I often think of the good life I have. By most common measures—say, type of work, income, health, leisure, and social status—I'm doing well. Despite the adage, 'call no man happy until he is dead', I wonder no less often: How much of my good life do I really deserve? Why me and not so many others?

The dominant narrative has it that I was a bright student, worked harder than most, and competed fairly to gain admission to an Indian Institute of Technology, where my promise was recognized with financial aid from a US university. When I took a chance after graduate school and came to Silicon Valley, I was justly rewarded for my knowledge and labor with a measure of financial security and social status. While many happily accept this narrative, my problem is that I don't buy it. I believe that much of my socioeconomic station in life was not realized by my own doing, but was accidental or due to my being at the right place at the right time.

---

1   An earlier version of this essay appeared on 3 Quarks Daily on March 28, 2011. It also appeared in *The Humanist*, May/Jun 2011, and was included in four college anthologies in the United States.

A pivotal question in market-based societies is 'What do we deserve?' In other words, for our learning, natural talents, and labor, what rewards and entitlements are just? How much of what we bring home is fair or unfair, and why? To chase these questions is to be drawn into the thickets of political philosophy and theories of justice. In this short essay, inspired by American political philosopher Michael Sandel's *Justice*, I have tried to synthesize a few thoughts on the matter by reviewing three major approaches to distributive economic justice: libertarian, meritocratic, and egalitarian, undermining en route the dominant narrative on my own well-being.

Three Models of Distributive Justice

The **libertarian model** of distributive justice favors a free market with well-defined rules that apply to all. 'Citizens are assured equal basic liberties, and the distribution of income and wealth is determined by the free market.'[2] It offers a formal equality of opportunity—making it a clear advance over feudal or caste arrangements—so anyone can, in theory, strive to compete and win. But in practice, people do not have real equality of opportunity due to various disadvantages, for example, of family income, social class, gender, race, caste, etc. So while the racetrack may look nice and shiny, the runners don't begin at the same starting point. What does it mean to say that the first to cross the finish line deserves his or her victory? Isn't the contest rigged from the start, based on factors that are arbitrary and derive from accidents of birth?

Take my own example. I was born into the upper-caste, riding on eons of unearned privilege over 80 percent of Indians. I was a boy raised in a society that lavished far more

---

2   Michael Sandel. 2009. *Justice: What's the Right Thing to Do?* Farrar, Straus and Giroux, p. 153.

attention on boys. My parents fell closer to the upper middle class, had university degrees, and valued education and success—both my grandfathers had risen up to claim senior state government posts. I lived in a kid-friendly neighborhood with parks, playgrounds, and a staff clubhouse. I had role models and access to the right schools and books, the right coaching classes, and peers aspiring for professional careers. My background greatly shaped my ambition and self-confidence and no doubt put me ahead of perhaps 96 percent of other Indians—the odds that I would perform extremely well on standardized academic tests were huge from the start.

The **meritocratic model**, often associated with the United States, recognizes such inequities and tries to correct for socioeconomic disadvantages. At its best, meritocracy takes real equality of opportunity seriously and tries to achieve it through various means: Head Start programs, education and job training, subsidized healthcare and housing, and so forth. Meritocrats admit that market-based distribution of rewards is just only to the extent to which we can reduce endemic socioeconomic disadvantages and bring everyone to the comparable starting points. But thereafter, they believe that we are the authors of our own destiny and whoever wins the race is morally deserving of the rewards they obtain from the market—and its flip side, that we morally deserve our failure too, and its consequences. Swiss writer Alain de Botton looked at this phenomenon in the United States in his 2004 documentary film, *Status Anxiety*.[3]

But is this entirely fair? Even if we somehow leveled socioeconomic disparities, the winners of the race would still be the fastest runners, due in part to a natural lottery. People are often born with certain talents and attributes—for instance,

---

3   A splendid essay on meritocracy in America is by Wilfred M. McClay, 'A Distant Elite: How Meritocracy Went Wrong', *The Hedgehog Review*, Vol. 18, No. 2, Summer 2016.

oratory, musical acumen, physical beauty and health, athleti-
cism, good memory and cognition, extroversion, etc.—that
give them unearned advantages. Are their wins not as arbitrary from a moral standpoint as of those born with silver
spoons in their mouths? Further, isn't it pure luck that our
society happens to value certain aptitudes we may have—
such as the leap and hand-eye coordination of Michael Jordan, sound-bite witticisms of talk show hosts like Jay Leno,
or the algorithmic wizardry of Sergey Brin in the Internet
age? A millennium ago, society valued other aptitudes, such
as sculpting bronze in Chola India, equine archery on the
Mongolian steppes, or reciting epigrammatic verse in Arabia. My own aptitude for science and math served me well
in an India looking to industrialize and a United States facing a shortfall of engineers. I might have done less well in
an earlier age where the best opportunities were perhaps in
mercantile pursuits or the bureaucracy of government.

But how can a system of distributive justice compen-
sate for random natural gifts that happen to be valued in a
time and place? We cannot level natural gifts across people,
can we? The mere thought is bizarre. The American political
philosopher John Rawls (1921-2002) had much to say about
this in his landmark 1971 book, *A Theory of Justice*, in which
he developed his **egalitarian model**. Since we cannot undo
the inequities of the natural lottery, he writes, we must find a
way to address the differences in the rewards that result from
them. We should certainly encourage people to hone and exercise their aptitudes, he says, but we should be clear that
they do not morally deserve the rewards their aptitudes earn
from the market. Since their natural gifts are not their own
doing, and are moreover profitable only in light of the value
a community places on them, they must share the rewards
with the community.

One might object here: Wait a minute, what about the role of the personal drive and effort we put into cultivating our talents? Do we not deserve the rewards that come from our striving? Not really, says Rawls. Countless factors beyond our choosing influence our ambition and effort, such as our upbringing, our family's work ethic, our childhood experiences, subconscious insecurities, social milieu, career fads, role models, parental and peer pressure, available life paths, lucky breaks, and other contingent factors. It is not clear how much of it is our own doing, however militantly we may hold the illusion that we create our own life story (an illusion not without psychological and practical payoffs). Even the accident of being firstborn among siblings can be a factor in how hard we strive. Each year, Sandel reports, 75-80 percent of his freshman class at Harvard are firstborns. Besides, effort may be a virtue but even the meritocrats do not think it deserves rewards independent of results or achievement. So, in short, we cannot claim to deserve the rewards on the basis of effort either.

Rawls deflates the idea that we morally deserve the rewards of meritocracy. If we accept this, it follows that the house of distributive justice cannot be built on the sands of moral desert (which, in simple terms, is a condition in which we are deserving of something, whether good or bad), but must be built on other grounds.[4] Notably, however, Rawls doesn't make a case for equal rewards. Instead, Rawls speaks of the 'Difference Principle' in dealing with the inequities of the natural lottery. This principle, says Sandel, 'permits income inequalities for the sake of incentives, provided the incentives are needed to improve the lot of the least advantaged.'[5] In other words, income inequality is justified only to the extent to which it improves the lot of the most

---

4   Some philosophers disagree. Look up Robert Nozick, for instance, for a libertarian critique.

5   Sandel, pp. 157-8.

disadvantaged when compared to an equal income arrangement. Only if society is better off as a whole does favoring inequality seem fair.[6]

Choosing the Rules of the Game

One might ask: Why should we uphold the Difference Principle at all? Is it not an arbitrary construct? No, says Rawls, and invites us to a thought experiment on creating 'a hypothetical social contract in an original position of equality'. Imagine, he says, that 'when we gather to choose the principles [for governing ourselves], we don't know where we will wind up in society. Imagine that we choose behind a 'veil of ignorance' that temporarily prevents us from knowing anything about who we are', including our race, gender, class, talents, intelligence, wealth, religion, etc.[7] What principles would we then choose to order our society? Rawls makes a powerful case that simply out of a desire to minimize our odds of suffering, we will always choose political equality, fair equal opportunity, and the Difference Principle.

Some have argued that the Difference Principle may not get chosen as is, not unless it has a clause to address the unfairness of propping up those who willfully make bad choices or act irresponsibly. Further, is it desirable, or even possible, to choose a social contract from behind the so-called 'veil

---

6 Does this approach diminish the role of human agency and free will when it comes to moral desert? Some say it does, yet the claim seems modest enough, that our achievements have many ingredients, and the contributions from agency/free will are intertwined with the contributions from social and random factors—to the point that it seems unreasonable to give by default all credit to agency/free will, which libertarians try to do in order to justify the rewards of the market. However, some philosophers find an unresolved tension in Rawls' approach to setting up the Difference Principle. See, for instance, *Egalitarianism, Free Will, and Ultimate Injustice* by Saul Smilansky.

7 Sandel, p. 141.

of ignorance', as if, in Rawls' words, 'from the perspective of eternity' with scant regard for context?[8] Doesn't Rawls implicitly presuppose a people who already value political equality, individualism, and resolving claims through public deliberation? Rawls later downplayed its universality but, argues Sandel, even in the United States, Rawls' thought experiment supports an arid secular public space detached from so much that is central to our identities. This includes historical, moral, and religious discourses, which, if squeezed out, often pop up elsewhere in worse forms, such as the religious right. If the point is to enhance the social contract, Sandel adds, political progressives should do so not by asking people to leave their deepest beliefs at home but by engaging them in the public sphere.[9]

Sandel's basic critique here is that Rawls' concern with the distribution of primary goods—which Rawls defines as 'things that every rational man is presumed to want'—is necessary but not sufficient for a social contract. As purposive beings, we should also consider the telos of our choices, such as our common ends as a community, the areas of life worth shielding from the market, the space we should accord to loyalty and patriotism, ties of blood, marriage, and tradition, etc. Still, Rawls' thought experiment retains a powerful moral force and continues to inspire liberals. His theory of justice, writes Sandel, 'represents the most compelling case for a more equal society that American political philosophy has yet produced.'[10]

---

8   See *Communitarianism* by Daniel A. Bell, SEP, 2009, for an introduction to communitarianism and its critique of Rawls. A different kind of critique comes from the Indian economist Amartya Sen, who finds a tension between Rawls' liberal idea of justice and 'the pluralism of reasons for justice.' See 'Justice and Its Critics', Adam Kirsch, *City Journal*, September 2009.

9   Jonathan Derbyshire. 2009. 'The NS Profile: Michael Sandel', *New Statesman*, June 04.

10 Sandel, p. 166.

Theories of justice may clarify and guide our thoughts, but we still have to figure out how to change the game we want to play and where to draw the lines on the playing field. An open society does this through vigorous public debate. As British philosopher Isaiah Berlin wrote, 'people who want to govern themselves must choose how much liberty, equality, and justice they seek and how much they can let go. The price of a free society is that sometimes, perhaps often, we make bad choices'. Thereafter, when the rules are in place, 'we are entitled to the benefits the rules of the game promise for the exercise of our talents'.[11] It is the rules, and not anything outside them, that create 'entitlements to legitimate expectations'. Entitlements only arise after we have chosen the rules of the competition. Only in this context can we say we deserve something, whether admission to a law school, a certain bonus, or a pension.

In Rawlsian terms, the problem in the United States is not that a minority has grown super rich, but that for decades now, it has done so to the detriment of the lower social classes. The big question is: why does the majority in a seemingly free society tolerate this, and even happily vote against its own economic interests?[12] A plausible answer is that it is under a self-destructive meritocratic spell that sees social outcomes as moral desert—a spell at least as old as the American frontier but long since repurposed by the corporate control of public institutions and the media: news, film, TV, publishing, and so forth. It parallels a religious spell in more ways than one. Here too, powerful social institutions are invested in clouding our notions of cause and effect. Rather than move towards greater fairness and egalitarianism, they promote a libertarian gospel of the free market with minimal

---

11 Sandel, p. 163.
12 One reason may be that for a lot of people who have reached basic economic security, cultural interests trump economic interests (such as nationalism, ethnic pride, religious chauvinism, etc.).

regulation, taxation, and public safety nets. They beguile us into thinking that the lifestyles of the rich and famous are within reach of all, and uphold rags-to-riches stories as exemplary ('if this enterprising slumdog can do it against all odds, so can you!' goes the storyline). All this gets drummed into people's heads to the point that they only blame themselves for their lot and don't think of questioning the rules of the game.

What would it take to break this spell? For starters, it would require Americans to realize that the distribution of wealth in their society is far less egalitarian than they think it is—a recent survey revealed that Americans think the richest fifth of them own 59 percent of the wealth, while the actual figure is 84 percent. Perhaps living on credit helps create the illusion that the average American has more than he or she does. Americans also believe that their odds of rising to the top are far better than they actually are; social mobility is quite low by international standards. A kid from the poorest fifth of all households has a 1 percent chance of reaching the top 5 percentile income bracket, while that of a kid from the richest fifth has a 22 percent chance. The task of breaking this spell, then, requires telling new kinds of stories, engaging in vigorous public debate, and employing our best arts of persuasion.

Section 4
The Discourse on Inequality

Ambedkar in the
Indian Imagination[1]

'Turn in any direction you like, caste is the monster that crosses your path,' wrote Bhimrao Ramji Ambedkar, India's foremost crusader for dignity and civil rights. That monster has always haunted Ambedkar's legacy, polarizing it along caste lines. On the one hand is his godlike presence in Dalit communities, who, out of affection and admiration, have built countless statues of him, usually dressed in a Western suit and tie, with a fat book under his arm, and in whose folk songs, poems, and calendar art he has long held pride of place. He is an inexhaustible source of inspirational quotations to them. They celebrate his birth anniversary late into the night with *dhol* and dance. On his death anniversary, 1.5 million assemble to pay their respects at his memorial in Mumbai. For generations, his bold, secular, and emancipatory ideas inspired many lower caste activists and writers, many of whom recall their lives in 'before-and-after Ambedkar' phases. When Omprakash Valmiki, the author of the memoir *Joothan: A Dalit's Life*, first read about Ambedkar's

1   An earlier version of this essay appeared as 'Caste Iron' in *The Caravan*, November 2013.

life and work, he 'spent many days and nights in great turmoil.' He grew more restless; his 'stone-like silence' began to melt, and 'an anti-establishment consciousness became strong' in him. Ambedkar gave voice to his muteness, Valmiki wrote, and raised his moral outrage and self-confidence.

On the other hand, there remains a longstanding apathy for Ambedkar among caste Hindus.[2] What respect he does get from India's elites is usually limited to his role as the architect of the constitution—important, but arguably among the least revolutionary aspects of his legacy. The social scientist and educationist Narendra Jadhav, interviewed in the *Times of India* in early 2013, described Ambedkar as the 'social conscience of modern India', and lamented that he has been reduced to being 'just a leader of Dalits and a legal luminary.'[3] Indeed, even thoughtful, liberal elite Indians are commonly ignorant about Ambedkar's life and social impact, both in his lifetime and in the decades since. As the scholar Sharmila Rege noted in *Against the Madness of Manu: BR Ambedkar's Writings on Brahminical Patriarchy,* not only lay readers, but Indian post-graduates and academics in the social sciences, humanities, and women's studies are also unlikely to have read him.[4] Or as the writer Anoop Kumar said in 2015, 'I have been in sociology seminars where caste was discussed but Ambedkar was not discussed. Some of us—we were very cruel to our teachers actually—we used to pop up this question about Ambedkar. Immediately, their facial expressions would change and we were looked down upon as if we were criminals.'[5] What explains this severe disjunction in how Ambedkar is received in India?

---

2   This refers to all castes within the top three varnas: Brahmins, Kshatriyas, Vaishyas.
3   Narendra Jadhav. 2013. 'Ambedkar's role is being belittled,' *The Times of India*, April 13.
4   Sharmila Rege. 2013. *Against the Madness of Manu: BR Ambedkar's Writings on Brahminical Patriarchy*. Navayana.
5   Anoop Kumar. 2015. 'The Collective Dilemma of the Left, Right

India's benighted historiography offers one explanation. In his provocative series of essays on modern Indian
history, published as *The Indian Ideology*, the historian Perry
Anderson deemed Ambedkar to be 'intellectually head and
shoulders above most of the Congress leaders'—a view that
abounds among Dalit intellectuals, but not one you will find
in the works of bestselling Indian historians and public intellectuals such as Ramachandra Guha, Sunil Khilnani, or Amartya Sen, who, despite polite words of respect for Ambedkar,
remain trapped in a worldview shaped by caste privilege, and
in whose books silences and evasions have often masquer-
aded as political moderation.[6] While these scholars acknowledge aspects of Ambedkar's value, they resist doing so at the
expense of Gandhi and Nehru—a specious position given
how much the two sides differed in their stance on matters of
great significance to a liberal democracy, such as advancing
equal opportunity, safeguarding minorities, and fighting systemic discrimination. Indeed, while Gandhi's social reform-
ism and Nehru's secular rationalism are considered by many
scholars as vital to India's self-image, it is Ambedkar who, on
both counts, demonstrated a deeper and more radical understanding of both in the Indian context.

While Ambedkar opposed British colonialism and its
economic exploitation of India, he didn't join the anti-colonial movement spearheaded by the Congress. 'Ambedkar
was for freedom,' writes scholar Braj Ranjan Mani, 'but he
held the view that as no country was good enough to rule
over another, no caste or class was good enough to rule over
another.'[7] On the prospect of self-rule for his people, Ambed-

and Centre: What to do with Ambedkar?', *Round Table India*, June
15.
6   For a significant critique of Amartya Sen's approach to Indian history, culture, and Hinduism, see Braj Ranjan Mani's essay, 'Amartya
Sen's Imagined India', *Countercurrents.org*, June 4, 2012.
7   Braj Ranjan Mani. 2015. *Debrahmanizing History: Dominance and*

kar wrote, 'It is only in a Swaraj constitution that we stand
any chance of getting the political power in our own hands,
without which we cannot bring salvation to our people ...
We are willing that it may happen, though the idea of Swaraj
[also] recalls to the mind of many the tyrannies, oppressions
and injustices practised upon us in the past.'[8]

More than any other leader of the nationalist movement, which would come to define almost all of independent India's heroes, Ambedkar understood that India's deeply
entrenched social inequities and caste loyalties were serious
obstacles to democratic participation and a shared sense of
citizenship and nationhood. Social tyranny in India, Ambedkar held, was far more vicious than political tyranny. 'A reformer who defies society,' he wrote in *The Annihilation of
Caste*, 'is a much more courageous man than a politician
who defies the government.' Forging a just and democratic
society, in his view, not only required political reform that
the nationalist elites emphasized but also extensive social reform—in short, not just political democracy but also social
democracy. Without the latter, he feared, the caste elites—
who had nothing but contempt for the 'servile classes'—
would simply replace the British and use the organs of state
to extend their domination over others. Focusing on political
democracy while doing little to achieve social democracy, as
he would later say in a related context, was 'to build a palace
on a dung heap.'

None of Ambedkar's contemporary reformers, not even
his great rival, Gandhi, located the fundamental challenges of
nation-building in the social realm so emphatically. Ambedkar had a singular sense of the urgency of emancipating the
'depressed classes' through anti-discrimination laws and
enabling equal access to public goods such as wells, schools,

Resistance in Indian Society, Manohar, pp. 353-4.
8   *Babasaheb Ambedkar Writings and Speeches* (BAWS): Vol. 2: 505-6.

temples, village squares, transportation, and crematoriums. He spoke forcefully about the raw deal women got under the traditional laws of Brahminical patriarchy, and how caste amplified the oppression of women. He saw the necessity of advancing equality of opportunity through reservations— still a bitterly contested issue in modern India. In her classic biography, *Ambedkar's World*, Eleanor Zelliot points out that Gandhi instinctively opposed the idea of reservations for the 'untouchables' in the legislature, until he was forced to compromise out of political expedience, while continuing his stubborn opposition to separate electorates at any cost, including his own life.[9] It led Gandhi to begin a fast-unto-death until the Poona Pact of 1932.

Ambedkar had called Gandhi's fast 'a foul and filthy act … the worst form of coercion against a helpless people to give up the constitutional safeguards (which had been awarded to them [by the British])'. Criticized for 'putting the Mahatma's life in danger', Ambedkar had compromised from a growing fear of 'terrorism by [Gandhi's] followers against the depressed classes', should something happen to him. Thereafter, the only Scheduled Caste nominees that would rise through the ranks of major political parties would be Uncle Toms— or *chamchas* ('stooges'), as the founder of the Bahujan Samaj Party, Kanshi Ram, memorably called them[10]—who wouldn't dare to confront caste Hindus in the party or the voting majority. But the Poona Pact, seen by Dalits as a blow to their struggle, is still routinely defended in history books. It often goes unsaid, especially in the works of mainstream Indian historians, that Jawaharlal Nehru was no better in this respect, claiming that in reservations for 'untouchables' lay 'not only folly but disaster ... How are we going to build our public sector or indeed any sector with second rate people?' Nota-

---

9   Eleanor Zelliot. 2013. *Ambedkar's World*. Navayana.
10 Kanshi Ram. 1982. *The Chamcha Age* (An Era of the Stooges), pamphlet, published by Kanshi Ram, New Delhi.

bly, this crucial detail about Nehru finds no mention in both Khilnani's *The Idea of India* and Guha's *India After Gandhi*, both of which established something as close to hero worship of Nehru as is possible for historians to get away with.

Such feeble liberalism and stubborn prejudice common among his contemporaries, far from being allied with Ambedkar's worldview, actively opposed it. But popular historians in the decades since independence focused almost entirely on a certain kind of nationalist politics, lionizing Gandhi and Nehru at the expense of other civil rights struggles and social reform movements (unless they were led by the 'upper castes'—the Bengal renaissance comes to mind—whose protagonists, including Ram Mohan Roy, the Brahmo Samaj, and other 'progressives' from the landowning bhadralok class, nevertheless stayed within the Brahminical fold, extolled the Vedic corpus and 'the pure spirit of its dictates', and attacked social ills that sometimes only afflicted upper-caste families, such as the practice of Sati and enforced widowhood, but never the caste system itself). Historians' reflexive bias for nationalist politics only deepened, given how long the Congress, largely a party of upper-caste nationalists that led the anti-colonial struggle, has ruled in the decades after 1947. Indeed, from whose social perspective, if not of the elites who replaced the British, would it seem that no significant struggles were afoot besides anti-colonialism, no other heroes?

Ambedkar has become more visible than ever in the new millennium. A growing number of scholarly and popular books, websites, magazine articles, and popular film, theatre, and artwork testify to this, such as films by Jabbar Patel (*Dr. Babasaheb Ambedkar*), Nagraj Manjule (*Fandry, Sairat*), and Pa. Ranjith (*Madras, Kabali*), Arvind Gaur's play *Ambedkar Aur Gandhi*, and *Bhimayana*, the critically acclaimed graphic novel by Subhash Vyam and Durgabai Vyam. Ambedkar even topped a poll ranking 'the greatest Indians' conducted by *Outlook* magazine in 2012. Over the last few years, parks, freeways, townships, schools and universities across India— even a football stadium in Delhi—have come to bear his name, not to mention countless new statues.

Much of the explanation for this resurgence in parts of 'mainstream' culture lies in the politicization of the 'lower castes' in recent decades, and in the success at the polls of political parties focused on their issues, whose leaders—most notably Kanshiram and Mayawati, leaders of the Bahujan Samaj Party—have used Ambedkar as a symbol for asserting their pride in public parks and plazas in various towns and cities. That he is still seen as a leader of only the 'lower castes' is evident both in the motivations that underlie any desecration of the symbol, and in which communities do and do not take offense to such desecration—witness recent incidents as far apart as Gyanpur in Uttar Pradesh, Mandya in Karnataka, and Keezhakappu in Tamil Nadu.

Also driving Ambedkar's visibility is a small class of educated and self-confident Dalit scholars, activists, and artists that has infiltrated the academy, civic institutions, media, and other elite cultural spaces, such as literary festivals, art galleries, and branded publishing.[11] Popular thinkers and writers like Narendra Jadhav, Anand Teltumbde, Sharankumar Limbale, Meena Kandasamy, Kancha Ilaiah, and Chandra Bhan Prasad often invoke Ambedkar in their social analysis and creative work, even as they continue to goad Brahminical India towards a long overdue reckoning with its past. And finally, the diffusion of Western modernity through the many pathways of globalization—including economic, cultural, and technological—has now produced a sliver of the caste elite whose embrace of an individualistic and egalitarian

---

11 An example here is Savi Sawarkar who has achieved high recognition for his visual art.

ethos causes them to sympathize more readily with Ambedkar's struggle.

Ambedkar did not endear himself to caste Hindus in his
lifetime. He berated upper-caste reformers for merely tinker-
ing around the edges of the caste system. He wrote closely
argued critiques of many Hindu scriptures and epics, evalu-
ating them for their morality, including views on caste and
gender. 'I have read the *Rigveda* and the *Atharvaveda* many
times,' he wrote. 'But what is there in them about societal and
human progress and ethical conduct that is persuasive, this
I cannot understand.' Despite the fact that 'all scholarship is
confined to the Brahmins,' he sharply asked, 'Why have the
Brahmins not produced a Voltaire?'[12] In 1927, when he was
thirty-six years old, he publicly burned a copy of *Manusm-
riti*. In 1935, he proclaimed: 'I was born a Hindu; I had no
choice. But I will not die a Hindu because I do have a choice.'
He studied several world religions and in 1956, months before his death, led a mass conversion to Navayana Buddhism,
which he claimed was better adapted than Hinduism for the
modern age.

Ambedkar also understood that caste made patriarchy
much worse, and rightly identified the causal connection
between the practice of endogamy and women's subordinate
status, including stringent controls over their marriage and
sexuality, especially for upper-caste women, leading to practices like child marriage, Sati, and the inferior status of widows and restrictions on their remarriage. He challenged the
defenders of Brahminical patriarchy with the Hindu Code
Bill, which sought to ban polygamy and advance the rights of
women. The bill included the rights to divorce, maintenance,
equal inheritance, removal of caste restrictions in marriage

---

12 The Ambedkar quotes in the preceeding three sentences come from
Sharankumar Limbale. 2004. *Towards an Aesthetic of Dalit Litera-
ture: History, Controversies, and Considerations*, Translated by Alok
K. Mukherjee. Orient Longman.

and adoption, and more—citing as justification not so much modern Western standards as the most liberal practices from the subcontinent's own past, as well as examples cherry-picked from the Hindu scriptures he knew thoroughly (though upper-caste feminists, barring exceptions, have yet to acknowledge his place in the history of Indian feminism). Ambedkar held that 'The relationship between husband and wife should be one of closest friends', though as Omvedt has argued, Ambedkar might not have seen 'very much farther than the ideal of a nuclear family typical of capitalist society, in which the woman provided support and help to the principal earner and worker, the man'.[13]

Ambedkar's radical ideas endeared him neither to the Indian right, nor the left. This was thrown into sharp relief in early 2013, when the Arvind Memorial Trust's conference on caste and Marxism in Pune occasioned fierce, news-making debates between participants on the relationship of Ambedkarite thought with communism. The human rights activist Anand Teltumbde, reflecting on the conference, pointed out in an essay that Ambedkar had once tried 'joining hands with the Communists but got a taste of their 'Brahmanism''.[14] This caused a bitter rift with Ambedkar, to whom, writes the scholar Gail Omvedt, 'eradicating caste was the precondition of a united working-class struggle.'[15] Ambedkar held that the working class in India, riven by distinctions of caste and religion, was far from ready for the communist revolution, adding, 'If Lenin had been born in India he would first eradicate casteism and untouchability from among workers'. His rift with the Communists never healed, which was unfortunate

13 Gail Omvedt. 2008. *Seeking Begumpura: The Social Vision of Anticaste Intellectuals*. Navayana, pp. 264-5.
14 Anand Teltumbde. 2013. 'To the Self-Obsessed Marxists And The Pseudo Ambedkarites,' *Sanhati.com*, April 2.
15 Gail Omvedt. 2008. *Ambedkar: Towards an Enlightened India*. Penguin Books Ltd. Kindle Edition, Location 1039.

because Ambedkar sympathized with some of their ideas and, more generally, with democratic socialism—evident in his role as labor minister in the Viceroy's Cabinet, where he developed policies on irrigation, power, and public works.

Ambedkar, however, was not doctrinaire about his socialist leanings—in the 1950s, for instance, he criticized Nehru's foreign policy and advocated closer ties with the United States based on whether they could help 'solve the problems of our own country'. He wanted the Indian state to remain central to people's lives but didn't want it to be ruled by dogma, including the Marxist-Socialist kind. Both nationalized and private enterprises had their place in economic development. Above all, he favored raising industrial production to reduce poverty, but held that any 'preconceived pattern of industry cannot be the primary or paramount consideration … [as long as there is] no exploitation of the working classes.' Problem-solving, especially the problems of the poor and marginalized, mattered to him more than ideological commitments—a fitting tribute to his beloved mentor at Columbia, John Dewey, a noted philosopher of Pragmatism (a philosophical school whose approach to truth and reality has strong affinities with Buddhism). Indeed, it was pragmatism that led Ambedkar, over the course of his life, to shift his economic thinking away from Marxism to something closer to welfare capitalism.

Emerging as the de facto leader of the 'untouchables' in the early 1930s, Ambedkar founded political parties and periodicals to articulate their interests, astutely represented them at Round Table Conferences, and organized mass protests and rallies to agitate for basic civil rights. At a conference in 1942, he exhorted them with these words: 'Educate, Agitate and Organize! Have faith in yourself. With justice on our side I do not see how we can lose our battle. The battle to me is a matter of joy. The battle is in the fullest sense spiritual.

There is nothing material or social in it. For ours is a battle not for wealth or for power. It is a battle for freedom. It is a battle for the reclamation of the human personality.'

Ambedkar's preferred mode of resistance—legal-democratic means, non-violence, and the shaming of opponents with principled argument—did not rule out collaboration with progressive caste Hindus. For instance, his Independent Labour Party, with its caste-sensitive socialist platform, included many Brahmins as well as Kayasthas, such as Anantrao Chitre and Surendranath Tipnis, who agitated alongside Dalits in their struggle for the right to public water tanks. GN Sahasrabudhe, a Brahmin, was appointed the editor of *Janata*, a weekly Ambedkar founded in 1930. He chose a Brahmin, Sharada Kabir, for his second wife, who became a companion and collaborator in many of his life projects.

Ambedkar continued to refine his anti-caste struggle even as Gandhi himself held out for a sanitized version of the existing caste system. Omvedt writes that Ambedkar's public debates with Gandhi represented 'not simply a confrontation of two idiosyncratic leaders but of two deeply divergent conceptions of the Indian nation itself.'[16] Perhaps it was inevitable, then, that rather than see him as Dalit intellectuals do, defensive elites would, for generations, marginalize him as a partisan man of his people. It is hard to avoid concluding that upper castes and their intellectuals have not yet done the kind of soul-searching necessary to embrace his ideas, which require an interrogation of ingrained habits of mind, sense of identity, and reflexive pride in Hindu civilization—hardly an easy task. In refusing to engage with him, they also limit their own intellectual emancipation.

In many ways, Ambedkar's afterlife in India parallels that of Martin Luther King, Jr. in the United States. Like caste

---

16 Gail Omvedt. 2008. *Ambedkar: Towards an Enlightened India*. Penguin Books Ltd. Kindle Edition, Locations 1878-1879.

Hindus with Ambedkar, White Americans did not see King as their benefactor. This despite the fact that in confronting White supremacy and its physical and emotional violence, King also humanized White Americans. Yet, a whole lot of them saw King's work as an intrusion into their way of life, even a violation of their individual liberty and rights. Though White Americans have come a long way since, even today the tenor and quality of King's reception and emotional resonance vary sharply across racial lines; more extremely so does Ambedkar's across caste lines.

Towards the end of his life, Ambedkar seems to have felt a sense of personal failure. His secretary, Nanak Chand Rattu, records him as saying, 'I have not been able to fulfill my life's mission. I wanted to see my people as a governing class, sharing political power in terms of equality with other communities. I am now almost crippled and prostrate with illness. Whatever I have been able to achieve is being enjoyed by the educated few, who with their deceitful performance, have proved to be a worthless lot, with no sympathy with their downtrodden brethren.'[17] Ambedkar lamented such failings among 'his people' and the selfishness of those vying to succeed him—human failings that have also plagued other communities and emancipatory movements.

His self-assessment now seems unduly harsh, more a sign of the exacting standards he had set for himself. As the political scientist Christophe Jaffrelot has written, Ambedkar's 'contribution to the making of modern India is possibly more substantial than that of any other leader of his generation.' Uniquely among leading national figures, Ambedkar not only overcame enormous personal odds (caste humiliation, poverty, the deaths of four of his five children, poor health), he also pioneered a critique of Indian society based

---

17 Nanak Chand Rattu. 1995. *Reminiscences and Rememberances of Dr. B.R. Ambedkar.* Falcon Books, p. 191.

on Enlightenment values of liberty, equality, and fraternity—values that he situated in India's own ancient traditions, most notably in Buddhism. He was more of a secular rationalist than even Nehru, with a far more sophisticated sense of history, economics, and philosophy. This aspect of Ambedkar—rooted in a worldly, inclusive, scrupulously reasoned, secular and radical egalitarianism, coupled with a bracing focus on equal dignity and social justice as foundations for civil rights—still hasn't received its due in mainstream scholarship and opinion. Which other leader of the 20th century is as relevant to every dream of a just, modern, liberal, secular, humane, and democratic society in India today?

The Rationalist and the Romantic[1]

In early 2014, the Indian publishing house Navayana released an annotated, 'critical edition' of Dr. BR Ambedkar's classic, *Annihilation of Caste* (AoC). Written in 1936, AoC was meant to be the keynote address at a conference but was never delivered. Unsettled by the scathing text of the speech and faced by Ambedkar's refusal to water it down, the caste Hindu organizers of the conference had withdrawn their invitation to speak. Ambedkar, an 'untouchable', later self-published AoC and two expanded editions, which included MK Gandhi's response to it and his own rejoinder.

AoC, as S. Anand points out in his editor's note, happens to be 'one of the most obscure as well as one of the most widely read books in India.' The Navayana edition of *AoC* carries a 164-page introduction by Arundhati Roy, 'The Doctor and the Saint'. The publisher's apparent strategy was to harness Roy to raise *AoC*'s readership among *savarna* (or caste Hindu) elites to whom it was in fact addressed, but who have largely ignored it for over seven decades, even as count-

1   An earlier version of this essay appeared on 3 Quarks Daily on March 31, 2014.

less editions of it in many languages have deeply inspired and empowered generations of Dalits.

However, this new edition has drawn a mixed response. Expressions of praise coexist alongside howls of disapproval and allegations of an ugly politics of power and privilege, co-option and misrepresentation. To many Dalit and a few *savarna* writers and activists, this 'Roy-Navayana project'— Navayana is a small independent publishing house run by Anand, a Brahmin by birth—is a bitter reminder that no Dalit-led edition of *AoC* can get such attention in the national media, that gimmicks are still needed in this benighted land to 'introduce' *AoC* and Ambedkar to the *savarnas*, that once again, caste elites like Roy, with little history of scholarly or other serious engagement with caste (as Anand himself suggested about Roy three years ago[2]), are appropriating *AoC* and admitting the beloved leader of Dalits into their pantheon on their own terms—all while promoting themselves en route: socially, professionally, and financially.

Such responses may seem provincial, hypersensitive, or even paranoid to some, but they should not be brushed aside as such. They point to a universally toxic dynamic of power and knowledge to which *savarna* elites are so alert and sensitive in colonial, orientalist contexts, yet so blind to its parallels within India, propagated by their own class. Is this because it's easier to see prejudice directed from above at one's own class, versus the prejudice it doles out below? Especially on a fraught topic like caste, one's social location shapes how one frames and conducts a debate on annihilating caste, its current state, and the heroes and villains in this fight. The folks at Navayana—a leading English language publisher of anti-caste books, including many by Dalit authors—would surely nod in agreement.

---

2   S. Anand. 2011. 'Lighting Out for the Territory', *The Caravan Magazine*, February 1.

What's notable in this case is the intensity of disapproval—and how it blindsided Navayana—even before many of the protesting Dalits, men as well as women, had read Roy's full introduction. It was clear that in their estimation, Roy simply had not earned the stripes to be the sole introducer of a 'critical edition' of *AoC*. Or perhaps, having read the excerpt and her interview, many Ambedkarites didn't like what they saw as Roy's facile and unjustified account of Ambedkar's weaknesses, as in his views on modernity, urbanization, and Adivasis. A legitimate fear is that this edition of *AoC*, given Roy's brand, might become the dominant interpretation of the text and its author. Would it not have been more prudent and honorable for Navayana to have also included in this book other 'introductions' by Dalits who have engaged the longest with *AoC* and relate to it differently? Or to publish Roy's essay as a standalone book? Only time will tell how this project impacts anti-caste struggles and academia's output in India and abroad. Meanwhile to Anand, a self-described 'Ambedkar zealot' who sees himself as a radical champion of the Dalit cause and who I believe published this edition in that spirit, this turn of events—with many Dalit friends and activists questioning his agenda and lumping him with caste Hindus he has ridiculed before—must feel like a sad and painful desertion.

However, it is worth remembering that Roy's introduction is also a subjective response of a writer to a text that clearly moved her. How good is her introduction, separate from the dubious politics and prudence of its pairing with *AoC*? Like all living classics, *AoC* too requires new readings in every age, including of celebrity writers relatively new to Ambedkar, as Roy evidently is. Just as W.E.B. DuBois can teach White folks what it means to be White better than any White person, Ambedkar serves a parallel role for upper-caste folks. That the upper castes will relate to him differently than Dalits do is a truism that should not surprise anyone.

And if this 'King of the Ghetto'—a status that Roy alleges history has forced on him—is to be appreciated more widely and accorded a richly deserved global stature, he will have to be read and analyzed by non-Dalits. In time, perhaps a big director like Richard Attenborough will even make a big film about him.[3] Non-Indian and *savarna* writers may be late but they too are entitled to make him their own as they see fit. Others, in turn, are entitled to critique such efforts, as many Dalits and non-Dalits have done with Roy, especially on the website *Round Table India*, on the YouTube channel *Dalit Camera*, and in offline forums on university campuses.[4] They have pointed out flaws of logic and empathy, and tried to show how a writer's analysis and assessments are shaped by her identity, ideology, and privilege. They have argued that this project is an attempt by caste elites to 'appropriate' Ambedkar, rather than the laudable sort of cross-fertilization in which the ideas of radical thinkers traverse social boundaries to find homes in new hearts and minds (fortunately, the Internet can now enable more democratic resistance to hegemonic narratives and appropriation). In what follows, I offer my own response to Roy's introduction and reflect on the portrait of Ambedkar I see in it—an exercise shaped no doubt by my own identity, ideology, and privilege.

* * *

Roy's strategy in her introduction is to first lower Gandhi from the high perch of reverence he still commands among caste Hindus (at least outside Hindutva organizations like the RSS where he is reviled for being an 'appeaser' of Muslims), a reverence evident in things as diverse as the iconography

---

3   Jabbar Patel's English Language film, *Dr. Babasaheb Ambedkar* (1999), was a good attempt, though it was funded by the government and did not reach a large audience.

4   Much of the commentary on *Round Table India* was compiled as a book, *Hatred in the belly: Politics behind the appropriation of Dr Ambedkar's writings*. The Shared Mirror, 2015.

of Anna Hazare's anti-corruption movement, popular Bollywood fare on 'Gandhigiri', and names of flagship government schemes like MGNREGA. This strategy, Roy reckons, is necessary to make room for Ambedkar. Here Roy differs from most mainstream historians who, even when they elevate Ambedkar, do not do so at the expense of Gandhi. 'They should both be heroes,' said Ramchandra Guha in 2012. 'Why must we diminish one figure to praise another? India today needs Gandhi and Ambedkar both.' In the essay, 'Ambedkar in the Indian Imagination', I have argued that Guha's is 'a specious position given how much the two sides differed on matters of great significance to a liberal democracy, such as advancing equal opportunity, safeguarding minorities, and fighting systemic discrimination.' Add to this their approach to caste, religion, politics, and economics. As the scholar Gail Omvedt noted, the two men represented 'not simply a confrontation of two idiosyncratic leaders but of two deeply divergent conceptions of the Indian nation itself.' Comparing them is to compare more than just two individuals. Roy too finds their major differences irreconcilable, where praising Ambedkar can imply diminishing Gandhi—and vice versa.

Roy revisits Gandhi's South African past to furnish a persuasive account of his life and mind that is nothing like the staple of history textbooks. Admitting that her account is purposefully selective, since 'Gandhi actually said everything and its opposite', Roy points out that in South Africa, Gandhi harbored a host of racial prejudices, identifying more with the Whites and upper-class Indians and looking down disdainfully on Black Africans and indentured Indians.[5] Roy's

---

5 Similar arguments appear in Ashwin Desai and Goolam Vahed. 2015. *The South African Gandhi: Stretcher-Bearer of Empire*, Stanford University Press. For an article that defends Gandhi against such arguments, see E. S. Reddy. 2016. 'Some of Gandhi's Early Views on Africans Were Racist. But That Was Before He Became Mahatma', *The Wire*, October 18.

portrait of Gandhi—with his views on race, caste (including 'the ideal Bhangi'), women, labor, religion, and more—helps establish continuity with his later attitudes in India, especially his faith in the varna system, his doctrine of 'trusteeship', and his empathy deficit for 'untouchables'. This deficit was evident in his patronizing stance towards them, opposition to legislative reservations and a separate electorate for them, and his attempts to tackle untouchability after the Poona Pact through the organization Harijan Sevak Sangh, which didn't admit any 'untouchables' in leadership roles (imagine setting up an organization to tackle gender discrimination but not admitting any women in leadership roles). Roy's focus on Gandhi seems excessive at times—the main body of *AoC* mentions Gandhi only once—even as it also helps illuminate many attitudes that Ambedkar was up against and the context of their exchange that Ambedkar later appended to the *AoC*. At least in part, Roy's essay seems like her way of making sense of, and coming to terms with, her own recent discovery of Gandhi's inconvenient truths, most of which have long been articulated by Dalit scholars, starting with Ambedkar himself.

Roy's essay, studded with soaring prose and rhetorical flourishes, also covers a lot more ground: how caste manifests itself in the modern economy and persists in so many professions and institutions of democracy, how the *savarnas* wield 'merit' as their 'weapon of choice' to protect their privileges, and the discrimination and violence Dalits still face today. She describes Ambedkar's family background, his early 'encounters with humiliation and injustice', his satyagrahas and other civil rights campaigns for 'untouchables' and women, his call for a separate electorate and the events that led to the Poona Pact, the causes of the historic rift between Ambedkar and the Left, and more.

Why has caste survived for so long? Roy cites Ambedkar who blamed it on a system of 'graded inequality' in which, he wrote, 'there is no such class as a completely unprivileged class except the one which is at the base of the social pyramid. The privileges of the rest are graded ... each class being privileged, every class is interested in maintaining the system.' Thus, she concludes, 'there is a quotient of Brahminism in everybody, regardless of which caste they belong to [and this] makes it impossible to draw a clear line between victims and oppressors.' While true, Roy might have added that those near the top of this pyramid of privilege and resources nevertheless deserve the greatest censure, for they have the fewest excuses for not reforming the system and the institutions they control. Eventually, she writes, such Brahminism 'precludes the possibility of social or political solidarity across caste lines' and that is why caste still survives.

More controversially, Roy faults Ambedkar for his views on the Adivasis, claiming that he did not understand them. He saw them as backward, in a 'savage state', and in need of civilizing. 'Ambedkar speaks about Adivasis in the same patronising way that Gandhi speaks about Untouchables', Roy said in an interview. He displayed against them 'his own touch of Brahmanism', she writes in the introduction. Quoting Ambedkar from *AoC*, she asks: 'How different are Ambedkar's words on Adivasis from Gandhi's words on Untouchables'? Many of these judgments feel gratuitous; I think more sympathetic readings are possible and warranted, but the case she makes, given Ambedkar's high standards, is at least a head-scratcher. 'Ambedkar's views [on Adivasis] were paternalistic and not too helpful,' Omvedt wrote in her review of Roy's introduction. '[But Roy] suggests that his views about Adivasis were similar to Gandhi's views towards Untouchables, which is a gross exaggeration.'[6] Roy however grinds the axe further and claims that Ambedkar's 'views on

6   Gail Omvedt. 2014. 'Ambedkar Needs No Introduction', *Indian Express*, May 17.

Adivasis had serious consequences. In 1950, the Indian Constitution made the state the custodian of Adivasi homelands', making them 'squatters on their own land.' Whether Ambedkar or anyone else—given the dominant mood of territorial consolidation in the new nation state—ever had any room to maneuver on this front, she does not say.

Also disconcerting is Roy's assessment that Ambedkar, in a 'troubling manner ... resorts to using the language of eugenics, a subject that was popular with European fascists.' This is not only a gross misreading of the text but also a deplorable juxtaposition. As early as 1916, Ambedkar had rejected any biological dimension to the hierarchy of caste and saw it as a social construct.[7] He reiterates this position in *AoC*: '[The] Caste system does not demarcate racial division. [The] Caste system is a social division of people of the same race.' Eugenics was then a major obsession in the US and Europe, and Ambedkar, in section 5 of *AoC*, used the then current language of eugenics in an argument—where he was playing devil's advocate—to debunk any biological superiority of the Brahmins.

* * *

Roy has, with great vigor and courage, championed a host of social justice issues in India and abroad, and her moral compass is rare and laudable. Not surprisingly, she extols Ambedkar's radical egalitarianism across caste, class, and gender, and his language of dignity and rights. She enters more contentious terrain when she evaluates Ambedkar's approach to modernity. This is the Roy who, in her non-fiction, has argued from positions that could be called anti-modern, anti-industrialization, anti-urbanization, anti-globalization, and even anti-statist. We could see these as pillars of her own utopia, reminiscent more of Gandhi than Ambedkar. Gan-

---

7   See BR Ambedkar. 1916. *Castes in India: Their Mechanism, Genesis and Development.*

dhi, she says, 'believed (quite rightly) that the state represented violence in a concentrated and organized form'. He was
'prescient enough to recognize the seed of cataclysm that was
implanted in the project of Western modernity.' Ambedkar
on the other hand, writes Roy, recoiling from the iniquities
of the past, 'failed to recognize the catastrophic dangers of
Western modernity.' The very existence of Adivasis, fighting
'the pitiless march of modern capitalism', she claims, 'poses
the most radical questions about modernity and 'progress'—
the ideas that Ambedkar embraced'. She adds,

> The impetus towards justice turned Ambedkar's gaze away
> from the village towards the city, towards urbanism, mod-
> ernism, and industrialization—big cities, big dams, big irri-
> gation projects. Ironically, this is the very model of 'develop-
> ment' that hundreds of thousands of people today associate
> with injustice, a model that lays the environment to waste
> and involves the forcible displacement of millions of people
> from their villages and homes by mines, dams and other ma-
> jor infrastructural projects.

Many will recognize this recurrent feature in Roy's writing: daring but simplistic, earnest but overstated, a purveyor
of partial truths. She might as well rail against modern medicine because of its side-effects, grossly unequal access, and
rampant malpractices. Roy concludes that 'The rival utopias
of Gandhi and Ambedkar represented the classic battle between tradition and modernity... both were right and both
were also grievously wrong'. But Gandhi's fond fantasy of an
idyllic village was very much a byproduct of modernity, so
a sharper framing of their differences might be Romanti-
cism vs. Enlightenment Rationalism. Gandhi raged against
machines, railways, hospitals, modern education, law courts,
and explained floods and earthquakes as divine punishment.
'Neither railways nor hospitals are a test of a high and pure
civilization. At best they are a necessary evil. Neither adds

one inch to the moral stature of a nation.'[8] Yet he himself
traveled the country by rail and relied on modern medicine
when he needed it, such as an appendicitis operation in 1924.
Unlike other nationalists, he also distrusted the enterprise of
writing history, 'I believe in the saying that a nation is happy
that has no history.' By contrast, Ambedkar eulogized 'reason, the purpose of which is to enable man to observe, medi-
tate, cogitate, study and discover the beauties of the Universe
and enrich his life.' He valued 'sufficient leisure' that allowed
humans to cultivate their minds, adding that 'Machinery
and modern civilization are thus indispensable for emancipating man from leading the life of a brute'. Gandhism 'is
merely repeating the views of Rousseau, Ruskin, Tolstoy and
their school.' Gandhism harks 'back to squalor, back to poverty and back to ignorance for the vast mass of the people.'
Ambedkar continued,

> The economics of Gandhism are hopelessly fallacious. The
> fact that machinery and modern civilisation have produced
> many evils may be admitted. But these evils are no argu-
> ment against them. For the evils are not due to machinery
> and modern civilisation. They are due to wrong social or-
> ganisation which has made private property and pursuit of
> personal gain matters of absolute sanctity. If machinery and
> civilisation have not benefited everybody the remedy is not
> to condemn machinery and civilisation but to alter the or-
> ganisation of society so that the benefits will not be usurped
> by the few but will accrue to all.[9]

Whether emerging nations like India ever had the option of rejecting modernity is not a question that Roy seems
to have considered. Did other viable models exist in a world
where power and prosperity accrued to those who embraced
modernism, industrialization, urbanism, a constitutional
state, science, public health, social security, and liberal edu-

---

8   MK Gandhi. 1909. *Hind Swaraj*. Navajivan Publishing House.
9   BR Ambedkar, 1945. *What Congress and Gandhi Have Done to the
     Untouchables*.

cation? Couldn't an alternative model have turned out to be
far worse? It is true that modernity has also spawned huge
new problems but, as always, the picture of gains and losses
is decidedly mixed and very intertwined. What do we make
of the fact that there is also a genuine mass appetite for modernity, which has spread not by diktat but by diffusion? If
this has set us on a collision course with nature, we might as
well blame it on the tragic human 'weakness' that has come
to seek greater dignity, pleasure, and freedom in the short
run of human lives. How voluptuously romantic and ultimately counter-productive for highly modern citizens of a
liberal state, such as Roy, to stand opposed to something as
manifold and irrepressible as 'modernity' itself, rather than
focusing on the only path that has been open to us: influence
its unfolding, use its tools to reduce its harms, make it more
equitable. Isn't that precisely what Ambedkar, a democratic
socialist, would have done?

Roy's critique of Ambedkar's fondness for 'Western
modernity' is of a piece with attitudes evident elsewhere in
her writing. It is one thing to cherish and want to preserve
certain 'traditional ways of life', 'cultural diversity', and 'eco-
logical harmony' for a people, and to shield the innocent and
the unprepared from the ravages of 'Western modernity'
and globalization. But it is another thing to want that *and*
to also want human rights, a better democracy, free speech,
feminism, gay rights, modern medicine, a caste-free society,
and 24x7 electricity (or other similar combinations). Our
tragedy is that these two desires are not entirely compatible.
Consider this: Can gay rights take root in a tradition-bound
patriarchal culture without causing or requiring other trans-
formations of the self, social attitudes, and secular law? Will
there be no cultural fallout if women start taking charge of
their reproductive cycles and life paths? Can the benefits
of modern medicine be widely distributed without science

education and research, industry, precision manufacturing, markets, competition, profit incentives, lawyers, tax surpluses via economic growth, and so on? Clearly, there are better and worse ways of doing all this (and India has a very poor record to show here), which is often the domain of social justice movements.

It's one thing to critique the worst aspects of the mixed track record of 'Western modernity', say, related to corporate capitalism, income inequality, or ecology—and Roy has frequently done that—but to do so while holding 'Western modernity' as the original sin seems not only a lost cause but also cognitively dissonant, for it relies on the same modernity to make its case. 'Democracy,' Roy has written, 'can perhaps no longer be relied upon to deliver the justice and stability we once dreamed it would.' What better alternative to democracy we could pursue, she has not said. Her disquiet with the trajectory of Indian democracy, which she claims 'has been hollowed out and emptied of meaning', coexists with a formless nostalgia for the pre-modern. 'We plunder the earth hoping that accumulating material surplus will make up for the profound, unfathomable thing that we have lost.'[10] Roy longs for a 'new modernity' but has not said what in it is not to be found in the capacious tent of 'Western modernity' (which, besides predatory strains of capitalism and economic globalization, also houses communism, socialism, environmentalism, zero-growth economics, and so on). All this may help explain why her political commentary—even as she takes on pressing issues with her heart in the right place—has often seemed closer to a loose wail of pain, filled more with the carping of the disillusioned and slogans of a globalized left than lucid analysis or viable solutions.

* * *

10　Arundhati Roy. 2009. 'What Have We Done to Democracy?', *The Nation*, October 12.

To question Roy's approach to modernity does not mean that Ambedkar's approach to modernity is beyond criticism. Dalit intellectual and social scientist DR Nagaraj offered some in *The Flaming Feet and Other Essays*. Nagaraj, like Roy, saw partial truths in both Gandhian and Ambedkarite responses to modernity. He held that the advocates of these 'contending visions are yet to comprehend each other fully.' Persuasive or not, Nagaraj's critique is a lot more nuanced than Roy's animus for modernity itself.

'The modern city and its development ethos', wrote Nagaraj, 'are bound to annihilate the memories of Dalits and leave them in almost a state of culturelessness. [But] this argument is not usually viewed with sympathy by the majority of Ambedkarites, for they believe there is nothing positive or precious in the memories of Dalits, there is only humiliation and pain.' Nagaraj argued that 'the disappearance of indigenous technology represents a big civilizational blow to the subaltern castes' but Ambedkarites, lured by the emancipatory potential of modernization and urbanization, failed to see 'the treacherous deal that was struck between the forces of modernity and the upper strata of the caste system.' This deal may not have been avoidable, and 'There is little wisdom in putting the blame at the door of the agents of modernity in India,' wrote Nagaraj. But Ambedkarities didn't fully realize, nor prepare to deal with the problematic fact that concentrated 'capital and high-tech-based models of development would in the Indian context inevitably lead to the hegemony of the upper castes over the lower.' Keen to escape 'certain professions and humiliation in traditional society', Ambedkar did not take a critical attitude towards 'the practices of erasure within modern development' and didn't factor into his analysis 'the nature of new technology and the social basis of its ownership.'

The same outlook, wrote Nagaraj, led Ambedkarites to also develop 'misgivings about traditional cultures', misgivings that tend to be 'shared by movements for radical social change.' This meant that even the worth of a community's cultural and 'social experience [were] judged from the viewpoint of radical politics.' According to Nagaraj,

> A sure way of enhancing the self-respect of humiliated communities like the Dalits is to revitalize their cultural forms. But modernists and radicals, particularly Ambedkarites, resent such efforts. For them, any attempt to see creativity in traditional Hindu folk culture is tantamount to supporting the unjust society it has sustained. ... [To them] the art of playing drums is linked with the humiliating task of carrying dead animals. The joy of singing oral epics is traditionally associated with the insult of an artist standing outside the houses of upper-caste landlords with a begging bowl. Old culture means humiliation and therefore self-respect essentially means repudiating one's cultural past. [Such] are the attitudes of the modernists and radicals who are products of historical change and the will to change.

And while it is true, wrote Nagaraj, that the lower castes, aided by reservations, are slowly entering 'the exclusive reserves of the upper castes within social administration and political management ... many a time such presence seems only of symbolic value', even as the material gaps continue to increase (a point that has assumed greater salience in the last two decades). While Nagaraj pointed out what he saw as blind spots in Ambedkar's vision, he did not say what alternative paths or policies Ambedkar might have pursued. Ambedkar had however realized 'the tragedy of a memoryless community'. Through his founding of, and mass conversions to, Navayana Buddhism—which Nagaraj called 'one of the most moving chapters of Indian history'—Ambedkar tried 'to build a new memory' for Dalits, marking 'a decisive break with a certain kind of modernization'.[11]

---

11 DR Nagaraj. 2013. *The Flaming Feet and Other Essays: The Dalit Movement in India*. Permanent Black. Kindle Edition.

* * *

'I did not have to read Ambedkar to understand caste,' Roy said at a launch event for this book. 'I just had to grow up in an Indian village.' This struck me as unusual. How many Dalit thinkers would say the same? I wish she had written about her own journey of awakening to caste iniquities. When did she start thinking about it deeply and seeing things afresh? Personal encounters and discoveries are an effective device in good storytelling. Nonetheless, Roy's essay, despite its many problems, has already proven useful for the debates it has provoked. It shows that there are indeed irreconcilable differences between Ambedkar and Gandhi. The same can also be said about Ambedkar and Roy.

On the Politics of Identity[1]

Our identity is a story we tell ourselves everyday. It is a selective story about who we are, what we share with others, why we are different. Each of us, as social beings in a time and place, evolves a personal and social identity that shapes our sense of self, loyalties, and obligations. Our identity includes aspects that are freely chosen, accidental, or thrust upon us by others.

Take an example. A woman may simultaneously identify as Indian, middle-class, feminist, doctor, Dalit, Telugu, lesbian, liberal, badminton player, music lover, traveler, humanist, and Muslim. Her self-identifications may also include being short-tempered, celibate, dark-skinned, ethical vegetarian, and diabetic. No doubt some of these will be more significant to her but all of them (and more) make her who she is. Like all of our identities, hers too is fluid, relational, and contextual. So while she never saw herself as a 'Brown' or 'person of color' in India, she had to reckon with that identity in America.

---

1   Earlier versions of this essay have appeared on 3 Quarks Daily on
    July 13, 2015 and in Raiot on May 19, 2016.

Identity politics, on the other hand, is politics that an individual—an identitarian—wages on behalf of a group that usually shares an aspect of one's identity, say, gender, sexual orientation, race, caste, class, disability, ethnicity, religion, type of work, or national origin. Any group—majority or minority, strong or weak, light or dark-skinned—can pursue identity politics. It can be a dominant group led by cultural insecurities and chauvinism, or a marginalized group led by a shared experience of bigotry and injustice (the focus of this essay). Both German Nazism and the American Civil Rights movement exemplify identity politics based on the racial identity of their constituent groups, as do the White nationalism of Donald Trump's presidential campaign and the activism of the Black Lives Matter movement in the US. Both Hindutvadis and Dalits are identitarians of religion and caste, respectively. As Eric Hobsbawm also noted in his essay 'Identity Politics and the Left', labor unions, too, have long pursued identity politics based on social class and the identity of being an industrial worker.

Life, and identity politics, can amplify certain aspects of our identity while suppressing others. During the Sri Lankan Civil War, the Tamil Tigers elevated Tamil national identity over that of caste. Gender identity turns secondary in some contexts: Indian women often close ranks with Indian men when White Westerners lecture them on sexual violence in India. Likewise, Dalit women often close ranks with Dalit men when upper-caste women expound on gender violence among them.[2] Especially after September 11, 2001, many European citizens and residents with complex ethno-linguistic roots faced a world hell-bent on seeing them as, above all, 'Muslims'.

---

2   In the 2016 presidential election in the US, White women discounted gender affinities with Hillary Clinton to vote in a majority for Donald Trump's party affiliation and White nationalism, despite his openly misogynistic remarks.

The Value of Identity Politics

Like all politics, identity politics too can be regressive or progressive, depending on its aims and methods. All social groups, whether dominant or marginalized, practice identity politics, but the term is now largely associated with groups that have been marginalized for an aspect of their identity (more on this sleight of hand later but in this essay too, for the sake of readability, I'll use the unqualified term 'identity politics' to refer to the marginalized).

That identity politics emphasizes one aspect of a person's identity above all others—and explains much about her life in terms of that identity—is a source of both strength and weakness. Especially for those marginalized by a single aspect of one's identity—whether race, caste, gender, class, religion, ethnicity, or another basis of discrimination—identity politics can empower both the individual and her group. It can challenge deeply ingrained habits of mind and weaken structural hegemonies. Its focused advocacy can help transform both popular opinion and bring about legislative reform, as with the granting of equal inheritance rights to women in India (2005) and the legalization of same-sex marriage in the US (2015). It can enrich democratic debate, help equalize opportunities, and awaken us to the value of diversity in public life. Identitarians have produced compelling new readings of our past and our literature and culture. They have given us new moral visions and greater self-knowledge.

For example, Steve Biko, the anti-apartheid leader, raised the slogan 'Black is beautiful' and founded the Black Consciousness Movement, awakening and mobilizing a generation of Blacks in urban South Africa. During the Civil Rights era, the assertion of Black identity and pride helped a historically oppressed people to organize and reclaim self-respect, raise their own and the public's consciousness, push for equal rights, and combat various social barriers and exclusions. In doing so, many Black identitarians, notably Martin Luther King Jr., also civilized White Americans, emancipating them from their own prison of inhumanity—a point rarely acknowledged. Much the same is true in India with many caste identitarians, notably BR Ambedkar. What still strikes us about them is the moral force and persuasiveness of their politics of identity, rooted in demands for equal human dignity and civil rights. Likewise, it was the politics of gender, raised by feminists, that brought about so many gains for women. In the former colonies of the West, the rise of nationalism—and a national identity—mobilized diverse groups behind the cause of ending colonization, though this same once-empowering politics of identity sadly later turned into a toxic majoritarianism in so many countries.

Indeed, if men or Whites or Brahmins or heterosexuals have long used whatever power and knowledge was tied to their identity in order to define, judge, and subjugate others (is this not identity politics?), can the latter fight back without politicizing those definitions, judgments, and subjugations? As long as socially constructed race remains a vector of discrimination, would it not also remain a source of social identity, around which people organize to reclaim their dignity and rights? If racism did not exist, would we still have our modern idea of race—or the identitarians' preoccupation with it?

Perhaps the most prominent movement for rights, equality, and other progressive change in the modern era has emerged from the political Left, from those who identify with various strands of Marxism and socialism. Yet, a great many of these leftists now complain about the rise of seemingly progressive identity politics of race, caste, gender, sexuality, ethnicity, and others. In large part this may be because leftists see these movements as divisive and threatening the solidarities of class, especially among workers as workers.

Ironically, among the factors that explain the rise of these movements is the Left itself. Marxism, like the monotheistic faith of its cultural ancestors, aspires to a universalism representing everyone. But theory is one thing, reality another. In reality, most leftists, being humans, did not care about every group equally. Consider the Left in America and India. The American Left was led by White men who were neither too ruffled by racism, nor accorded it the centrality it deserved in their social analysis, and conveniently remained blind to their own privilege.[3] The Indian Left was similarly blind to the reality of caste; was it a coincidence that its leadership was entirely upper-caste (and is still largely so)?[4] Marxist-socialists in both countries, for all their economic radicalism, did not even pursue voluntary affirmative action to include marginalized groups in their leadership ranks. 'There hasn't been a single Dalit in the Communist Party of India (Marxist) politburo since its formation in 1964.'[5] Despite Dalits constituting 22 percent of the population of West Bengal (2011 census), its Chief Minister from 1977-2000, Jyoti Basu of CPI(M), told the Mandal Commission that he knew of only two castes in West Bengal: rich and poor. Older Indian Marxists meanwhile recall that Brahmins and Dalits in their organizations maintained separate pitchers of water.

Clearly, the Left failed to recognize that the very real divisions among workers, such as of race and caste, were a major obstacle to working-class solidarity; the identity of be-

3   This argument has been developed by Michael C. Dawson in *Blacks In and Out of the Left* (The W. E. B. Du Bois Lectures). Harvard University Press, 2013; and by Richard Iton in *Solidarity Blues: Race, Culture, and the American Left*. The University of North Carolina Press, 2003.
4   See Anand Teltumbde. 2013. 'To the Self-Obsessed Marxists And The Pseudo Ambedkarites', *Countercurrents.org*, April 3.
5   Shoaib Daniyal. 2016. 'How Mamata Banerjee brought identity back into West Bengal politics (and why that's a good thing)', Scroll. in, April 30.

ing 'a worker' may have been the most common but it wasn't necessarily the most important and could easily be trumped by other identities that also shaped one's material realities. When leftists chide identity politics, they reveal their poor grasp of the human material—especially of the fact that humans are not rational beings, that even card-carrying comrades cannot easily transcend many aspects of their social identity and ties of blood, kinship, and culture. Even the big stars of the Left, including Hobsbawm, failed to see this reality and maintained a stodgy opposition to identity politics in the name of an idealized, universal politics of the Left.[6] This 'universal' focus of the Left helped drive various groups, whose particular concerns they had glossed over, to organize for themselves.

In other words, identity politics is an expression of a human need for justice, a need largely unaddressed, and perhaps unaddressable, by traditional Marxist-socialists.[7] The Left in India and the US will likely remain small, unless it learns and becomes more inclusive in its leadership and concerns (parts of the Indian Left could also increase their relevance by abandoning their doctrinaire aversion to capitalism and instead promoting a 'welfare capitalism' that harnesses the power of markets to raise living standards with strong regulatory oversight and redistribution to reduce economic inequality). The Left needs to accept that economic class is not the only arena of injustice, that declining wages aren't necessarily more worrisome than rising racial discrimination, sexual violence, or religious persecution.[8] As Ambed-

6   Eric Hobsbawm. 1996. 'Identity Politics and the Left', *New Left Review*, No. 217.
7   Linda Martín Alcoff, Satya P. Mohanty, Michael Hames-García, Paula M. L. Moya. 2006. *Identity Politics Reconsidered*. Palgrave Macmillan.
8   Nancy Fraser. 1998. 'Social justice in the Age of Identity Politics: Redistribution, Recognition, Participation', *WZB Discussion Paper*, No. FS I 98-108.

kar wrote about the 'untouchables', 'The want and poverty which has been their lot is nothing to them as compared to the insult and indignity which they have to bear as a result of the vicious social order.'[9]

Indeed, the origins of identity politics lie in oppressive social beliefs and practices that may overlap with but are not subsumed under a class conflict conceived in economic terms. Any politics that doesn't target such social beliefs and practices, focusing instead on 'the common good', may end up perpetuating them. Identity politics, above all, enables a persecuted people or group to champion their own cause, which no one else will do. Rather than disdain particularist struggles as a burden, the Marxist-socialist Left would do well to recognize in them our collective emancipation.[10] As citizens, we ought to embrace identity politics when it's both progressive and pragmatic. Rejecting everything about identity politics makes no more sense than rejecting everything about politics.

Even the charge of essentialism, invoked by critics to malign identity politics, is vastly overblown and a straw man. Essentialism is the idea that certain people have a primary social identity that derives from an innate and immutable essence within them. But how many identitarians actually believe this?[11] Do many feminists accept gender essentialism as explanation for why women pursue science less often than men or earn less than men? Do many Black rights activists see their primary identity or their community's socioeconomic outcomes as rooted in biological difference? Isn't

9   *Babasaheb Ambedkar Writings and Speeches* (BAWS): Vol. 9: 212:13.
10 For more on this line of argument, see Robin D. G. Kelley. 'Identity Politics & Class Struggle', *New Politics*, Vol. 6, No. 2, Winter 1997.
11 See Roger White. 2004. 'Identity Politics and Essentialism' in *Post Colonial Anarchism: Essays on Race, Repression and Culture in Communities of Color 1999-2004*. Jailbreak Press, 2004. http://www.coloursofresistance.org/326/identity-politics-and-essentialism/

identity politics largely driven by shared and contingent social experiences? Isn't that why their narratives have much explanatory power and emancipatory potential in a given time and place? Caste is entirely a social construct, Ambedkar held, yet he cited its reality to persuasively explain a host of social phenomenon, including people's outcomes in life. Rejecting the charge of essentialism, bell hooks called us to recognize that 'black identity has been specifically constituted in the experience of exile and struggle.'[12]

Moreover, unlike the identity politics of dominant groups, that of marginalized groups arguably dissipates with rising parity. As marginalized groups emerge into the mainstream as significant equals with other groups, the appeal of identity politics to their younger generations also changes. Of course, as with all public politics, identity politics is not without its problems, but I think these problems are not so much of essentialism.[13] To recognize its limitations and excesses, we ought to at least hear some of the better criticisms of it.

The Limitations of Identity Politics

It's much easier for social liberals like me to criticize the partisan identity politics of dominant groups (Sinhalese, Hindutvadi, KKK, Zionist) than of marginalized groups (feminist, Black, Dalit, Palestinian). This is partly because the former are widely seen as natural targets in my circle, but perhaps also due to liberal guilt, which has its positive side even as it can, at times, cloud reason, clarity, and good judgment. But no public politics, however well-meaning, ought to be

---

12 bell hooks. 1990. 'Postmodern Blackness'. http://www.africa.upenn. edu/Articles_Gen/Postmodern_Blackness_18270.html

13 Nancy Fraser. 1998. 'Social justice in the age of identity politics: Redistribution, recognition, participation', *WZB Discussion Paper*, No. FS I 98-108

beyond criticism, so why should the identity politics of marginalized groups get a free pass? Most liberals will agree that
even such identity politics can sometimes lose its marbles
and begin to eat its own tail, though they may disagree on
when and how often this happens.

Many critics argue that identity politics, by focusing on
only one aspect of identity, ignores too many key differences and similarities among people. 'To see a person primarily as a 'white male' or a 'black female', one critic writes, 'is
to diminish both their humanity and their individuality.'[14]
Some consider this an aspect of essentialism and object to its
disciplinary function in dictating how members of a group
ought to see themselves. Feminist critic Gayatri Chakra-
vorty Spivak has however called this 'strategic essentialism',
where identitarians 'act *as if* an identity were uniform only to
achieve interim political goals, without implying any deeper
authenticity.' But it often doesn't work out like that. Identitarians, with their own narrow lens of social analysis, often
end up oversimplifying the categories of oppressor and oppressed, privileged and unprivileged, and avoid nuances and
shades of grey. Ethnic identitarians forget what they have in
common with their neighbors; gender identitarians down-
play class and caste divisions among women;[15] class identitarians fail to see race and caste divides among workers; caste
identitarians overlook the oppressive hierarchy within Dalit
Bahujans.[16] And so even the revisionist histories written by

---

14 Graham Good. 2013. 'Identity Politics is Killing College Life',
   Spiked, September 23.
15 Elen Turner. 2014. 'Reconciling Feminist and Anti-Caste Analyses
   in Studies of Indian Dalit-Bahujan Women', *Intersections: Gender
   and Sexuality in Asia and the Pacific*, Issue 34, March.
16 According to Bathran Ravichandran, founder of *Dalit Camera*: 'The
   violence or oppression on Dalits is no more carried out only by the
   Brahmins or upper-caste people. As in Khairlanji or even in my
   case, where I was beaten up by SC/ST members of ABVP, it is carried out by others from lower castes. But this discussion hasn't be-

identitarians, though valuable for many of their insights, may not be much better than the mainstream one, since they exaggerate the impact of a single aspect of social life, whether economics, gender, caste, race, or religion.

Indeed, critics claim that despite their advocacy and concern for social justice, identitarians too remain impervious to many kinds of pain and progress around them. What they see is largely along the lines of the identity and ideology they subscribe to. There's often hypocrisy in their reluctance to look within for discriminatory habits of mind similar to those of their rivals. Male identitarians of race and caste, for instance, have a poor record of addressing patriarchy in their midst.[17] Indeed, their equanimity towards injustices in other domains—of class, gender, sexuality, environment, animal welfare, and more—usually fails to distinguish them from their rivals.[18]

Furthermore, progressive identitarians usually focus on parity between groups, which is not the same as an egalitarian society, as Adolph Reed Jr., professor of political science, has pointed out. They seek proportional representation for their group in existing power structures (say, via positive discrimination, or voting based on identity[19]). This may help

---

come a part of the Dalit discourse yet.' Dipti Nagpaul. 2016. 'Write back in anger', *Indian Express*, January 31. For another perspective on the complex dynamics and the often-adversarial relations between Dalits and Bahujans, see Vidya Bhushan Rawat. 2017. 'Days of Identity in Dalit Politics Are Over, We Need to Focus on Ideology: A conversation with Bhanwar Meghwanshi, Dalit activist from Rajasthan'. *The Wire*, January 3.

17 Kimberle Crenshaw. 'Mapping the Margins: Intersectionality, Identity Politics, and Violence Against Women of Color', *Stanford Law Review*, Vol. 43.

18 Consider, for instance, that most meat-eating identitarians further a systemic cycle of great suffering and cruelty towards sentient farm animals. In averting their gaze and in their self-serving justifications, how different are they from those they criticize?

19 Stanley Fish. 2008. 'When 'Identity Politics' Is Rational', *New York*

make social institutions more representative of a society's demographics, but it often also means not agitating for a more egalitarian society for all. So in a highly unequal society where, say, 5 percent control 90 percent of the resources, having the right proportion of Blacks, Latinos, or women in the 5 percent becomes the primary goal and yardstick of fairness for many identitarians (usually those who're new to, or aspiring to, this 5 percent).[20] This, Reed suggests, comes at the expense of joining hands with others to reform the system itself, one that is now producing inequality on an ever-larger scale.[21]

Identitarians of race, for instance, mostly employ a racialist frame to explain the plight of African-Americans, and insist on race-based affirmative action to address historical injuries and current racism. In doing so, Reed argues, they often sacrifice solidarities of class and strengthen neoliberalism, making it harder to secure even those class-based redistributive policies—higher minimum wage, more safety nets, and public spending on job creation, healthcare, environment, and higher education, etc.—that would help a wide cross-section of African-Americans (along with poor Whites and Latinos). An obvious response to Reed—a leftist to whom 'class' seems to be the only meaningful social category for analyzing inequality[22]—is that these two approaches are not necessarily mutually exclusive, and identitarians, despite their adversarial rhetoric, do in fact make pragmatic compromises. Reed's point, however, is still worthy of reflection

Times, February 17.
20 Adolph Reed, Jr. 2015. 'From Jenner to Dolezal: One Trans Good, the Other Not So Much', *Common Dreams*, June 15.
21 Ujval Nanavati. 2015. 'Compared to China, India has far greater wealth disparity', *Forbes India*, February 2; Rukmini S. 2014. 'India's staggering wealth gap in five charts', *The Hindu*, December 8.
22 Adolph Reed. Jr. 2014. 'Nothing Left: The long, slow surrender of American liberals', *Harper's Magazine*, March.

since the two camps often pursue their agendas in ways that impede progress for the other.[23]

Indeed, some critics, including Reed and Marxist scholar and sociologist Vivek Chibber, see this conflict rooted in the very sociology of today's social justice movements, many of which, they posit, have been captured by upwardly mobile, urban middle-class identitarians. These identitarians disdain Left politics not only for its failures in fighting, but for also practicing biases of race, caste, or gender. However, they unwittingly elevate the interests of their own class within their identity groups, and see prejudices of race, caste, or gender animating nearly every problem faced by the members of their identity groups. In other words, the accusation goes, these middle-class identitarians do not necessarily represent the interests of the less privileged members of their identity groups—wage laborers, small peasants, rural migrants to urban slums, and so on—whose interests often have more in common with the traditional concerns of the Left, such as minimum wage, labor unions, workplace safety, land reform, food security, minimum support price for crops, equal pay for equal work, minority rights, access to micro finance, clean water, primary healthcare and education, clean cooking fuel, and social security. Nor does this class of identitarians agitate much about issues of environmental degrada-

---

23 According to Reed, identitarians of race are comfortable with neoliberalism and practice a 'politics that's hinged in material terms ultimately on race relations administration as a career path'. They're invested, above all, in maintaining 'the dominance of the racialist interpretive frame of reference' to explain the plight of African-Americans. He sees this not as a practical alternative to class-based politics but its divisive subset 'because part of the material foundation of the class has been … a claim to be representatives of the aspirations of and of the voice of black people writ large'. Source: 'Adolph Reed on Sanders, Coates and Reparations', Doug Henwood in conversation with Adolph Reed (transcribed by John Halle), *Outrages and Interludes*, January 25, 2016.

tion and injustice, whose victims especially abound in their identity groups. This has parallels in the feminist movement, which doesn't ably speak for all women. White feminists in the US, the most vocal subgroup among feminists, submerge or sell out the concerns of women of color. Much the same is true with upper-caste feminists, who are unable or unwilling to represent the concerns of marginalized Dalit women.

It is one thing to criticize various leftist organizations for their blind spots and failures. Leftist critics however allege that rather than building a better Left or forging alliances, middle-class identitarians are unable or unwilling to see the baby in the leftist bathwater; in effect, their politics is frequently anti-Left and pro-neoliberal.[24] They prefer politicians and intellectuals of their own identity groups who push for socioeconomic justice through affirmative action, mainly in public-sector jobs and college admissions, which disproportionately benefit their own class. In India, for instance, middle-class identitarians are most concerned with caste-based reservations in jobs that currently reach less than 1 percent of Indians when nearly 70 percent are theoretically eligible,[25] and in college admissions that currently reach less than 4 of this 70 percent.[26] Even counting second-order beneficiaries

---

24 For more on this line of argument, see Nancy Fraser. 2017. 'The End of Progressive Neoliberalism', *Dissent*, January 2.

25 Only about 4% of jobs in India are in the public sector, with 1-2% being entry level jobs where reservations apply (promotions are not based on quotas). Of these jobs, about half are for various reserved categories.

26 According to the 'All India Survey on Higher Education (2011-12)', Ministry of Human Resource Development, 58% of colleges—serving about half of all students in India—were private, with no aid from the government, and so not obligated to provide reservations. Given the Gross Enrollment Ratio of 20% in the 18-23 age group in 2012, about 10% were in colleges where reservations applied. So at most 5% of the enrollment was from reserved categories, though it's quite rare for colleges to fulfill its quota requirements and even 4% seems too high.

(e.g., their families), the percentage benefited is small—and it is not the worst-off segment. The oppressive social order, in effect, perpetuates itself by throwing sops to a small but vocal middle-class among the marginalized. One could call this a trickle-down model of social justice. Chibber has argued that 'the Dalit movement, like identity movements across the world, has really narrowed its focus to forms of oppressions that are very real, but which still constitute only a small subset of the oppressions that the Dalits face.'[27]

Critics also lament identitarian solidarity based solely on group membership, especially when solidarity trumps even evidence of public corruption, incompetence or ethical and legal wrongdoing by that group's privileged members.[28] Take the case of Devyani Khobragade, a Dalit and Deputy Consul General of India in the New York consulate.[29] Her arrest and strip-search for visa fraud and violation of labor laws in Manhattan in early 2014 caused a major diplomatic row. Curiously, identitarians of both caste and nation rallied behind her in India—and not behind the Indian maid she had allegedly abused.

Meanwhile the same caste identitarians often inflate the 'sins' of even sympathetic allies in the rival group. Many jumped on an ill-worded, out-of-context remark by Ashis Nandy at the Jaipur Literature Festival 2013, which I attended.[30] It was a provocative remark but one that I thought was closer to intellectually 'provocative speech that forces you to think' rather than 'provocative speech that is intended to

---

27 Vivek Chibber. 2016. 'Dalit movement has to see itself as part of a class-wide movement', *The Hindu*, March 3.
28 For an example, see Feminista Jones. 2015. 'Why Black Women Are Jumping to Bill Cosby's Defense–and Why They Should Stop', *Time Magazine*, January 9.
29 Aakar Patel. 2013. 'India's disproportionate Devyani Khobragade tantrum', *Firstpost*, December 23.
30 'What Ashis Nandy Actually Said At JLF', *Outlook Magazine*, January 30, 2013.

hurt, denigrate' or incite violence.[31] But it did offend some people, who, in a lapse of judiciousness, demanded Nandy's arrest under the Prevention of Atrocities Act, never pausing to think that such objectionable speech is best tackled by more speech, not a ban or jail by the State.[32] The right to free expression, including the right to offend, is not just good for the elites. It's at the heart of what makes a liberal democratic order. This right, with as few exceptions as possible (for speech that incites direct violence, for instance), needs defending even by identitarians, for it's also a precondition for their own social justice activism.[33] P. Sivakami, Dalit author and activist, made precisely this point in defending free speech at the Jaipur Literature Festival 2016.

Then there is what Tim Lott recently called 'assumption creep', wherein identitarians assume 'that if you believe one thing you probably believe another thing, which you are hiding.'[34] So an upper-caste man who praises yoga or Advaita may be seen as endorsing all of Hinduism, including caste. Ethical objections to the non-essential raising of animals for meat may be seen as a covert defense of Brahminism. Finding anything admirable in Gandhi is to make suspect one's commitment to social justice for Dalits. To say that caste and race prejudices have declined in recent decades (which also acknowledges the hard work of many before us) may be understood to mean that all is well now and no more work is needed. To praise any aspect of Narendra Modi's regime may be seen as being soft on Hindutva. To wonder aloud if biology (the capacity and experience of childbirth, for instance)

---

31 Shvetal Vyas. 2013. 'The corruption of a republic', *MnM Commentary 26.*

32 Ashis Nandy booked for 'casteist' comment, BSP demands arrest', Zee News, January 26, 2013.

33 This point was argued well by Ronald Dworkin. 2006. 'The Right to Ridicule', *New York Review of Books*, March 23.

34 Tim Lott. 2015. 'If leftwingers like me are condemned as rightwing, then what's left?' *The Guardian*, March 11.

makes men and women somewhat different might signal to some that one also discounts the flexibility of gender roles.

Additionally, many identitarians are seen as extrapolating an objectionable part to the whole: the fact of caste damns all of Hinduism, including the entire diversity of beliefs and practices that people and historians associate with that label; Nandy's clumsy remark in Jaipur means a rejection of his entire scholarship by people who haven't read him; all of Heidegger is *verboten* due to his early intellectual flirtation with the Nazis. This is akin to certain Leftists who see corporations and globalization as almost entirely evil. Then there's the matter of erasing distinctions between lesser and greater evils, of ignoring nuance when convenient. Take an example. It's a truism that unearned (or inherited) privileges increase one's blindness towards (a) the systemic obstacles others face in life and (b) the social institutions that perpetuate those privileges. But identitarians often collapse the distinction between prejudices born of such unthinking complacency and the more deliberate forms of racism, casteism, or sexism (conflating, say, those who swear by the ideal of being caste-blind in a caste-ridden society with those who plainly see members of their caste as superior to others by birth). Of course, to some extent such extrapolating and conflating tendencies exist in all of us, but the above are all examples of how they can cause identity politics to go haywire, or to at least lose some of its moral allure.

Critics also allege that many identitarians deploy strong labels too readily. Their knee-jerk reaction to a disagreeable article or book is to declare it racist, sexist, casteist, fascist, or imperialist—often without reading it and while discarding the entire progressive record of its author or publisher. This may produce smug satisfaction but it soon gets tiresome and loses its rhetorical power. Indeed, many identitarians pursue the least charitable reading of their rivals and their condemnation is often permanent and collective (made easier by social media). Sanctimony rules as they habitually indulge in online tirades, argumentative jousting, and competitive displays of armchair radicalism. Much of it is performative, where individuals primly signal their own 'pure' politics. They implicitly assume that their rivals are incapable of a deeply felt and introspective yearning for social justice. Hyperbole multiplies; words like 'violence', 'brutality', and 'atrocity' are used to describe an ever-widening range of narratives and verbal slights. Facile accusations of 'cultural appropriation' proliferate on college campuses and online forums, in an age so defined by hyper-globalization and intense cultural promiscuity.[35]

In time, the lofty goal of hating bad ideas, not their espousers, gets diluted or lost. Outsider opinions and scholarship—unless they bow to in-group codes, symbols, and orthodoxies—are dismissed on identity grounds. The chimerical perfect is made the enemy of the incremental good. Relatively small intellectual differences lead to harsh labels and a severing of ties. Somewhere a critic wonders: Can this be anyone's road to emancipation?

Such closed political orthodoxy breeds anxiety, self-censorship, and unreflective political correctness among their rivals—the kind that also raises the cost of calling a spade a spade—while fostering groupthink, cynicism, and separatism among identitarians. Cross-identity conversations trail off. It gets harder to respectfully agree to disagree, since the interlocuters one disagrees with are not also seen as complex individuals but largely as embodiments of narrow identities of privilege, with black and white moralities. For a critique to be heard by identitarians in this milieu, it often has to be

---

35 For an engaging essay that questions the very idea of cultural appropriation, see Fredrik deBoer. 2016. 'no one has the slightest idea what is and isn't cultural appropriation', fredrikdeboer.com, December 1.

authored by brave insiders—brave because it can cost them the comfort and solidarity of their group. Such insiders often succeed in unsettling dogmas, building alliances across identities, and helping advance social justice more effectively. One critic, Douglas Williams, writes:[36]

> Look, I am Black. Also, sometimes, I can be wrong. Those two things are not mutually exclusive, and yet we have gotten to a point where any critique of tactics used by oppressed communities can result in being deemed 'sexist/racist/insert oppression here-ist' and cast out of the Social Justice Magic Circle. And listen, maybe that is cool with some folks. Maybe the revolution that so many of these types speak about will simply consist of everyone spontaneously coming to consciousness and there will be no need for coalitions, give-and-take, or contact with people who do not know every word or phrase that these groups use as some sort of litmus test for the unwashed.

Critics complain that identitarians' hostile, scorched earth dismissal of their rivals, often laced with rage and sarcasm, creates a hypersensitive public space that inhibits discussion and debate—as well as learning and mutual understanding. Vitriolic responses even to interlocutors who speak more from ignorance than malice, or who make genuine errors in judgement, are sometimes paralleled only by the identitarians' inability to accept even modest criticism of their own gods and heroes, the quickness of their claim to hurt sentiments, and an immoderate fear of appropriation of their movement by dominant elites and academics. All this may be understandable in light of history and human nature, but how laudable or helpful is it in advancing the larger cause of social justice?

---

36 Williams, Douglas. 2015. 'The Dead End of Identity Politics', *The South Lawn*, March 10.

A Rejoinder to the Critics

In response to such criticisms, identitarians might argue that their rivals have long been hostile to them and caused enormous damage already. Why should they play by the oppressors' debating rules and decorum, or stoically educate them to notice the systemic exclusions they face at every step? Protecting the delicate feelings of the privileged can't be more important than asserting equal rights and opportunities for discriminated groups. The time for niceties is past, they might say. Nothing short of hostile sarcasm and loud agitation will expose the blindness and hypocrisy of dominant elites and force open new spaces for marginalized groups.[37]

And if Reed, Chibber, and others on the Left allege that middle-class identitarians focus only on 'a small subset of the oppressions that the Dalits face', is that not evidence that the Left still doesn't get it? First, in complaining that reservations in public-sector jobs benefit too few people, the Indian Left fails to see that the primary goal of such reservations is not mass employment but to ensure that a wider cross-section of people have a say in the governance of their nation. Second, the Indian Left even resents the emerging scholarship and activism from middle-class identitarians that has exposed the long collusion between Brahminical knowledge and power, opening compelling new vistas on India's history and culture. Why doesn't the Indian Left—as might appear to their rivals—recognize that these two developments can make life better for even the least fortunate members of marginalized groups? Finally, caste identitarians might call the allegation by the Left an oversimplification, arguing that they do in fact target a wide range of caste oppressions, that what

---

37 An early example of this approach is Frederick Douglass' speech, 'The Meaning of July Fourth for the Negro' (July 5, 1852). A marvelous reading by James Earl Jones is on YouTube: https://www.youtube.com/watch?v=8tTkHJWxfP0

they'd really like is a caste-sensitive Left, which largely remains an illusion.

As for cross-identity conversations, they won't get any easier until many more members of dominant groups not only recognize the equal humanity of others but also use their inherited privileges to undo the very systems that grant and perpetuate such privileges. That the members of dominant groups—whose dominance was built and is sustained no less through identity politics—see problems with their rivals' tactics is predictably partisan. They feel threatened, so they pick on parts of identity politics and complain as if the whole of it were worse than what it tries to combat. Identitarians no doubt see their own tactics as raising consciousness and courage among their own—a prerequisite for their personal growth and emancipation. As Martin Duberman, historian and gay rights activist, has explained,[38]

> Yet we hold on to a group identity, despite its insufficiencies, because for most non-mainstream people it's the closest we have ever gotten to having a political home—and voice. Yes, identity politics reduces and simplifies. Yes, it is a kind of prison. But it is also, paradoxically, a haven. It is at once confining and empowering. And in the absence of alternative havens, group identity will for many of us continue to be the appropriate site of resistance and the main source of comfort.

As for the sleight of hand that sees identity politics only in the politics of minorities—and puts the burden on them to curtail it in order to reduce the nation's divisiveness and promote 'the common good', as we see in calls arising even from liberals and leftists in the US after Donald Trump's election[39]—Nigerian writer Chimamanda Ngozi Adichi offers this sharp reminder:

---

38 Martin Duberman. 2001. 'In Defense of Identity Politics', *In These Times.com*, July 9.

39 See an example of this from the political scientist Mark Lilla. 2016. 'The End of Identity Liberalism', *The New York Times*, November 18.

Now is the time to recalibrate the default assumptions of American political discourse. Identity politics is not the sole preserve of minority voters. This election is a reminder that identity politics in America is a white invention: it was the basis of segregation. The denial of civil rights to black Americans had at its core the idea that a black American should not be allowed to vote because that black American was not white. The endless questioning, before the election of Obama, about America's 'readiness' for a black President was a reaction to white identity politics. Yet 'identity politics' has come to be associated with minorities, and often with a patronizing undercurrent, as though to refer to nonwhite people motivated by an irrational herd instinct. White Americans have practiced identity politics since the inception of America, but it is now laid bare, impossible to evade.[40]

Navigating Identity Politics

Some of the critiques above of identity politics of marginalized groups are more warranted than others, but no call for its dissolution is warranted. Rather, given the stakes, we should hope that it becomes more effective, that it moves away from its self-indulgent and illiberal manifestations— what we might call 'instances of *imperfect activism*'.[41] After all, some of the best impulses behind identity politics are animated by the quest for equal human dignity, opportunity, and civil rights, which deserves our unwavering support. A key challenge for left-liberal groups in both India and America is how to pursue a progressive politics of common cause while also addressing the genuine disadvantages of particular groups—without the latter, the unity required for the former will remain elusive too.[42]

---

40 Chimamanda Ngozi Adiche. 2016. 'Now is the time to talk about what we are actually talking about', *The New Yorker*, December 2.

41 For an illuminating discussion on 'political correctness' and identity politics, see Julia Serano. 2016. 'Prejudice, "Political Correctness," and the Normalization of Donald Trump', *Medium*, November 23.

42 To understand why identity politics is integral to any meaningful

It's worth noting here that I, too, inhabit a politics of identity that waxes and wanes based on context, such as to whom, about what, and where I'm speaking. Indeed, is it even possible for anyone to not partake in identity politics at all? Those inclined to say 'yes' likely practice the invisibilized or unmarked form of identity politics common among those of privilege and power (for instance, patriarchy may be so normalized that many men are unable to see their own politics of gender identity in their daily lives, and may pretend they are above it all). As American writer Matthew Yglesias has written, 'The idea that gendered or ethnic claims are despoiling a liberalism of pure selves and neutral rationality is little more than an unselfconscious form of identity politics.'[43] It is the identity counterpart of that old Band-Aid commercial that long promoted its soft-pink colored product as 'flesh-colored, almost invisible'.

I also realize that however much I want, I should not expect to be heard solely as a freethinker with an autonomous conscience and mind. Others will impose on me a social identity, whether I embrace it or not, and history will invade our interactions. Until the many past wrongs of groups against groups are redressed or forgotten, I will be seen as a member of a group with a certain history versus other groups—often of mutual suspicion, exploitation, or prejudice. It is part of the filter through which others will see me and try to interpret me. In different local and global contexts—say, between India and the United States—I will be placed on different rungs in the hierarchy of social beings.

Some members of dominant groups tend to quote people from marginalized groups as support for their own arguments. This in itself is not brave or noble, nor does it make

pursuit of liberty, see Jacob T. Levy. 2016. 'The Defense of Liberty Can't Do Without Identity Politics', *Niskanen Center*, December 13.

43 Matthew Yglesias. 2015. 'All politics is identity politics', *Vox*, June 5.

their arguments more solid. That depends on the arguments themselves. The truth is that intellectuals in any group have a wide range of views, some of which we will find more judicious and pragmatic than others. Consider the views of women on women's rights, Muslims on political Islam, Blacks on race in America (contrast WEB Du Bois with Booker T. Washington, MLK Jr. with Malcolm X, Adolph Reed Jr. with Ta-Nehisi Coates), and Dalits on caste (contrast Kanshi Ram with Jagjivan Ram on politics, Anand Teltumbe with Chandra Bhan Prasad on economics, Urmila Pawar with Ajay Navaria on the prudence of mass conversion to Buddhism,[44] DR Nagaraj with many Ambedkarites on MK Gandhi and Indian modernity, and so on). Our lives are constrained by imperfect knowledge and subjective experience; no two humans are identically sensitized towards the many vectors of injustice in social life. Within every identitarian group too, individuals will differ on who, and to what degree, they see as the 'enemy' and what strategies and alliances make sense.

How then to navigate the turbulent waters of identity politics? The first step is to work on recognizing both its value and its excesses. This is best done by trying to see the world from the vantage point of others and listening carefully and humbly. But empathy is not enough; what is also needed is a critical sensibility informed by historical and statistical literacy—to help keep things in context, and to more judiciously assess the many injustices of the world and ways of addressing them. To see the lives of others more clearly, including of those more privileged than us, especially re-

---

44 See Urmila Pawar's introduction to her 2002 autobiography, *Aaydan*, translated by Maya Pandit and published as *The Weave of My Life*, Stree, 2008. While Pawar doesn't directly argue for mass conversion to Buddhism, she fondly remembers her own and describes its value in giving her and her besieged community 'a [new] way of life, with tremendous social strength.' An actively vocal advocate of conversion to Buddhism is the scholar Kancha Ilaiah.

quires us to work on our blind spots, irrational fears, and prejudices, many of which are byproducts of group privileges, normative identities, and mental colonization. Prejudices are not just the overt kind that we—well-meaning progressive liberal folk—believe we no longer possess. They also lurk beneath our everyday awareness. It is in the nature of human socialization to imbue us with unconscious biases that hurt others and require conscious effort to undo. We may never be able to transcend all systemic biases within our social institutions—as new ones, so often, replace the old—but it is a mark of our humanity to not abandon this effort.

Alongside, it is also important to reflect on our own tendency to self-censor, to avoid challenging 'our own side'. Poseurs and self-promoters surround us in every camp, each moved by his/her inner demons and drives. Who among any group, marginalized or not, deserves to speak for the whole is always an open question, to be best settled by each of us, not automatically by claims of identity. Social truths are subjective and contingent. As the Buddha advised, there is no better guide to making sense of our world than our own reason and compassion. We would also do well to realize that dismissing identity politics wholesale is part of the problem, not the solution.

No Saints or Miracles
Revisiting the Idea of India[1]

'Nations without a past are contradictions in terms,' wrote Marxist historian Eric Hobsbawm. Precursors to every modern nation are stories about its past and the present—stories full of invention, exclusion, and exaggeration—which help forge a 'national consciousness'. Historians, wrote Hobsbawm, have 'always been mixed up in politics' and are 'an essential component of nationalism'. They participate in shaping a nation's mythos and self-perception. In his vivid analogy, 'Historians are to nationalism what poppy-growers in Pakistan are to heroin addicts: we supply the essential raw material for the market.' The more nationalist a historian, he held, the weaker his bid to be taken seriously as a historian.

But not all historians are equally complicit. Some are deeply skeptical of the dominant national histories and claims of nationhood. 'Getting its history wrong is part of being a nation,' wrote the scholar Ernst Renan. The skeptical historian may even see positive value in certain aspects

---

1 An earlier version of this review appeared in the *Himal Southasian* print quarterly 'Are we sure about India?' (January 2013), and the common text is reproduced with permission.

of nationalism—its potential to bind diverse groups and inspire collective action, for instance—but she always sees a pressing need to inspect and critique its claims, assumptions, omissions, myths, and heroes. Scrutiny may reveal that a 'cherished tradition' is neither cherished, nor a tradition; likewise, for supposedly 'ancient' origins and customs, traits and virtues, arts and culture, and other qualities of life and mind said to define the essence of a nation and its people. This approach is especially common among Marxist historians (their analytical orientation defines the genre, not their views on communism). The best of them know that there is no ultimately objective history, but who yet seek to write history from below and attempt to expose the actual conditions of social life, including the divisions, conflicts and oppressions that plague any nation. [2]

This, then, is the vantage point of Marxist historian Perry Anderson's magnificent and lucid new work, *The Indian Ideology*. What does the title refer to? In his own words, it 'is another way of describing what is more popularly known as 'The Idea of India', which celebrates the democratic stability, multi-cultural unity, and impartial secularity of the Indian state as a national miracle.' Anderson offers a critique of this idea.

Nationalism in India arose in the 19th century. A native elite, responding to British colonialism, began articulating a consciousness based on a new idea of India. Until then, despite civilizational continuities, the Subcontinent had no sense of itself as 'India', no national feeling based on political unity or a shared identity. Rival political units and ethnic

---

2 But as Benedict Anderson rightly reminds us, it's not true that 'Marxists as such are not nationalists' (*Imagined Communities: Reflections on the Origin and Spread of Nationalism*. Verso, 2006, pp. 165-166.). Twentieth century Marxist regimes have frequently resorted to nationalism and its symbols to bolster their power and prestige.

groups abounded, divided by language, faith, caste, geography, history, and more. There was no historical awareness of the ancient empires of Mauryas or Guptas, or that the Buddha was Indian. This and much more of the Indian past would emerge via European scholarship, profoundly shaping 'Hinduism' and Hindu self-knowledge. Anderson surveys the rise of Indian nationalism and offers sharp vignettes of the minds and matters that drove Gandhi, Jinnah, Nehru, Bose, Ambedkar, Mountbatten and others. His analysis of the forces that led to Partition is astute and provocative. He assesses the performance of the independent nation-state and subjects Indian intellectuals to a withering critique for what he diagnoses as their comfort with 'the Indian ideology'. Though not without shortcomings, Anderson has given us a masterwork of critical synthesis—trenchant, original, and bold—that should fuel discussion and debate for years ahead.

Gandhi the Hindu Revivalist

A major site of early Indian nationalism was the Indian National Congress, a political party that began with a group of secular-minded professionals—mostly children of Macaulay's English education system—hoping only for more representative colonial rule. Despite some success, it wasn't until after Gandhi's arrival from South Africa that Congress became a popular political force. What distinguished Gandhi from most leaders of nationalist movements, writes Anderson, were three political skills:

> He was a first-class organiser and fundraiser ... who rebuilt Congress from top to bottom ... [Secondly,] though temperamentally in many ways an autocrat, politically he did not care about power in itself, and was an excellent mediator between different figures and groups both within Congress and among its variegated social supports. Finally, though no great orator, he was an exceptionally quick and fluent com-

municator ... To these political gifts were added personal qualities of a ready warmth, impish wit and iron will. It is no surprise that so magnetic a force would attract such passionate admiration, at the time and since.[3]

Gandhi's success however came at a huge cost, writes Anderson, mostly due to his religiosity. To him 'religion mattered more than politics', more so even than to Ayatollah Khomeini. Anderson presents a fresh portrait of Gandhi, including the peculiar grab-bag of Hindu beliefs, inflected with Christian ones, that he embraced. These would also inspire his odd ideas about sexuality and abstinence that have caused much head-scratching ever since. Would it were that his faith had played out only in the bedroom. Instead, it was part of a worldview that despised the social changes wrought by modernity—machines, railways, hospitals, and modern education—and defended all manner of atavisms. To 'real intellectual exchange he was a stranger' and 'rarely disavowed directly anything significant he had once said or written'. Gandhi, Anderson continues, had 'limited knowledge of, or interest in, the outside world', as evident in his extreme misreading of Hitler. Floods and earthquakes were punishments for human failings. Allergic to socialism, his political ideal was a nebulous *Ram Rajya*.

While Gandhi despised untouchability and even campaigned against it, he naively held that 'the caste system is not based on inequality', that its discrimination and hierarchy was an aberration that ought to be fixed by transforming minds while preserving castes. 'I do not believe in caste in the modern sense', he wrote in 1933. 'It is an excrescence and a handicap on progress.' But the 'spirit behind caste is not one of arrogant superiority' and it is really 'the best possible adjustment of social stability and progress' since the 'beauty of the caste system is that it does not base itself upon dis-

3 Perry Anderson. 2012. *The Indian Ideology*. Three Essays Collective, p. 17.

tinctions of wealth possessions', as class-based systems in the West did. He held that the 'hereditary principle [of caste] is an eternal principle. To change it is to create disorder'. Gandhi even believed that Hinduism had a built-in mechanism for social justice since misbehaving Brahmins would be demoted in the next life. Over time, faced by Ambedkar's attacks, he would tone down his views. Anderson observes that Gandhi knew little about Islam and warned his son to never marry a Muslim for it was against dharma. He claimed to revere the cow, reflexively imagined India as a Hindu nation, and was really a 'Hindu revivalist'.

The basic facts here are not new; what is striking is Anderson's choice of material and the narrative he weaves out of it. One tragic impact of Gandhi's takeover of Congress, writes Anderson, was that he 'injected a massive dose of religion—mythology, symbology, theology—into the national movement'. Despite his sincere belief in the parity of all religions, Gandhi's was inevitably a Hindu imaginarium. This increased the popular appeal of Congress to Hindus but also sowed the seeds of Muslim alienation in Congress, culminating eventually in Partition. Behind the rhetoric, only 3 percent of Congress members were Muslims in the 1930s, when a quarter of the population was Muslim. Gandhi's beliefs inspired his 'thoroughly regressive' Khilafat campaign, opposed by secular-minded Muslims like Jinnah.

Gandhi's Hindu sensibility also led him to sabotage the British agreement to a separate electorate for the 'Untouchables', championed by Ambedkar. This leader of the 'Untouchables', Anderson writes, was 'intellectually head and shoulders above most of the Congress leaders' and held that 'No matter what the Hindus say, Hinduism is a menace to liberty, equality and fraternity'. Gandhi saw things differently. For him, tackling untouchability did not merit a fast unto death, but blocking political approaches to empowering the 'Untouchables' did. After all, Anderson observes,

> If Untouchables were to be treated as external to the Hindu community, it would be confirmation that caste was indeed, as its critics had always maintained, a vile system of discrimination ... and since Hinduism was founded on caste, it would stand condemned with caste. To reclaim the Untouchables for Hinduism was an ideological imperative for the reputation of the religion itself. But it was also politically vital, since if they were subtracted from the Hindu bloc in India, its predominance over the Muslim community would be weakened. There were 'mathematical' considerations to bear in mind, as Gandhi's secretary delicately reported his leader's thinking on the matter. Most menacing of all, Gandhi confided to a colleague, might not Untouchables, accorded separate identity, then gang up with 'Muslim hooligans and kill caste Hindus'?[4]

More contentiously, Anderson argues that 'contrary to legend, [Gandhi's] attitude to violence had always been—and would remain—contingent and ambivalent.' Nor did he have much success with Satyagraha, or non-violent resistance, for 'each time Gandhi had tried it, the British had seen it off.' Anderson claims that success in the nationalist struggle came not from the mass mobilization of Satyagraha, but from Gandhi's rebuilding of Congress, its rise as a popular political force, and the steady expansion of the electoral machinery after 1909.

But even if Anderson is right, surely Gandhi's Satyagraha amplified the success of the struggle by raising mass consciousness. Moreover, was non-violence still not preferable to violent resistance? Anderson seems unconvinced. He admires the secular-leftist leader Bose, his 'fearless militancy and commanding intellectual gifts', his commitment to intercommunal alliances, and criticizes Gandhi's undemocratic eviction of him from the Congress. In Anderson's view, the

---

4   Anderson. *The Indian Ideology*, p. 40.

violence that Satyagraha 'spared the British was decanted among compatriots', only to show itself later in communalism and Partition. This argument might be more persuasive if it weren't truly an imponderable. Anderson claims that Gandhi's infusion of Congress with Hindu religiosity—of which Satyagraha was a part—'was the origin of the political process that would eventually lead to partition.' But did Gandhi's compatriots see Satyagraha as a part of Hindu religiosity? We know that it was adopted and practiced to good effect by oppressed populations of many non-Hindu nations, and even by the Pashtun Muslim leader Khan Abdul Ghaffar Khan, aka the 'Frontier Gandhi'. Martin Luther King, Jr. was influenced by it, noting that 'The ultimate weakness of violence is that it is a descending spiral, begetting the very thing it seeks to destroy. Instead of diminishing evil, it multiplies it.' It is plausible, however, that in much of India and especially in Congress, Satyagraha, simply by its association with Gandhi, was seen as part of the Hindu political matrix that was alienating and sometimes even threatening to non-Hindus. But what if Gandhi had not transformed Congress in such a way? Anderson writes,

> ... the question remains whether even without him, the logic of mass organisation in populations as steeped in the supernatural as those of South Asia would not have transformed Congress into the Hindu party it became. For everywhere in the region, political awakening was intertwined with religious revival.

What is lacking in Anderson's portrait of Gandhi? Sharp as it is, it leaves out many non-religious dimensions of his appeal. For instance, the cultural critic Vinay Lal has pointed out Gandhi's 'extraordinary ability to nurse the wounded, minister to the sick, nurture the young, and bring into the orbit of everyday life those, such as victims of leprosy [including 'untouchables'], who had been shunned by society.'[5]

---

5   Vinay Lal. 2008. 'The Gandhi Everyone Loves to Hate', *EPW*, Octo-

Gandhi also led by example, as when he cleaned a public latrine to assert the dignity of labor. A rare and courageous
honesty pervades his autobiography. Marxist historian Irfan
Habib sees Gandhi as a social reformer and has argued that
his worldview was less a defense of tradition than an 'assertion of modem values in traditional garb'. He accorded
greater parity to men and women in many walks of life, as in
his attempts to include more women in the freedom struggle. His was an ahistorical and creative re-reading of Indian
culture, evident in his original take on the *Bhagavad Gita*.
Gandhi was a deeply religious man yet he wrote that 'Every
true scripture only gains by criticism. After all we have no
other guide but our reason to tell us what may be regarded as
revealed and what may not be.' According to Lal, he seldom
visited temples and though he was a devout, if unorthodox,
Hindu and devotee of Ram, he 'unequivocally rejected pas-
sages in [the Ramacaritamanas of] Tulsidas that he found
offensive or degrading to women and the lower castes.' His
'message of tolerance and inclusiveness between Hindus and
Muslims', writes Arundhati Roy, 'continues to be Gandhi's
real, lasting and most important contribution to the idea of
India.'[6]

Some defenders of Gandhi have argued that his views
on caste too evolved late in his life. By the 1940s, they claim,
Gandhi not only saw inter-religious marriage as 'a welcome
event', he also advocated, in historian Mark Lindley's words,
'intermarriage between Brahmins and Untouchables in order to dismantle the caste system 'root and branch."[7] 'When
all become casteless', Gandhi wrote, 'monopoly of occupations would go.' The earlier Gandhi did not say such things

---

ber 4.

6   Arundhati Roy. 2014. 'The Doctor and the Saint', an introduction to
    BR Ambedkar's *Annihilation of Caste*, Navayana, p. 82.

7   Mark Lindley. 'Changes in Mahatma Gandhi's Views on Caste and
    Intermarriage', *Academia.edu*.

but instances of such views are few in number and it is hard to assess to what extent they reveal a genuinely progressive turn in his vision.

Gandhi is therefore rightly criticized for his long-held views on caste, because even if he had begun to think differently late in his life, it seems too little, too late. By then his approach to caste had caused enough damage already, not the least by thwarting Ambedkar. His writings defending the varna order are too numerous to whitewash. In 1922, Gandhi wrote, 'The caste system is a natural order of society.'[8] In 1933, at age 64, he wrote that 'the caste system has a scientific basis. Reason does not revolt against it ... Caste creates a social and moral restraint—I can find no reason for its abolition. To abolish caste is to demolish Hinduism.'[9] The law of varna, he wrote in 1934, 'has universal application. The world may ignore it today but it will have to accept it in the time to come.'[10] The scholar Braj Ranjan Mani has argued that anti-caste radicals like 'Ambedkar and Periyar saw Gandhi as an orthodox moralist whose pacifism actually enhanced his authoritarianism, and whose renunciations rid none of his desire to control and coerce the traditionally subjugated. Gandhi's defense of caste and Brahmanism under the cover of spiritual-cultural nationalism was the secret of his popularity among the elite intelligentsia.'[11]

Gandhi's voluminous writings, and the open book that his life was, continue to both provoke and resist a definitive assessment. Nonetheless, Anderson's bracing analysis

8   Quoted in BR Ambedkar. 1945. *What Congress and Gandhi Have Done to the Untouchables*. Gautam Book Center, p. 265.
9   Published in 1933 in *Harijan*, an English language journal published by Gandhi from 1933-48. Archived at https://www.gandhi-heritageportal.org/journals-by-gandhiji/harijan
10   MK Gandhi. 1962. *Varnashramadharma*. Navjivan Publishing House, Chapter 8.
11   Braj Ranjan Mani. 2015. *Debrahmanizing History: Dominance and Resistance in Indian Society*. Manohar, pp. 47-48.

of Gandhi's impact on the nationalist struggle is a singular achievement. It strikes hard at hagiographies of the Father of the Nation and raises unsettling questions about the nation he helped shape, which in turn shaped him and continues to define his legacy today.

Cry, the beloved nation

Perhaps no single event has had a greater impact on the politics of modern South Asia than Partition, which created the nation-states of India and Pakistan, and later Bangladesh. The genocide it triggered forced the migration of 12-18 million people, the largest in world history, a million deaths, and a poisoned well of politics in the region. What were its causes? Which key players deserve more blame than others? Could it have been averted? Not only do perceptions differ sharply but most Partition narratives are steeped in nationalist posturing, demonization, and layers of taboo.

In 2011, for instance, Jaswant Singh, a leader of the Indian right-wing party BJP and former Defense and Foreign Minister of India, caused a storm with his biography of Jinnah. In it Singh assigned greater blame for Partition to Nehru and even praised Jinnah for his sundry qualities. No BJP official attended the book launch, after which Singh was summarily expelled from the BJP and his book banned in Gujarat. So while emotions still run high on the topic, it's also true that at least among scholars today, such as Pakistani historian Ayesha Jalal and Indian Jurist HM Seervai, Singh's interpretation has gained ground. Yet few historians have offered a sharper account of it than Perry Anderson, who humanizes many icons of Indian nationalism, restoring to them their rightful share of human follies.

One such icon is Nehru, a disciple of Gandhi with a crippling 'psychological dependence' on him, but whose 'intellectual development [was] not arrested by intense religious belief'. Nehru, a Brahmin, was born into a higher social class than Gandhi, a Bania. Anderson notes that Nehru was not religious, had extramarital affairs, and 'had acquired notions of independence and socialism Gandhi did not share'. That said, Nehru's 'advantages yielded less than might be thought' and he 'seems to have learned very little at Cambridge', becoming 'a competent orator' but never acquiring 'a modicum of literary taste'. To Anderson, *The Discovery of India*, 'a steam bath of *Schwärmerei*' with a 'Barbara Cartland streak', reveals 'not just Nehru's lack of formal scholarship and addiction to romantic myth, but something deeper ... a capacity for self-deception with far-reaching political consequences.' He combined qualities like 'hard work, ambition, charm, some ruthlessness' with 'others that were developmentally ambiguous: petulance, violent outbursts of temper, vanity.'

Unwilling to challenge Gandhi's ideas or his tactics in Congress, even Nehru reflexively associated Hinduism with the nation. Anderson cites historian Judith Brown's view of him as 'an 'utterly reliable' prop of the old guard within the party'. Many a times, writes Anderson, Nehru presented the caste system in 'a roseate light': a division of labor with advantages, not a division of laborers in a discriminatory hierarchy. 'Untouchability, as Ambedkar would note bitterly, Nehru never so much as mentioned.' Not only did he stay mum when Gandhi blackmailed Ambedkar on the issue of separate electorates, he would later, with a coldness unbecoming a *chacha*, also oppose reservations on the grounds that they would '[lead] to inefficiency and second-rate standards'. A poor judge of character, writes Anderson, Nehru surrounded himself as Prime Minister with 'a court of sycophants', and launched the dynasty with the elevation of his daughter—devoid of any obvious qualifications for the role—to Congress presidency. He was nevertheless a liberal democrat by conviction, writes Anderson,

> As prime minister, he took his duties in the Lok Sabha with
> a conscientious punctilio that put many Western rulers to
> shame, regularly speaking and debating in the chamber, and
> never resorted to rigging national elections or suppressing
> a wide range of opinion. So much is incontestable. But lib-
> eralism is a metal that rarely comes unalloyed. Nehru was
> first and foremost an Indian nationalist, and where the pop-
> ular will failed to coincide with the nation as he imagined
> it, he suppressed it without remorse. There, the instruments
> of government were not ballots but, as he himself blurted,
> bayonets.[12]

Anderson's portrait of Nehru has omissions, but backed
by telling examples from Nehru's writings, speeches, and actions, it provides a much-needed counterpoint to the par-
oxysms of adoration more common among liberal Indian
historians.

* * *

What key events led to Partition, and what was Nehru's role
in them? In 1909, the Minto-Morley Reforms introduced
limited self-rule in British India based on a franchise of
two percent of the population (comprising 'aristocratic ele-
ments in society and the moderate men', stated the legislation). Those reforms also introduced separate electorates for
Hindus and Muslims. This, on one hand, was a progressive
safeguard to a minority community in a first-past-the-post
voting system. On the other hand, it enthroned religion as
the defining element of political identity, which would later
take on a life of its own.

Anderson recounts how the secular-minded Jinnah, 'a
member of Congress long before Gandhi' as well as a member of the Muslim League—and hailed by Gokhale as an am-
bassador of Hindu-Muslim unity—left the Congress in 1920
in 'dismay at the radicalisation of its tactics and disgust at the
sacralisation of its appeals, once Gandhi took over.' In 1927,

---

12 Anderson. *The Indian Ideology*, pp. 132-133.

Jinnah even 'proposed a pact that would reserve Muslims one-third of the seats in a central legislature in exchange for a single rather than separate electorates.' Nehru dithered, tried to negotiate down, until Congress scuttled the proposal. 'A penultimate chance of unity between the two communities was cast to the winds,' writes Anderson.

One might argue that from here on, the exigencies of competitive electoral politics would inevitably have led to Partition, but many more real opportunities to avert it arose and were lost—a story Anderson tells very well. The Muslim League, despite being a national party, had its primary base in the United Provinces. For decades, it competed unfavorably with other Muslim parties in Punjab and Bengal, which made it easier for Congress to regard the Muslim League with hubris. Meanwhile, Anderson writes, Congress was 'monolithically Hindu' in the 1930s, 'commanded the loyalty of an overwhelming majority of the Hindu electorate, but had minimal Muslim support'. Given the demographics, free elections would grant it absolute control of any future central legislature. Drunk on its position of strength, Congress blew every chance to make concessions 'to ensure that the quarter of the population that was Muslim would not feel itself a permanently impotent—and potentially vulnerable—minority.'

By the late 1930s, the League had increased its following among Muslims and the England-educated Jinnah had become the sole spokesperson of Muslim parties at round table conferences. Even then he 'probably aimed at a confederation rather than complete separation'. In 1940, he did voice the two-nation theory in Lahore, demanding 'autonomy and sovereignty' to Muslim majority areas but he spoke even then 'of constituent 'states' in the plural and did not mention the word 'Pakistan'—which Jinnah subsequently complained was being pinned on him by Congress.' As late as 1943, Anderson holds, Jinnah was opposed to the creation of Pakistan. Down to the end, writes Anderson,

> [Jinnah] seems to have calculated that the British, confronted with the incompatibility of the aims of League and Congress, would ... impose a confederation ... on the two parties, in which the Muslim-majority zones of the subcontinent would be self-governing, with a central authority weak enough not to impinge on them, but strong enough to protect Muslim minorities in self-governing Hindu-majority zones. In the event, the cabinet mission produced a plan close enough to this vision. But for Nehru, such a scheme was worse than partition, since it would deprive his party of the powerful centralised state to which it had always aspired, and he believed essential to preserve Indian unity. Congress had insisted on its monopoly of national legitimacy from the start. That claim could no longer be sustained. But if the worst came to the worst, it was better to enjoy an unimpeded monopoly of power in the larger part of India than to be shackled by having to share it in an undivided one. So while the League talked of partition, Jinnah contemplated confederation; and while Congress spoke of union, Nehru prepared for scission. The cabinet mission plan was duly scuppered.[13]

Similar accounts have been offered by scholars Ayesha Jalal, HM Seervai, and AG Noorani. Jinnah was apparently nothing like the glowering scoundrel that bore his name in Richard Attenborough's biopic *Gandhi*.

If Nehru comes off smelly in Anderson's account, so does Louis Mountbatten. 'British imperialism did not favour partition' in South Asia, writes Anderson; Mountbatten, that 'mendacious, intellectually limited hustler', gave in when no deal could be reached. For partition to have a chance of being fair and peaceful, 'at least a year—the year London had originally set as the term of the Raj—of orderly administration and preparation was needed. Its conveyance within six weeks was a sentence of death and devastation to millions.' Mountbatten, having lit the fuse, 'handed over the buildings

---

13 Anderson. *The Indian Ideology*, p. 67.

to their new owners hours before they blew up, in what has
a good claim to be the most contemptible single act in the
annals of the empire.' When the smoke cleared, a genocide
had taken place, a 'moth-eaten' Pakistan had come into being
on little more than a religious identity, and the major goal of
building political safeguards for Muslims in Hindu-majority
regions—Jinnah's core constituency—had not been realized.

If Congress leaders were largely responsible for Partition,
is Anderson too soft on British imperialism? He posits that
during the initial phase of imperial rule, the British applied
divide-and-rule to 'more favourably fragmented political,
ethnic and linguistic units' than religion. Only when modern
nationalism made Hinduism a source of political identity,
'the British accommodated the initial Muslim reaction to it
with alacrity, granting separate electorates. But after that, no
viceroy stoked religious tensions deliberately.' Is this true? It
could be; after all, no viceroy wanted a law-and-order problem on his hands. However, was it not in the British interest
to at least keep the two communities divided and competing
with each other for the master's attention? Was there no element of imperial venality in the decision to create separate
electorates—which arguably sowed the seeds for Partition
before Gandhi even joined Congress? Indeed, wasn't this
outcome made likelier by the imperial state's mission to socially categorize its subjects, a process initiated by the census of 1871-72 that made religion a primary site of political
conflict and rivalry? Nor does Anderson go back far enough
to consider the role the British and their idea of religion unwittingly played in shaping the emergent Hindu identity and
nationalism, especially the muscular Hinduism imagined on
monotheistic lines (see the essay, 'The Moral Universe of the
Bhagavad Gita': Part 1). These should be included, if our goal
is to catalogue all factors that contributed to the gathering
of the communal impulse in the Subcontinent. Anderson
however proposes a far more provocative factor: that even

without the 'soft Hindutva' of Congress, political awakening may have, sooner or later, made bloody conflict between the two religious communities inevitable. He adds,

> Such a conclusion, however, is not more palatable to polite opinion in India than the alternative. Confronted with the outcome of the struggle for independence, Indian intellectuals find themselves in an impasse. If partition could have been avoided, the party that led the national movement to such a disastrous upshot stands condemned. If partition was inevitable, the culture whose dynamics made confessional conflict politically insuperable becomes a *damnosa hereditas*, occasion for collective shame. The party still rules, and the state continues to call itself secular. It is no surprise the question it poses should be so widely repressed in India.[14]

Investigating the 'miracles'

Why did democracy survive in India? India famously had none of the conditions thought to be necessary for the flourishing of democracy, such as an egalitarian social order and an ethos of individualism. Elite Indian men of Congress followed the White men, inheriting the colonial 'machinery of administration and coercion'. They made little 'effort to meet even quite modest requirements of social equality or justice.' Instead, writes Anderson,

> Nehru's regime, whose priorities were industrial development and military spending, was barren of any such impulse. No land reform worthy of mention was attempted ... Primary education was grossly neglected.[15]

The masses voted but didn't organize for collective action due to the deep social stratification of caste, along which lines they would later be mobilized in politics. The caste system, concludes Anderson, combined with a polity that preferred otherworldly explanations for their earthly misery 'is

---

14 Anderson. *The Indian Ideology*, p. 100.
15 Anderson. *The Indian Ideology*, p. 110.

what preserved Hindu democracy from disintegration'. There is truth in this observation, if also a serving of reductionism and cultural determinism. Did no other contingent factors play a role, such as the taste for representative self-rule that an elite class of Indians had acquired in the closing decades of the Raj? Is it not possible that India's massive ethnic diversity made democracy particularly suitable as a means of resolving conflict among communities with competing claims and ways of life?

Anderson examines in some detail the Indian idea of secularism in which the state is not presumed separate but is an impartial patron to all religions, at least in theory. In reality, the fortunes of Muslims, which he quantifies, have worsened sharply, even in state institutions. Even the 'Indian armed forces are a Hindu preserve, garnished with Sikhs'—only one percent of them are Muslim, practically none in the secret services. Despite official secularism, the state rests, 'sociologically speaking, on Hindu caste society', writes Anderson. 'The continued dominance of upper castes in public institutions—administration, police, courts, universities, media—belongs to the same matrix'. He contextualizes the rise of BJP and sees it more as an inflamed tumescence on a body of Hinduized secularism, which, he correctly notes, exists 'by default, not prescription'. In other words, the gap between the ideal and the reality of secularism is large.[16] Many even hold that 'India is secular because it is Hindu'. Pride in such feeble secularism, Anderson quotes an Indian critic, is self-congratulation that 'overlooks or rationalises the sectarian religious outlook pervading large areas of contemporary social and political practice'.[17]

---

16 Andre Beteille. 2001. 'Secularism re-examined', *The Hindu*, September 3.
17 Anderson. *The Indian Ideology*, p. 151.

Anderson points out that India's preservation of its territorial unity, often spoken of as a miraculous feat, is far from unique; hardly any post-colonial states have broken up. This unity, often held to be a sacred value in India, is also a dubious thing since massive coercive force has gone into preserving it, whose cost the Indian intelligentsia self-censors. Anderson's account of Nehru's wily seizure and mishandling of Kashmir is morally astute; even in Indian academia today, any talk of self-determination is 'garlic to the vampire' and risks repression by the state. The bureaucracy that rules Kashmir 'under military command contains scarcely a Muslim, and jobs in it can be openly advertised for Hindus only.' No less astute is his account of the insurgencies in the Northeast, large parts of which have long been under brutal military repression. He recounts how Nehru's vanity and delusions led to the disastrous war with China. His regime also 'made it a crime to question the territorial integrity of India' and enacted the Armed Forces Special Powers Act (AFSPA)—one of a 'barrage of liberticide laws in India', and a 'licence to murder ... [by which] Indian troops and paramilitaries were guaranteed impunity for atrocities'. Indeed, as Anderson writes, the Indian government has since made ample use of the AFSPA against its own citizens in ways that make the British massacre at Jallianwala Bagh look like a mere trifle.

> For what is perfectly obvious, but never seen or spoken, is that the hand of AFSPA has fallen where the reach of Hinduism stops. The three great insurgencies against the Indian state have come in Kashmir, Nagaland-Mizoram and Punjab—regions respectively Muslim, Christian and Sikh. There it met popular feeling with tank and truncheon, pogrom and death squad. Today, the same configuration threatens to be repeated [with] pre-Aryan tribal populations with their own forest cults ...[18]

---

18 Anderson. *The Indian Ideology*, p. 144.

Anderson also discusses the Indian Constitution, caste politics, public corruption, activism of the Supreme Court, social welfare schemes, and more. Perhaps his most damning critique is of the lack of intellectual dissent as it relates to the dominant idea of India. He approvingly cites from the work of some Indian scholars, but a clear subtext of *The Indian Ideology* is that the leading historians and public intellectuals in India—and also the media—are not critical enough, present too sanguine a view of India, and are unable or unwilling to make obvious sociological connections. In 'patriotic reveries' they 'fall over themselves in tributes to their native land'. He cites telling examples from Ramachandra Guha, Amartya Sen, Sunil Khilnani, Pratap Bhanu Mehta, and others. Driven perhaps by the slights of colonial scholarship, they have created new half-truths, silences, and evasions in accord with the idea of India—'a late mutant of Indian nationalism'—and are failing in their duty to adequately represent the Third Estate.

One might ask if public intellectuals in other nations are more responsible, but can an answer here dent the validity of Anderson's claim about *these* individuals? He acknowledges the work of many dissenting, self-critical Indians, but insisted in a recent interview that 'as an overarching set of tropes about India, the ideology remains in place, and I believe hasn't yet been the object of a systematic critique. The hope of the book would be to set the ball rolling for less general piety about them.'[19]

Such accusations, and the hauteur and irreverence Anderson delivers them with, are bound to cause pain and provoke angry, defensive reactions.[20] Detractors will claim to

19 Praful Bidwai interviews Perry Anderson, 'Respect Gandhi If You Will, Don't Sentimentalise Him', *Outlook India*, November 12, 2012.
20 See Partha Chatterjee, Sudipta Kaviraj, Nivedita Menon. 2015. *The Indian Ideology: Three Responses to Perry Anderson*. Permanent

find in this work the ghosts of the Raj and Orientalism, or the rant of a Hindu-hating Marxist. Others will latch on to a particular argument or fact in the book and erect a straw man in an attempt to demolish the whole. Limiting oneself to such responses would be a grave mistake. The task of the intellectual historian is not to give pleasure or to get every answer right; it is to help clear some cobwebs of the mind, challenge orthodoxies, and stimulate debate.[21] All national histories peddle fictions and lies—some more damaging than others—and so does India's. Trying now to get to a better future behooves us to better understand our past. Anderson's 'dance of destruction' has also opened up new avenues of self-knowledge in the Subcontinent. We would do well to engage with it calmly and honestly.

Black, in association with Ashoka University.
21 For an example, see AG Noorani. 2009. 'Indian historians are absolutely dishonest or simply opportunistic', *TwoCircles.net*, November 17.

About the Author

Namit Arora grew up in the cow-belt city of Gwalior, famous for its fort and the first epigraphic evidence of zero and the decimal system. Following IIT Kharagpur (1989) and a Master's in Computer Engineering from Louisiana State University, USA (1991), he played a cog in the wheel of Internet technology in Silicon Valley for nearly two decades. This didn't make him wise but it enabled him to attend lectures of dubious practical value at Stanford University and to live, work, or travel in scores of countries, including yearlong stints in London and Amsterdam, as well as extended stays in India. In 2013, he quit his high-tech profession and moved back to India. In 2015, he began volunteering for the Dialogue and Development Commission, an advisory body of the Delhi government tasked to find innovative solutions to civic problems.

Namit wrote a column on 3 Quarks Daily for many years. His essays have also appeared in venues like *The Humanist*, *Philosophy Now*, *The Times Literary Supplement*, *The Caravan*, *The Kyoto Journal*, *The Philosopher*, *Himal Southasian*, and four college anthologies in the US. His review of *Joothan* won the 3 Quarks Daily 2011 Arts & Literature Prize.

Namit's photography has been licensed by over 15 museums, 30 academies, 50 media and publishing houses, and many government agencies and NGOs. His videography includes *River of Faith*, a documentary film about the Kumbh Mela. He lives with his partner Usha Alexander and mutually chose to be childfree. His home on the web is Shunya.net.

Acknowledgements

I wrote the essays in this book over the last seven years. They have benefited from readings, conversations, encounters, and influences too numerous to mention. Foremost among the latter is Usha Alexander, my amazingly smart, kind, and insightful partner who has enriched my life in countless ways. She also read and critiqued these essays, which sometimes led to long, animated exchanges that have made my thinking more sensitive and grounded, especially on gender and race.

I'd like to thank S. Abbas Raza, founding editor of 3 Quarks Daily and now my friend, for offering me a column in 2009. I intensely dislike pitching my work to publishing outlets, and my *3QD* column saved me from that trouble. A lot of what's in this book first appeared there in earlier versions. I was fortunate to get many discerning readers who engaged with my writing on *3QD*, encouraging and challenging me. Some have become my friends and continue to exert a salutary influence on my thoughts.

I'm grateful to many other friends for being part of a long conversation and their spirited jousting with me, online and in living rooms, on topics I've covered in this book. They include Sandeepan Banerjee, Shreyasi Chatterjee, Pran Kurup (sadly, no longer with us), Vijay Poduri, Aditya Dev Sood, Nita Soans, Rahul Nair, Jayant Mahto, Ravi Verma, Ruchira Paul, and several other friends. Indeed, it's hard to even be fully aware of all the ways in which friends bring goodness into our lives. I'm grateful to my elder sister, Juhi Luthra, for her encouragement, despite our differences, and to my younger sister, Nupur Arora, for being there. I couldn't begin to recount my lifelong debt to my parents. I'll only say that I'm thankful that they have finally begun to see that my quitting a lucrative career in Silicon Valley and moving back to India at 45, without much of a career plan, hasn't turned out to be entirely for the worse.

Finally, my deepest gratitude to friends Asad Zaidi and Nalini Taneja, who run Three Essays Collective, for seeing value in publishing this book and for their editorial critiques. Together they combine poetry, scholarship, a cosmopolitan ethos, professional integrity, and a commitment to social justice in deeply alluring ways—altogether rare in today's publishing industry.

Index